ALCOHOL AND SUBSTANCE ABUSE

Alcohol and Substance Abuse

A CLERGY HANDBOOK

Stephen P. Apthorp

Morehouse-Barlow
Wilton

Morehouse-Barlow Co., Inc.
78 Danbury Road
Wilton, Connecticut 06897

ISBN 0-8192-1375-6 (cloth)
ISBN 0-8192-1372-1 (paper)

Library of Congress Catalog Card Number 85-061215

Composition by The Publishing Nexus Incorporated
1200 Boston Post Road, Guilford, Connecticut 06437

Printed in the United States of America

2 4 6 8 10 9 7 5 3 1

To THE GLORY OF GOD, in grateful thanksgiving
for a life ransomed, healed, restored, forgiven.

To my children, GEOFFREY and LISA,
who were there before as well as after.

And to my wife, MARY MURRAY,
who loved the pieces when there was yet no person.

Thank you

CONTENTS

PREFACE

If you don't care for drunks or druggies, then this book is for you.

If you don't like dealing with family problems that are the result of chemical use, then this book is for you.

If you don't know how to address the issues of substance use and abuse in your community, then you can use this book.

If you think chemical dependency is a sin or the result of a moral weakness, a character flaw, or a lack of inner strength, you will find this book useful.

If you feel frustrated because you can't get a drunk sober or a druggie straight, this book will help.

If you are concerned about the chemical-using society in which you live, want to learn what you can do about it, but don't have the time or the inclination to become proficient, then this book is especially for you.

If you fit into any of these categories, or all of them, this book is for you.

My primary purpose is to provide you with as much practical information as you must have to deal effectively with the complex issues of substance use, misuse, and abuse. Consider this book an "operations manual" to supplement your ministry. It is not designed to make you an expert in the chemical-dependency field; rather it is, in computer parlance, an access code that offers user-friendly material so you can be friendly and useful in a chemical-using and chemical-abusing society.

Combing through the literature on the topic, the first thing I found was that there was an overwhelming mass of excellent, up-to-date information on all aspects of alcohol and drug use and abuse. It expressed the viewpoints and served the purposes of every imaginable discipline. Next it became apparent that everything was written with a particular reader in mind, a reader supposedly very interested in the subject. In almost every case the author (or authors) assumed that because he or she had something cogent to say, the target audience would be interested to read it.

In researching the material on alcohol and drugs written for the clergy, the same assumption was apparent. There was an abundance of excellent information that represented every conceivable point of view, or at least answered most questions. Again, it was written *by* those who were interested *for* those supposedly interested. Whether I reviewed a book on the subject of alcoholism or a denominational manual on chemical health or listened to tapes on the treatment of drug abuse or attended a conference on the Church and chemical dependency, I found both the explicit and implicit purposes were to provide useful information to people who either wanted to know or needed to know. This thought raised some questions in my mind:

What about those who do not want to know? What about those who have no need to know? What about those who are not interested? I was at a loss to find anything written for the minister who was not ready, willing, or able to address the issues of substance use or abuse. Nothing was available for the clergyperson who had a reason for disregarding this aspect of God's ministry. There was documentation of the clergy's pervasive lack of interest, but there was nowhere to be found material written specifically for those who *did not, would not, could not* care. With the profound shock only a major discovery can trigger, I realized the churchpeople who addressed alcohol and drug abuse and the chemical-dependency experts who wrote for the clergy were all operating on a false premise—that ministers who were not involved would be as interested in the subject as those who were. Briefly, that because ministers were shepherds, they would also want to be veterinarians. My research, however, revealed the opposite: Ministers want to be ministers, *not* chemical-dependency specialists.

Minneapolis is the Mecca of help for the chemically dependent, and the Johnson Institute is its training center. Before beginning to write this book, to be certain my knowledge was current, I trained at the Johnson Institute. It was while I was studying there that I first wondered why the clergy shunned the subject of substance abuse, and what information was available for the uninvolved—or, more to the point, the disinterested—clergy. My investigation led to the discovery that those of us who were concerned about alcohol- and drug-related problems were having a grand time talking to ourselves. Not only was it erroneous to expect pastors to be practitioners, it was unrealisitc (given the priorities and time constraints of managing the ministry) to ask them to become passionately involved. They have neither the time not the inclination. It was unfair of local churches and denominational leaders to expect this involvement of them. The question was: What *could* they do?

It is one thing to write an "operations manual" for those who are interested;

it is quite another to do so for those who definitely are not. Yet as far as the clergy is concerned, there *is* a need; it is *theirs. Chemical dependency is the greatest single cause of pastoral problems in the Church today. Behind cancer, it is the number two killer in America.* Ministers, priests, and rabbis are the only care-giving professionals who have standing invitations to enter their parishioners' homes on any day of the week. Not only are they confronted by the problem daily, they have *access* to it daily. But, as the evidence suggests, they are not responding.

Of all pastoral problems it is ironic that we, the clergy, should be the least interested in alcohol- and drug-related problems when, in fact, we don't have to be. It is well known that the more dispassionate his or her approach to the complexities of substance misuse and abuse, the more effective a care-giver or professional is. Unlike the treatment of other pastoral problems, to become personally involved is to perpetuate the problem, not to solve it. The unique contention of this book is, therefore, that we need not be experts in alcohol- and drug-related problems to be effective instruments of God's redeeming power. It is a radical notion that our lack of interest is exactly what is needed to serve God's purpose, but God wants you and me to be ministers—spiritual leaders— not chemical-dependency specialists. We can be most useful to Him if we stick to what we are called to do, what we are trained to do, what we like to do best— to act as shepherds, *not* as veterinarians.

Others in the parish can be chemical-dependency specialists. One out of eight adults in America is an alcoholic, so there are any number of parishioners who would be willing to help or become involved. Our job is to tap the resources available to us, to claim that energy and enthusiasm, and to turn them into forces for chemical health. Our responsibility is to know where we can get the specialized help and to use it. Our ministry is to interpret, in light of the totally reliable hope God offers, the hopes of a world that has come to rely on the momentary gratification of chemicals. Therein lies the reason for this book. It is an "operations manual" written specifically for the clergyperson who wants to be an effective instrument of God's peace, but doesn't want to be involved in the complexities of alcohol and drug use and abuse.

I have tried to make the book itself a model for clergy and parish use. Its purpose is not so much to preach or proclaim as it is to describe a methodology that can serve the minister's purposes. I hope this book, like the irritant grain of sand in the pearl-producing oyster, will prompt both the Church and the clergy to capitalize on the new idea that ministers do not have to be veterinarians to be successful shepherds. To that end, it offers practical procedures, advice, materials, models that have proven successful; insight, encouragement, and theological concepts that confirm it is through God's grace that we are all ransomed, healed, restored, forgiven.

The work of a parish minister is now, and will continue to be, affected by the problems of alcohol and drug use. With one out of eight adults in the U.S. suffering from alcohol dependency and one out of four families distressed by someone's abuse of chemicals, a clergyperson must deal with problems whether he or she is capable of it or not.

After clarifying why the clergy are not now (and need not be) the local alcohol and drug experts, this book suggests a suitable role and a proven model the minister can use to promote a parish program of chemical health. Acting as a catalyst, using the redemptive principles of Alcoholics Anonymous, the minister enlists enthusiastic parishioners to create a fellowship in which learning, sharing, and growth can occur. His or her method is to tap into the vested interests of experienced people through the leadership of a "spark plug" (defined later).

There is still controversy in the Church over whether alcoholism is a sin or a sickness. A pastoral answer is found in the medical definition, and the disease's symptoms are described to identify it as a family illness.

Many ministers are unaware that there is as much misuse of licit prescriptions as there is abuse of illicit drugs. Both aspects are discussed, and a definite theological stand on adolescent drug use is proposed.

How does a minister respond to a cry for help when the concern is alcohol or drug abuse? Applying the principles of "problem-solving therapy," the book offers practical, effective answers. Three diagnostic instruments with which to identify chemical dependency are provided. Once that preliminary problem is solved, treatment resources are suggested and a referral network is outlined.

Finaly, this book summarizes theological and biblical perspectives on chemical use and abuse which can help the minister proclaim God's message of hope to His people.

A word about language. At the risk of irritating some readers, I shall use the personal pronouns "he," "him," and "his" for gender-free references to unidentified individuals or where the antecedent may be either male or female. I once gave a seminary talk called "Substance Abuse and the Pastor's Role." Moments afterward, my use of the masculine personal pronouns to mean both male and female was challenged. The entire point of the talk was lost to my critic because I had not established the ground rules by which I would be referring to members of both sexes. My fault, not my listeners; the responsibility for communication lies with the communicator, not the communicatee—always! Because I had been insensitive to my audience, I had not conveyed vital information to someone who had taken the time to come and listen. How many lives may have been affected by that breakdown in communication! It is for this reason that at the outset I claim the use of the masculine pronouns to mean both male and female.

For much too long now, you who are parish ministers have been criticized for avoiding problems related to alcohol and drugs. For too long you have been reproached for not having an answer that prevents the damage of substance abuse. I believe the judgments against you are unwarranted. The sphere of substance use, misuse, and abuse demands that the interested person or professional be enlightened. The complexities of chemical dependency require that the care-giver, to be successful, have specialized preparation. You were not called into the ministry to be alcohol and drug specialists. You were never equipped to address the issues, nor to cure the problems. Finally, there are no agreed-upon moral or ethical positions you can avow to help solve the problem. In brief, you have been impaled on the twin spires of the local church's expectations and the denominational leaders' demands. You have been trans-fixed on these cruel horns because of the demands of your professional calling and your limited qualifications.

If you are not involved, if you are not enlightened, if you are not prepared, do not give up hope. You do not need to be proficient to minister to alcohol and drug misusers or abusers. Use this book; it was written especially for you. With it you can be a very successful pastor without having to be a practitioner. With it you can serve God's purpose without sacrificing your own.

S. P. A.

ACKNOWLEDGMENTS

Of the many, many people to whom I am indebted, I would like to give special recognition to:

Carl R. Apthorp, Jr., my father, who taught me the benefits of hard work and perseverance.

Mary Louise Apthorp, my mother, whose love of me was the basis of health.

Bonnie O. Apthorp, my former wife, who traveled with me from husband, father, and businessman to clergyman. Her sacrifice was my gain.

Eleanor, Worth, Emily, Mary Murray—the Coleman children—who lost their own father, had no alternative, and accepted me as substitute.

The Right Reverend John B. Coburn, Bishop, Diocese of Massachusetts, whose pastoral care allowed me to heal at my own pace.

The Reverend David A. Works, who put a name to my disorder, listened and laughed without judgment.

Meredith B. Handspicker, professor of Practical Theology at Andover Newton Theological School, whose idea it was that I write this much-needed book to fulfill my Doctor of Ministry project for the Department of Church and Ministry. His charity allowed me the opportunity.

George Bass, my friend, whose generosity made it possible for me to study at the Johnson Institute.

Barbara Sims, who volunteered long hours of deciphering my cursive and typing it. Her patience with a project much larger than we expected was priceless.

Joan Kaufman, who gladly gave me her proofreading and editing skills at a moment's notice.

Finally, I owe a debt of gratitude to Sharon Wegscheider, for permission to quote extensively from her beautiful book *Another Chance*, which is a literary masterpiece as well as an excellent pastoral course in family care. I am also deeply grateful to T. Furman Hewitt for his permission to quote from his excellent booklet *A Biblical Perspective on the Use and Abuse of Alcohol and Other Drugs*.

To all I offer my deepest gratitude.

ALCOHOL AND SUBSTANCE ABUSE

CHAPTER 1

The Minister's Dilemma

THE SIN OF ACEDIA

The phone on my desk rang at about 9:45 p.m. I had just concluded a long, tiring vestry meeting at the church and was about to go up to the rectory when the shrill sound stopped me.

God, I thought, *who could that be?*

I tried to comfort myself with the thought it was my wife calling to find out how soon I would be home. No such luck. It wasn't her cheery voice on the other end. It was the distraught cry of a parishioner.

"Reverend, could you please come over? John is drunk or drugged or something. He's banging around and I'm terrified of him."

Instinctively my whole body tensed in readiness to respond to the crisis. *Not again*, I thought. *This is the third time this week.*

I was sick of Mrs. Smith and her son John. Nothing I tried seemed to do any good, and when I told her or John what to do, neither of them followed through or acted on my advice.

"How much has he had this time, Mrs. Smith?" I asked, emphasizing the tiredness in my voice in the hope she would get the hint I wanted to go home.

"I don't know, but he's worse than before. Won't you come?" she pleaded.

Drunks, druggies, I thought. *What a lost cause! Getting involved takes too darned much time. Then when I do get the family put back together, the drunk gets drunk again or the druggie gets stoned and I'm back where I started. Worse, I'm exhausted. And I'm the one who feels guilty because I've failed them and I haven't solved their hopeless problem.*

"I told you if it happened again to call the police," I said in my most official, authoritative, professional voice.

"I can't, I just can't," she cried. "I can't bring myself to do that. I know the

1

police. What will they think? What will the neighbors think if a police car pulls up here this time of night?"

I wondered what the neighbors would think if I pulled up at ten o'clock for the third time this week.

"Look, Mrs. Smith," I said, "this has been going on ever since John got back from the service over a year ago. I've suggested you throw him out. I've told you to send him to AA. I've recommended you lock him out when he comes home high. I've said to call the police. I've suggested several other ministers to call. You haven't done any of those things. Until you do, my coming over will do no good. We just keep going over and over the same ground. I'm sorry, but tonight I can't come. I've got to get some rest."

"Please Reverend, I'm embarrassed to call the police," she said tearfully. "And the ministers you recommended say I'm not a member."

This guy is a blemish on my record, I thought. *He's giving me a bad name. People are talking. They're wondering why I'm not doing more to help that poor, long-suffering saint, Mrs. Smith. If they only knew the real truth; she's just as weak as that irresponsible son of hers.*

"But what do you want me to do?" I asked impatiently.

"Just come and help me calm John down and get him to bed," she said.

Put him to bed? I thought. *The guy isn't even a member of my parish. He's never set foot in my church and she wants me to put him to bed. Thank God I don't have any problems like this in my parish.*

"Mrs. Smith," I said, "putting him to bed is exactly the wrong thing to do. Let him stay where he is. Don't even try to help him. He doesn't want our help. He isn't ready for it, and until he is, there is nothing you or I can do. He's got to hit bottom!"

"But he'll be furious with me when he wakes up and . . . "

I didn't hear the rest of her plea. I was tired. I was frustrated. I was angry. I had tried my best to rescue John, but he had been defiant. He went right out and got wasted. The guy had an out-and-out moral problem—selfishness!

"Mrs. Smith," I said. "Do you want help?"

"Yes, please," she answered.

"Do you trust me to give you that help?"

"Yes, I do. I really do."

"Will you do what I suggest to help John get the inner strength to stop hurting himself?"

"Oh, yes, I promise."

"All right, here is what I want you to do." I said. "Tomorrow morning I want you to call a man named John Kelly. He's an authority on these problems. He's the one to help you . . . "

"But I don't want Mr. Kelly's help," she interrupted, "I want yours. You're

my rector! Why won't you or any other minister help me with my son's alcohol
and drug problem?"

"I'm sorry Mrs. Smith," I replied. "You'll just have to call Mr. Kelly. I can't
help you. Good night."

As I walked up the dark path to the rectory to get a much-needed, much-
deserved drink, I looked up at the black sky, filled with bright, glistening stars,
and I prayed aloud.

"Why me, Lord, why me?"

Today, as I reflect on that phone call, I realize I did the right thing for Mrs.
Smith, but in the wrong way and for the wrong reasons. I simply did not have a
creative way of dealing with alcohol or drug problems.

In seminary I had six pastoral-theology courses that addressed every
conceivable problem a human being can face; all, that is, but one—alcohol and
drug abuse. Or so I thought.

When I look back at the required reading lists and bibliographies of those
counseling courses, I see many books on alcoholism and drug abuse were
listed, many that were the best available then and several that remain so today.
I also see from a quick review of the class schedules that lectures and seminars
were assigned to the topic.

Where was I during those classes? Why didn't I do the related homework
and study the required reading? The answer is, I didn't like those problems.

The truth in a nutshell is: I didn't like "drunks and druggies." I believed
they were hopeless. I did not want to minister to them. I remember, however,
feeling guilty. By my own judgment I was being condemned by the sin psychiatrist Karl Menninger called "the heart of all sin . . . the Great Sin . . . the Sin of
Sloth." He called it "acedia."

> *Acedia*: inactivity—unresponsiveness—indifference." In some indi-
> viduals it can be an egocentricity— already mentioned—born of
> fearfulness and uncertainty, or of a lack of imagination. It appears as a
> "don't care" attitude which no amount of sentimentalizing as "con-
> tentedness," "minding one's own business," and "living and letting
> live" can cover up. A common excuse for inaction, indifference or
> lukewarm response is the "fear of becoming involved." Exactly, yet all
> life is a matter of involvement somewhere with something, many
> somethings, and this chronic fear and consequent withdrawal is surely
> a common sin. It is a kind of "being scared to death"—at least to
> nonlife.[1]

I was neither caring about nor caring for a large population of God's
suffering people. I knew that those who were alcoholics or drug abusers were
every bit as much children of God as those who never touched the substances or

those who drank responsibly. My heart, however, did not go out to them, for I felt the ones who really suffered were the people related to the abuser. Deep down inside I knew the drunk and the druggie were in pain too, but something kept me from caring about them. Even though I knew they were children of God, even though they were causing themselves and their families untold pain and destruction, even though they desperately needed my time and professional attention, nevertheless I felt that by some twist of fate they were getting exactly what they deserved. They were being required to pay for their sins. Poetic justice! Still, my hardhearted disinterest bothered me. Not enough to do anything about it, though, not enough to learn how to be helpful or useful, just enough to make me mad. I did not like feeling guilty about my indifference. Why should I feel guilty? I was not an alcohol or drug counselor.

Just as ignorance of the law is no excuse, neither was my dislike of drunks and druggies a valid reason to perpetuate my disregard. By my refusal to become involved, by my reluctance to learn about alcoholism and drug abuse, by my insistence on judging drunks and druggies as deserving of their problems, and by my unwillingness to respond to the suffering of family members, I was not only denying the problem of alcohol and drug abuse but contributing to it! Not to decide was to decide. My discomfort suggested I needed to care. My guilt proclaimed that God was calling me to care. But I answered God's call with indignation and complaint. "Why me, Lord, why me?"

THE CHURCHES' RESPONSE: INVOLVED OR UNINVOLVED?

During the late 1960s and early 1970s, when I was dodging God's call by asking, "Why me?" there were other clergy who were saying yes to it. One was Vernon E. Johnson, an Episcopal minister whose pioneering service in the field of alcohol abuse led him in 1973 to write *I'll Quit Tomorrow*, one of the most useful books on the practical aspects of treating alcoholism. Two other clergypersons troubled by the problems of alcohol abuse were The Reverend David C. Hancock, president of Prevention of Alcohol Problems, in Minneapolis, and The Reverend David A. Works, president of the North Conway Institute, in Boston. As a result of a quarter century of working separately and together to establish training programs on alcoholism for laypeople and professionals, both men felt the Church could be more involved in ministering to people suffering from alcoholism.

In January 1978, Works, an Episcopal minister, and Hancock, a United Presbyterian pastor, suggested to pollster George Gallup, Jr., president of the Gallup Poll, that he conduct a survey to ascertain the extent of alcohol problems in America. Mr. Gallup, in turn, asked Hancock to prepare the questions he could ask the American public about its feelings and attitudes toward alcohol.[2]

That spring the Gallup poll surveyed 1,523 adults nationwide. The results were surprising. The most startling statistic was that in one out of every four families across the U.S. drinking was causing trouble. When the adults were asked, "Has liquor ever been a cause of trouble in your family?" 24 percent said yes. What made this alarming was that in 1974, in another survey, only 12 percent answered affirmatively. In four years, therefore, the number of people distressed by alcohol-related problems had doubled. Furthermore, the poll revealed another unsettling fact: Forty-seven percent of the adults surveyed had no guidelines for their use of alcohol, and 51 percent had no guidelines for their children's use. (A year later Gallup would find that adults are not even able to decide for themselves if drinking is right or wrong, much less establish guidelines. Gallup reported that half of America's population basically disapproves of drinking even though some of them, of course, are drinking. And one in five would like to see a return to prohibition.)

Finally, the poll directed its attention to the resources most often used by people or families in need of help. It asked, "If you or someone else in your family had a drinking problem, where or to whom would you turn for help?" Twenty-five percent said they would turn to some kind of religious resource. Only Alcoholics Anonymous was named more often as a source of help. This raised the thought, "Was the church making itself available as a resource?" A documented answer was not forthcoming until Hancock and the Research Division of the United Presbyterian Church asked the question.[3]

In June 1979 David Hancock and his denomination addressed the issue of the Church's involvement with alcohol problems. It sent out a four-page questionnaire to four thousand Presbyterians, both clergy and laity. No other Church had conducted such a survey. The returns were gratifying, but the responses were alarming. Knowing the Gallup Poll had revealed that one in four families were distressed by someone with an alcohol problem, the Presbyterian survey asked, "Is the consumption of alcoholic beverages a problem in your community?" Forty-four percent of the laity said yes, and 72 percent of the clergy said yes. To test the extent of Church involvement with the problem, the survey asked, "Do you feel that the abuse of alcohol is a problem in which the church should be involved?" Forty-six percent of the members said yes; 83 percent of the pastors, however, said yes. Obviously, there was a discrepancy between the views of the leaders and the membership. When the survey asked its population, "Is your congregation currently involved in programs which address the issue of alcohol abuse?"— in other words, are you working on the problem or are you part of the problem?—81 percent of the lay members said their Church was not involved, and 76 percent of the clergy agreed. It was an open admission by both groups that there was very little interest or concern. When asked why, three-fourths answered, "Other congregational programs have higher priorities." Two-thirds said, "Alcohol problems have not surfaced as an issue in the congregation." Yet this was said at a time when the Gallup poll showed 24 percent of the population—one in four families— troubled by alcohol problems. The vast majority in the United Presbyterian poll (two-thirds) felt that alcohol problems "should be left to other community agencies or to AA and Al-Anon."[4] Little did they know then that their instincts that a problem existed were right and their complacency was unwarranted.

Next question. In an effort to learn whether the clergy was a resource for those suffering from alcohol problems, the survey asked the pastors, "During the past twelve months how many persons have sought help from you specifically about their own drinking problems or those of family members?" This question would reveal the involvement of the professional leaders. Sixty-nine percent of the clergy saw no one or no more than three alcohol-related cases a year. With the Gallup Poll reporting 25 percent of its adults willing to turn to religious resources for help, the Presbyterian pastors were seeing no one or at most three a year?[5]

Still concentrating on the ministers' concern and leadership, the United Presbyterian poll asked, "During the past twelve months have you preached about any subject related to the use of alcoholic beverages?" and "Have you spoken in public about any such a subject?" The goal was to learn if pastors were initiating any preventive or educational programs. The responses were disquieting. Sixty-three percent had not preached on any subject related to the use or misuse of alcohol, and 71 percent had not talked, taught, or lectured about it in any public setting. Not only were they unresponsive to the problem in terms of pastoral ministry, they were not even preaching about it. Though 83 percent had said earlier the Church should be doing something about alcohol problems, it was evident no pastor was.

Though 72 percent of the clergy had previously answered that consumption of alcohol was a problem in their community and 83 percent had said the Church should be doing something about it, the figures showed the United Presbyterian ministers were not responding to it. Because they were not working on the problem, they were therefore a part of the problem. *Acedia*! The one redeeming factor was, of all the denominations, the Presbyterians were the only ones to identify their sin and the extent of it.[6] What is particularly revealing about the survey is that so many of God's ministers were resisting a rampant problem. The question not asked was, "What is God saying in this mass resistance of His chosen leaders?"

One might look at the United Presbyterian survey and condemn that Church for disregarding one in four families in its denomination. The fact is, however, every other religious body has as many problems with alcohol and drug abuse, each proclaims that the churches and synagogues should address the issue, but there is still a lack of local involvement.

In 1963 a researcher named Harold Mulford conducted a study entitled "Drinking and Deviant Drinking in the United States." The data, which Mulford presented in the *Quarterly Journal of Studies: Alcohol*, included percentages of drinkers, classified by religious denomination:

Jewish	90%
Catholic	89%
Lutheran	85%
Presbyterian	81%
Episcopalian	81%
Methodist	61%
Baptist	48%

Mulford found that the denominations with the highest number of problem drinkers were the abstainers: the Baptists, with 16 percent, and the other small Protestant denominations, with 15 percent. He found the denominations with the lowest percentage of problem drinkers were the Lutherans, the Presbyterians, and the Episcopalians, with 5 to 6 percent.[7]

According to the National Council on Alcoholism, one out of eight adults in America is an alcoholic, as are 10 to 20 percent of all drinkers. Given Mulford's figures, it is clear, therefore, that every religious body in the U.S. has its proportionate share of alcohol-related problems. As to whether the clergy are doing anything about it, the answer is still no. The present response is no better than what the United Presbyterian Church found. This finding is demonstrated by a survey recently completed by the Johnson Institute of Minneapolis, the world-famous alcohol and drug education, counseling, and consulting center founded by Vernon E. Johnson.

In August 1982 the Johnson Institute questioned seven agencies in the Minneapolis-St. Paul area to ascertain who referred teenagers to the area's adolescent chemical-dependence assessment programs. The sample was 1,713 assessments of youngsters aged 13 to 18 years. It was found that the source of the highest number of referrals was schools, 28 percent; the courts were second, 25 percent; other social services agencies a close third, 21 percent; physicians in fourth place, 11 percent; families in fifth, 5 percent; and sixth, the clergy, referring a mere 2 percent, 1 percent above self-admissions, 1 percent.[8] Clearly the clergy was not a significant referral resource. Yet the Gallup Poll had established that 25 percent of the adult population was willing to turn to religious resources for help with an alcohol-related problem. The care-giving professions of the Minneapolis-St. Paul area are more highly sensitized to chemical dependency than any other comparable group in the U.S.; their area is the capital of chemical-dependency consultation, treatment, education, and training. Considering the 2 percent clergy referral rate there, what does that signify about the response of ministers and other religious leaders in less knowledgeable, much less sensitized communities?

A NATIONAL CRISIS

Though organized religion has direct contact with over half the families in America, it is apparent that one of the country's most alarming (and growing) problems is being ignored by churches and synagogues, laity and clergy alike. The Church's involvement hasn't improved since David Hancock and David Works first raised the issue. Yet the problem has grown into a national crisis. In 1982 the Churchmen's League in Massachusetts asked clergy and laity throughout the Commonwealth to select the ten issues they considered most important. Alcohol abuse was listed as the number one concern, with 71 percent of the votes, nuclear war was second, with 69 percent, and in third place was drugs, with 60 percent. Two years prior, the White House had sponsored a National Conference on Families in three areas of the country—Baltimore, Minneapolis, and Los Angeles. "Developing an agenda to strengthen and support families" was the basic conference objective. To the surprise of many, the delegates from all three cities agreed, listing as their number one recommendation, "New efforts to prevent alcohol and drug abuse." The vote was nearly unanimous—92.7 percent of the delegates considered it the most important issue facing America today.[9]

Alcohol and drugs are now involved in almost every pastoral problem a minister must face. One hundred twenty million Americans drink! One out of every eight adults is an alcoholic. Each one of these alcoholics has a damaging effect on three to four other people. With one in four families in America suffering from alcohol- or drug-related problems, the impact on parishes is undeniable. What is even more alarming to a pastor is the following: Except for cancer, alcohol is the leading killer in the U.S. According to the National Conference on Alcoholism, it is involved in:

80% of all fire deaths
65% of all drownings
65% of all murders
60% of all teenage highway fatalities
60% of all child-abuse cases
55% of all physical fights in the home
55% of all arrests

50% of all fatal car accidents
46% of all divorces
45% of all surgical/medical hospital admissions
40% of all problems brought before probate courts
40% of all assaults
36% of all pedestrian accidents
35% of all rapes
30% of all suicides

Many more women are drinking today than ever before; others are combining alcohol with tranquilizers, amphetamines, or antidepressants. It is estimated that four million women in the U.S. are alcoholic. Young people also are using alcohol as their number one drug of choice. The most recent figures from the National Institute on Alcohol Abuse and Alcoholism (NIAA) classify 15 percent of students in grades ten to twelve as heavy drinkers, i.e., those who drink "at least once a week and have five drinks or more in a typical drinking occasion."[10]

The National Council on Alcoholism's 1982 survey reports that: 31 percent of high-school students are considered alcohol misusers (drunk at least six times a year); 8 percent of all high-school students are daily users of alcohol; the average age children begin to drink is thirteen; and drunk driving is the leading cause of death among fifteen- to twenty-four-year-olds. It is estimated that 3.3 million teenagers, ages fourteen to seventeen, are showing signs they may develop serious alcohol problems.

With regard to the use of other drugs: "The National Institute on Drug Abuse (NIDA) through a 1981 study by the University of Michigan Institute for Social Research has determined that 7 percent of high school seniors are daily users of marijuana."[11] Owing to this drug's use, adolescents are the only age group in the U.S. with rising health problems. And one has only to pick up any newspaper or magazine or tune into a TV news show and there will be stories about cocaine use in every aspect of American life—among businessmen, athletes, nurses, doctors, lawyers, housewives, bankers, social workers, secretaries, teachers, gas station attendants, anyone who can afford it (and many who can't).

There is now general alarm about drug use by athletes—"uppers" to give them a competitive edge, steroids to give them bigger bodies and more strength, and cocaine to get high on after the contest. These people are the role models, the heroes of the younger generation. What they do becomes acceptable for every idol-worshiping child. The uncovering of drug use—for example, of amphetamines and cocaine— in the National Football League proclaimed to every aspiring athlete that the way to the top, to become number one, is through the use of licit and illicit drugs. A new wave of young abusers is expected as a result.

The motto of today is, "Better living through chemistry." No matter what the feeling, no matter what the emotion, no matter what the physical condition—pain or boredom, tension, fatigue, too much pressure or loneliness, or the discomfort of a headache, hemorrhoids, sore muscles, ulcers, rheumatism, or a broken leg—there is a prescription or nonprescription drug to bring relief. No one need suffer any pain from anything ever again, the multi-billion-dollar pharmaceutical industry promises. The alcoholic-beverage industry agrees! It spent $1,049.9 billion on its 1981 advertising to offer escape from all personal and social problems, to coax the common man and woman into drinking like the elite, to entice the social user and the misuser into drinking more (even though more creates more abusers). The illicit drug marketeers take advantage of the brainwashing accomplished by these legitimate drug pushers and rake in millions offering the illegal highs with which Americans of all ages, races, colors, and creeds get wasted.

To reemphasize: In 1982, the issues of alcohol and drug abuse were listed as the number one and the number three concerns, respectively, by the clergy and laity surveyed in the Commonwealth of Massachusetts. The number one concern among parents across the U.S. in 1980 was the prevention of drug abuse. Alcohol is the number two killer in America today. The use, misuse, and abuse of chemicals is involved in nearly every pastoral problem a minister, priest, or rabbi must face. But the 1978 Gallup poll and the 1979 United Presbyterian survey have demonstrated that churches across the land are not addressing the national crisis. The question that has not been answered is the one Mrs. Smith asked over the phone so many years ago— and it still cries for an answer: "Why won't the clergy help with the problems of alcohol and drug abuse?" In short, why *acedia*?

A 1975 study by the Reverend Karl A. Schneider, consultant for Alcohol and Drug Services to the Southeastern Pennsylvania Synod of the Lutheran Church of America, offers one answer. Schneider suggests that basically there are "ten roadblocks to clergy involvement in early intervention and training in alcohol and drug problems":

1. The "good guy" syndrome. This is the minister who wants everyone to like him, the pleaser who doesn't want to upset anyone.

2. The professional "perfect pastor." This person with high standards feels alcohol or drug abuse couldn't exist among his people because its a sickness of the weak.

3. Personal drinking pattern. Here is the clergyperson who drinks with his parishioners, tolerates drunken behavior, accepts the social pressures to drink, and doesn't think his own drinking pattern is a problem.

4. "Let George do it." This one finds a way to avoid problems altogether, doesn't want to be involved, is known to say, "He's not my parishioner."

5. "I haven't had an alcohol problem in years." The ostrich, himself a problem because he thinks there is no problem.

6. Fear of failure. This person won't touch a possible lost cause, counsels only the beautiful people, and addresses only the safe, easily managed problems.

7. Therapeutic nihilism or frustration. "Once an alcoholic, always an alcoholic" is the belief of this pastor. He tries to control the problem with his solutions, gets mad when they aren't carried out, and dislikes alcoholics because of it.

8. "It's a moral problem. All you need is will power." To this person, inner discipline is the answer. Alcoholism and drug abuse are sins that require self-control.

9. "What can I do about adolescent drinking in my neighborhood?" Though his concern is real, this minister focuses on the young to avoid adult attitudes and behavior.

10. The need to be a "rescuer." This pastor tries to rescue the alcoholic. He picks up the pieces for the family, relieves everyone of their hurt and distress, and as a result, he prolongs the sickness. When his saving efforts fail, he gives up on the alcoholic and the family. [12]

SHEPHERDS, NOT VETERINARIANS

Though Karl Schneider's study helps us identify the roles ministers fall into when avoiding substance-abuse problems, it does not answer Mrs. Smith's original question. The answer cannot be found in vocational roadblocks to involvement, nor in personal characteristics that hamper one's professional efficacy. The explanation for the *acedia* is found primarily in that both the local congregations and the institutional hierarchy have expected the clergy to fulfill unrealistic leadership roles. The Church has expected its clergy to serve as the parish experts on alcohol- and drug-related questions; it has supposed them to be chemical-dependency counselors and consultants; and it has admonished them to become knowledgeable enough to educate their congregations. This fundamental misconception of the clergy's role is evident in every effort to improve the Church's ministry to those affected by chemical abuse.

Nearly all the existing denominational position papers on the issues of alcohol and drugs, the institutional guidelines, the interchurch policy statements, the clergy resource manuals, the congregational plans and strategies, the study programs, the curricula, the pastoral books, the educational booklets, pamphlets, and tracts are grounded in these basic presuppositions: (1) that the clergy are interested in the issues of substance use, misuse, and abuse; (2) that because their parishioners are affected, ministers necessarily will educate themselves or obtain training in alcohol and drug problems; and (3) that they will be motivated to educate their parishes about these issues. A quick review of any of these documents reveals the assumption that because the authors were vitally interested in their specialized material, it would be of interest to the clergy as well. Furthermore, the authors assumed that because ministers were "shepherds," they would also want to become "veterinarians." Ironically, the Church has misjudged its ministers in supposing this; it has miscalculated the clergy's priorities and time constraints.

In 1956, Samuel W. Blizzard conducted a now famous survey of a carefully selected cross section of 670 Protestant ministers. The study was entitled "The Minister's Dilemma." Its function was to discover what parishioners expected of their minister as compared to the minister's own picture of his role. For purposes of analysis, six practitioner roles were distinguished: three traditional roles—preacher, priest (liturgist), and teacher; a neotraditional one—pastor; and two contemporary rolls—administrator and organizer. The ministers were asked to evaluate themselves in these six capacities from three perspectives— those of importance, effectiveness, and enjoyment. The ministers rated their roles as follows:

Order of importance	Sense of effectiveness	Feeling of enjoyment
Preacher	Preacher	Pastor
Pastor	Pastor	Preacher
Priest (Liturgist)	Teacher	Teacher
Teacher	Priest	Priest
Organizer	Administrator	Organizer
Administrator	Organizer	Administrator

When Blizzard then asked for an order of priority based on the functional demands of the parish ministry from most time spent in a role to least time, he found the ministers had to spend the most time as administrator, a role they felt was the least important and the least enjoyable, the one they rated second to last in personal effectiveness. Their time allocation was: administrator, 37 percent; pastor, 26 percent; preacher and priest, 18 percent; organizer, 11 percent; and teacher, 8 percent. In essence, the most fulfilling aspects of their ministry were not fulfilling them! They had to spend most of their time doing things they felt were the least important, the least meaningful, and the least enjoyable.

Finally the clergy were asked to evaluate their seminary education in light of their experience in the parish ministry and to list their priorities for additional training. They answered: pastor, administrator and organizer, preacher, teacher, priest. They felt most equipped in the traditional roles. The roles they found troublesome were the neotraditional (pastor) or contemporary (administrator/organizer) ones. The value of Blizzard's study was to point up "The Minister's Dilemma":

> No matter how different ministers' ideas of what is important in the ministry, all wind up doing substantially the same thing. . . . The minister is urged to spend much time organizing and administering programs. The national church body is at the same time failing to give him an adequate theological understanding of these offices.[13]

Rabbis are interested in being rabbis, priests are interested in being priests, ministers are interested in being ministers; they do not go to seminary to become alcohol and drug experts. By and large their reason for going is to become instruments of God for purposes of faith development. Nevertheless, in spite of this original intention, as Lewis D. Anderson and Ezra Earl Jones point out in their book *The Managment of Ministry*, ministers are still confronted with the same dilemmas Samuel Blizzard listed.

> They are to be prophets, priests and teachers. They have the responsibility of interpreting God's will for His people on the one hand and relating people in their sin and existential concerns to God on the other. . . .

> Aware of the ideals for which the church was established, ministers are nevertheless daily confronted with the need for merely preserving the institution itself. They recognize that the church exists to extend itself outside of its own walls, but they must give attention to membership growth, finances, and building repairs.

> They are sometimes caught between the demands of the denominational organization and the distinctive needs of the people who make up their congregation.

> They are managers whose first responsibility is to the congregations they serve, but who cannot limit their concern to the "insiders" who pay their salaries.

> They are people who must come to terms personally with the ambiguities of their roles as clergy on the one hand and as private citizens on the other—roles that are not always clearly defined and differentiated and appear at times to be in conflict.

> The task of synthesizing the many demands of ministry is enormous. It

would almost seem that the job of parish pastor is impossible for one person.[14]

That the minister does not have the time or the inclination to be the parish drug expert, and therefore cannot reasonably be expected by the Church to fulfill that role, is substantiated by the United Presbyterian Church's 1979 survey. Though 83 percent of the pastors felt alcohol abuse was a problem with which the Church should be involved, 71 percent admitted they had not talked, spoken, or lectured on it in any public setting.

That the Church at large, and denominational leaders in particular, expected the clergy to be interested in alcohol/drug problems, that they believed the clergy "should" be involved in chemical abuse when in fact the ministers had all they could do to meet the demands of their contemporary roles was and is a costly misjudgment. There may have been good reason to expect the clergy to be so engaged (given the chemical-dependency problems in the parishes), but considering the demands of managing the church and the responsibilities of managing the ministry, to suppose pastors to be practitioners of alcohol/drug education or counseling or consulting was then, and is today, unrealistic. The tragedy is that years of chemical education and substance-abuse prevention might have occurred and countless lives may have been redeemed if only the ministers' basic dilemma had been considered. Instead it was overlooked by the leaders of the religious denominations and the leaders in the alcohol/drug field. These leaders simply did not perceive that the resistance was the clergy's way of saying, "We are shepherds, *not* veterinarians!" Furthermore, neither profession noted that stressing such obligations and expecting compliance most often leads to indifference, resistance, and unwillingness to be involved—*acedia*.

The chemical-dependency field is not the clergy's profession. Substance-abuse prevention is not solely the minister's responsibility. From the local congregation's point of view there is good reason why the minister should not be asked to take on the role of chemical educator, counselor, or consultant. He is a sojourner in that community. In most cases he will move to another congregation after some years. The parishioners remain, by and large, while ministers come and go. Confronting the issues of chemical abuse is a continual process that cannot wax or wane depending on the interest, enthusiasm, or knowledge of the minister. To be most effective, the consciousness-raising and educational programs need to be promoted by parishioners with expressed or vested interest. According to the Johnson Institute, chemical education, especially the communication of attitudes, values, and lifestyles that promote responsible decisions, works best when there is a commitment to learn, when the students themselves determine what, when, and how they will learn, when new insights and increased awareness grow out of the people's own discovery, and when the intellectualizing or philosophizing is grounded in personal experience.

MINISTER TO THE MINISTERS

Since the task of synthesizing the many demands of the ministry makes it unrealistic to expect the clergy to be the local drug experts, this raises the most pertinent question of all: "What, then, *is* the minister's role?" Anderson and Jones, in *The Management of Ministry*, provide the answer:

> The pastor's role in the process of ministering is an enabling one. It is not his or her ministry—ministry belongs to the whole congregation—nor his or her responsibility to do the ministry—all members carry out the ministry. The pastor's role is to minister to the ministers and to be a catalyst in the church—one who causes and facilitates the process of ministry but who is not personally "used up" by it. A catalyst, by definition, participates in a process of transformation and facilitates its occurrence, but it is not itself changed or harmed in any way by the process. In the church, when the role of the congregation and the role of the pastor is confused, so that the pastor assumes the responsibilities of the congregation, ministry does not occur and the pastor becomes frustrated, harried and ineffective. The ministry is to those who come to church to be related to God. It is the pastor's job to manage their coming and their going out. The church's ministry is performed by those who come and then return to society.[15]

> The primary task of the church is to receive people as they are, enable them to submit their lives in dependence upon the ground and source of their being and to return to society renewed and strengthened for participating in other social institutions. . . .

> All of life is the church's concern. The task of the church in the community is to enable people to find direction and meaning for the whole of their lives, to provide a value system for their diverse relationships in society and to relate them to God who alone is able to provide strength for the weak. . . .

> The church must gauge its successes by the quality of lives redeemed and the characteristics of the social milieu where those lives are lived. When the primary task of the church is perceived to be that of accepting people in weakness to return them to the world in strength, success is measured in terms of the quality of the lives that have been renewed. . . .

The purpose of the church is to enable "members of society in their role as citizens to engage with the real human needs of their community, by helping them in their role as worshippers to realize their full potential. . . . "[16]

Recognizing the immediate and critical need for the promotion of chemical health in families, and acknowledging that churches are in a unique position to respond to the task of substance-abuse prevention, the minister's role is that of catalyst. As such he can initiate a program of chemical-health education without having to be the drug expert. He can do so by drawing on his greatest resource—his parishioners. As was shown, the interest and energy for an educational program are already in place; scarcely a parish family is untouched by someone's misuse or abuse of chemicals. As catalyst the minister is free to do what he is trained to do and what he likes to do best, that is, create a spiritual fellowship of interested persons and families, a fellowship in which caring and sharing, exploring and growing can occur. Historically, one of the true functions of a church or synagogue was to be a fellowship. Creating one that is open to addressing the issues of chemical health combines a congregation's historical purpose with the parishioners' interest in preventing alcohol and drug abuse.

Dr. Keith Schuchard, director of research for the National Parents' Resource Institute for Drug Education, Inc. (PRIDE), in Atlanta, Georgia, believes that building a nuclear family is the key to drug education and drug-abuse prevention. Drawing on the model of the strong, extended Greek family wherein the children grow up with strong bonds of affection and obligations to many generations of people, she says:

We are seeing increasing evidence in America, from the many parents' groups being formed, that despite the fragmentation of American family life, we can deliberately build an artificial extended family around a child, construct a "do-it-yourself" Greek family out of the parents of a child's friends, neighbors, coaches, pediatricians, etc., until a youngster knows clearly that many adults care about him (or her) and that his actions, especially negative behavior, will affect many people beside himself.[17]

What organization is better equipped to promote and facilitate the establishment of such do-it-yourself families as the local church or synagogue? What body of people espouses as its faith the principles that nurture individual and family health as does the religious community? What organization already promotes as its purpose the establishment and maintenance of fellowship? What person is better prepared to enable all this to occur among his parishioners and fellow community members than the minister? As far as the minister's own priorities are concerned, he does not have to act as drug expert, educator, counselor, or consultant; instead, he is the catalyst that creates the fellowship. In so doing he is in a position to fulfill the role God called him to, the one he believes is most important, in which he feels most effective and which he himself finds most enjoyable: "Minister to the ministers."

CHAPTER 2

The Clergy as Catalyst

We, the clergy, shall not be the alcohol or drug educators of the parish. Our role is to be the catalyst that creates an environment in which caring, sharing, learning, and growth can occur. Our hope is to prevent problems before they begin and to enable parishioners to choose lifestyles based on responsible decisions about the use of chemicals. This goal can be achieved only when individuals and families devote their time and interest to the requisite learning, not when we "inject" them with our knowledge. Building a do-it-yourself "Greek family," as described by Dr. Keith Schuchard, requires that we devote ourselves to promoting and maintaining an atmosphere of openness, honesty, and caring that minimizes or eliminates judgments, fear, denial, and prejudice. As catalysts, we are most effective when we stick to our business, the business no one else in the parish is trained or set aside to do—that is, ministering to the ministers. We can initiate the process, and we can participate in the process by preaching, inviting professionals, welcoming an Alcoholics Anonymous group, sitting in on classes, and helping the chemical-education chairperson, but we *are not* the process. If there is to be permanent change, it cannot be accomplished by one person pushing against the status quo; it must grow out of a common interest in, and commitment to, learning, growth, and change.

Our parishioners do not need us to be drug experts; they need us to interpret the issues of chemical use, misuse, and abuse in light of theology that has a practical application to their lives. They look to us to describe religious standards they can use as a basis for their own behavior and to suggest guidelines they can use to define their children's behavior. They want to know if their lives make a difference, if they are important, and just how their faith can help them find meaning in the face of a growing sense of obscurity. They want to know they can turn to us and that we will know what to do or where they can get help should trouble, sorrow, need, sickness, or other adversity arise. Our congregations look to us for leadership;

whether we like it or not, whether we have a religious stand on alcohol and drug abuse or not, we are their spiritual, moral, and ethical leaders.

In 1981 the Connecticut Mutual Life Insurance Company sought to ascertain what influenced Americans' values. It asked the New York firm of Research and Forecasts to conduct a study. All were surprised to learn that Americans' religious commitment has a greater impact in determining differences in values than age, race, sex, income, or political viewpoint. It also found that religious leaders were the group most admired by the public and closest to the public's views.[1] The public not only looks to us for direction in dealing with the number one *religious issue* of today (alcohol) and the number three issue (drugs), it has confidence in our leadership and it trusts that we shall address the family's major concern. Honesty and intelligence are the top qualities Americans look for in their leaders. The Connecticut study revealed the clergy is the group most trusted because of these two characteristics. It showed that our people believe in us and believe us. That is an awesome responsibility!

A MODEL FOR A "GREEK FAMILY"

Creating a fellowship, an extended Greek family, takes time and planning. Depending on the size of the congregation and where it is located (inner city, suburbia, or country), the methods will vary. Nevertheless, there are proven principles by which to facilitate the building and maintenance of a spiritual fellowship; they are found in one of the greatest spiritual movements of all times, Alcoholics Anonymous (AA). It is ironic that AA should now be a model for a fellowship because some of its roots are in the Church. Today its precepts of personal sharing, caring, and support are the basis of many major health-restoring organizations and groups, e.g., those within the Church—Faith at Work, Marriage Encounter, Cursillo, and those outside the Church—Al-Anon, Ala-teen, Narc-Anon, Overeaters Anonymous, Smoke Enders, Gamblers Anonymous, and most forms of group therapy. In each, the theological formula of confession, repentance, reconciliation, and redemption is the basis of new health and wholeness. The Reverend Samuel M. Shoemaker, an Episcopal minister much beloved for his lifelong work with alcoholics in the New York City area, described these fundamental principles in a tract entitled "What the Church Has to Learn from Alcoholics Anonymous." Because it provides the basis for building a fellowship, it is presented here in its entirety.

God chose what is foolish in the world to shame the wise, God chose what is weak in the world to shame the strong. . . . I Corinthians 1:26

During the weekend of the Fourth of July last, I attended one of the most remarkable conventions I ever expect to attend. It was a gathering in St. Louis of about five thousand members of the movement called Alcoholics Anonymous. The occasion was the celebration of their twentieth anniversary, and the turning over freely and voluntarily of the management and destiny of that great movement by the founders and "old timers" to a board which represents the fellowship as a whole.

As I lived and moved among these men and women for three days, I was moved as I have seldom been moved in my life. It happens that I have watched the unfolding of this movement with more than usual interest, for its real founder and guiding spirit, Bill W_____, found his initial spiritual answer at Calvary Church in New York, when I was rector there, in 1935. Having met two men, unmistakable alcoholics, who had found release from their difficulty, he was moved to seek out the same answer for himself. But he went further. Being of a foraging and inquiring mind, he began to think there was some general law operating here, which could be made to work, not in two men's lives only, but in two thousand or two million. He set to work to find out what it was. He consulted psychiatrists, doctors, clergy and recovered alcoholics to discover what it was.

The first actual group was not in New York, but in Akron, Ohio. Bill was spending a weekend there in a hotel. The crowd was moving towards the bar. He was lonely and felt danger assailing him. He consulted the church-directory in the hotel lobby, and found the name of a local clergyman and his church. He called him on the telephone and said, "I am an alcoholic down here at the hotel. The going is a little hard just now. Have you anybody you think I might meet and talk to?" He gave him the name of a woman who belonged to one of the great tire-manufacturing families. He called her, she invited him out at once and said she had a man she wanted to have meet him. While he was on his way, she called Dr. Bob S_____ and his wife Anne. Dr. Bob said he'd give her five minutes. He stayed five hours and told Bill, "You're the only man I've ever seen with the answer to alcoholism." They invited Bill over from the hotel to stay at their house. And there was begun, twenty years ago, the first actual Alcoholics Anonymous group.

The number of them now is beyond count. Some say there are 160,000 to 200,000 recovered alcoholics, but nobody knows how many extend beyond this into the fringes of the unknown. They say that each alcoholic holds within the orbit of his problem an average of fourteen persons who are affected by it. This means that conservatively two and a half million people's lives are different because of the existence of Alcoholics Anonymous. There is hardly a city or town or even hamlet now where you cannot find a group, strong and well-knit, or struggling in its infancy. Prof. Austin McCormick, of Berkeley, California, former Commissioner of Correction in the city of New York, who was also with us at the St. Louis Convention, said once in my hearing that AA may "prove to be one of the greatest movements of all time." That was years ago. Subsequent facts support his prophecy.

On the Sunday morning of the convention, I was asked to talk to them, together with Fr. Edward Dowling S.J., a wonderful Roman Catholic priest who has done notable service for AA in interpreting it to his people, and Dr. Jim S_____, a most remarkable black physician of Washington, on the spiritual aspects of the AA program. They are very generous to non-alcoholics, but I should have preferred that it be a bona fide alcoholic that did the speaking.

In the course of what I said to them, I remarked that I thought it had been wise for AA to confine its activity to alcoholics. But, I added, "I think we may see an effect of AA on medicine, on psychiatry, on correction, on the ever-present problem of human nature; and not least on the Church. AA indirectly derived much of its inspiration from the Church. Now perhaps the time has come for the Church to be reawakened and re-vitalized by those insights and practices found in AA."

I think some of you may be a little horrified at this suggestion. I fear you will be saying to yourself, "What have we, who have always been decent people, to learn from a lot of reconstructed drunks?" And perhaps you may thereby reveal to yourself how very far you are from the spirit of Christ and the Gospel, and how very much in need of precisely the kind of check-up that may come to us from AA. If I need a text for what I say to you, there is one ready to hand in I Corinthians 1:26, ". . . God chose what is foolish in the world to shame the wise. God chose what is weak in the world to shame the strong." I need not remind you that there is a good deal of sarcasm in that verse; because it must be evident that anything God can use is neither foolish nor weak, and that if we consider ourselves wise and strong, we may need to go to school to those we have called foolish and weak.

The first thing I think the Church needs to learn from AA is that nobody gets anywhere till he recognizes a clearly-defined need. These people do not come to AA to get made a little better. They do not come because the best people are doing it. They come because they are desperate. They are not ladies and gentlemen looking for a religion, they are utterly desperate men and women in search of redemption. Without what AA gives, death stares them in the face. With what AA gives them, there is life and hope. There are not a dozen ways, there are not two ways, there is one way; and they find it, or perish. AA's each and all have a definite, desperate need. They have the need and they are ready to tell somebody what it is if they see the least chance that it can be met.

Is there anything as definite for you or me, who may happen not to be alcoholics? If there is, I am sure that it lies in the realm of our conscious withholding of the truth about ourselves from God and from one another, by pretending that we are already good Christians. Let me here quote a member of AA who has written a most amazing book: his name is Jerome Ellison, and the book is "Report to the Creator." In this (p. 210) he says, "The relief of being accepted can never be known by one who never thought himself unaccepted. I hear of 'good Christian men and women' belonging to 'fine old church families.' There were no good Christians in the first church, only sinners. Peter never let himself or his hearers forget his betrayal in the hour the cock crew. James, stung by the memory of his years of stubborn resistance, warned the church members: 'Confess your faults to one another.' That was before there were fine old church families. Today the last place where one can be candid about one's faults is in church. In a bar, yes, in a church, no. I know; I've tried both places." Let that sting you and me just as it should, and make us miserable with our church Pharisaism till we see it just as definite and just as hideous as anybody's drunkenness can ever be, and a great deal more really dangerous.

The second thing the Church needs to learn from AA is that men are redeemed in a life-changing fellowship. AA does not expect to let anybody who comes in stay as he is. They know he is in need and must have help. They live for nothing else but to extend and keep extending that help. Like the Church, they did not begin in glorious Gothic structures, but in houses or caves in the earth,—wherever they could get a foot-hold, meet people, and gather. It never occurs to an AA that it is enough for him to sit down and polish his spiritual nails all by himself, or dust off his soul all by himself, or spend a couple of minutes praying each day all by himself. His soul gets kept in order by trying to help other people get their souls in order, with the help of God. At once a new person takes his place in this redeeming, life-changing fellowship. He may be changed today, and out working tomorrow—no long, senseless delays about giving away what he has got. He's ready to give the little he has the moment it comes to him. The fellowship that redeemed him will wither and die unless he and others like him get in and keep that fellowship moving and growing by reaching others. Recently I heard an AA say that he could stay away from his Veteran's meeting, his Legion, or his Church, and nobody would notice it. But if he stayed away from his AA meeting, his telephone would begin to ring the next day!

"A life-changing fellowship" sounds like a description of the Church. It is of the ideal Church. But the actual? Not one in a hundred is like this. The laymen says this is the minister's job, and the ministers say it is the evangelist's job, and everybody finds a rationalized excuse for not doing what every Christian ought to be doing, i.e., bringing other people into the redeeming, life-changing fellowship.

The third thing the Church needs to learn from AA is the necessity for definite personal dealing with people. AA's know all the stock excuses—they've used them themselves and heard them a hundred Times. All the blame put on someone else—my temperament is different—I've tried it and it doesn't work for me— I'm not really so bad, I just slip a little sometimes. They've heard them all, and know them for the rationalized pack of lies they are. They constitute, taken together, the Gospel of Hell and Failure. I've heard them laboring with one another, now patient as a mother, now savage as a prize-fighter, now careful in explanation, now pounding in a heavy personal challenge, but always knowing the desperate need and the sure answer.

Are we in the Church like that? Have you ever been drastically dealt with by anybody? Have you ever dared to be drastic in love with anybody? We are so official, so polite, so ready to accept ourselves and each other at face value. I went for years before ever I met a man that dared get at my real needs, create a situation in which I could be honest with him, and hold me to a specific Christian commitment and decision. One can find kindness and even good advice in the Church. That is not all men need. They need to be helped to face themselves just as they are. The AA people see themselves as they really are. I think many of us in the Church see ourselves as we should like to appear to others, not as we are before God. We need drastic personal dealing and challenge. Who is ready and trained to give it to us? How many of us have ever taken a 'fearless moral inventory' of ourselves, and dared make the depth of our need known to any other human being? This gets at the pride which is the hindrance and sticking-point for so many of us, and which, for most of us in the Church, has never even been recognized, let alone faced or dealt with.

The fourth thing the Church needs to learn from AA is the necessity for a real change of heart, a true conversion. As we come Sunday after Sunday, year after year, we are supposed to be in a process of transfor-mation. Are we? The AA's are. At each meeting there are people seeking and in conscious need. Everybody is pulling for the people who speak, and looking for more insight and help. They are pushed by their need. They are pulled by the inspiration of others who are growing. They are a society of the "before and after," with a clear line between the old life and the new. This is not the difference between sinfulness and perfection, but it is the difference between accepted wrongdoing and the genuine beginning of a new way of life.

How about us? Again I quote Jerome Ellison in his report to God (p. 205): " . . . I began to see that many of the parishioners did not really want to find You, because finding You would change them from their habitual ways, and they did not want to endure the pain of change . . . For our churchmanlike crimes of bland, impenetrable pose, I offer shame . . ." I suppose that the sheer visibility of the alcoholic problem creates a kind of enforced honesty; but surely if we are exposed again and again to God, to Christ, to the Cross, there should be a breaking down of our pride and unwillingness to change. We should know by now that this unwillingness, multiplied by thousands and tens of thousands, is what is the matter with the Church, and what keeps it from being what God means it to be on earth. The change must begin somewhere. We know it ought to begin in us.

One of the greatest things the Church should learn from AA is the need people have for an exposure to living Christian experience. In thousands of places, alcoholics (and others) can go and hear recovered alcoholics speak about their experiences and watch the process of new life and outlook take place before their eyes. There you have it, the need and the answer to the need, right before your eyes. They say that their public relations are based, not on promotion, but on attraction. This attraction begins when you see people with problems like your own, hear them speaking freely of the answers they are finding, and realize that such honesty and such change is exactly what you need yourself.

No ordinary service of worship in the Church can possibly do this. We need to supplement what we do now by the establishment of informal companies where people who are spiritually seeking can see how faith takes hold in other lives, how the characteristically Christian experience comes to them. Some churches are doing this, but not nearly enough of them. One I know where on Sunday evenings laymen and women speak simply about what has happened to them spiritually; it is drawing many more by attraction. This needs to be multiplied by the tens of thousands, and the church itself awakened.

As I looked out over that crowd of five thousand in Kiel Auditorium in St. Louis, I said to myself, "Would that the Church were like this— ordinary men and women with great need who have found a great Answer, and do not hesitate to make it known wherever they can—a trained army of enthusiastic, humble, human workers whose efforts make life a different thing for other people!"

Let us ask God to forgive our blindness and laziness and complacency and through these re-made people to learn our need for honesty, for conversion, for fellowship and for honest witness![2]

The value of Samuel Shoemaker's tract is that it offers us vision and insight we can tailor to our own congregations. Our aim is to build a sense of community, a family in which parishioners can satisfy their "need for honesty, for conversion, for fellowship and for honest witness." This is the minister's ministry. Each of us must decide how to implement these principles, but some practical ideas in each of Samuel Shoemaker's categories are useful.

"The first thing I think the Church needs to learn from AA is that nobody gets anywhere till he recognizes a clearly-defined need."

1. We can legitimize people's need for each other by preaching about the disintegration of family life and individual lifestyles.

2. . . . promote sharing of needs by being openly honest about our own frailties and mistakes.

3. . . . ask members of the congregation to witness publicly on "the worst or most painful thing that ever happened to me" or "the greatest mistake I ever made" or "my deepest regret"—i.e., confess faults to one another.

4. . . . hold parish suppers or a common Thanksgiving Day dinner for those without relatives or apart from family.

5. . . . pray for needs of specific individuals, friends, group causes, etc.

"The second thing the Church needs to learn from AA is that men are redeemed in a life-changing fellowship."

1. We can list those in trouble, sorrow, need, sickness, and adversity and ask parishioners to call on, write, or phone them.

2. . . . put suffering people in touch with those (inside or outside the congregation) who have had similar experiences.

3. . . . ask specific youngsters to respond to the needs of shut-ins or older people by shopping, snow shoveling, lawn mowing, or running errands.

4. . . . set up a committee to telephone those parishioners who are absent for a long time.

5. . . . open our facilities to AA and other such groups.

"The third thing the Church needs to learn from AA is the necessity for definite personal dealing with people."

1. We can establish in our churches or synagogues a "peer-counseling" or a "peer-tutoring" program for adolescents. Create a substitute father/mother program for children of single-parent families.

2. . . . teach a course on how to minister to one another—a "School of Pastoral Care for Lay People."

3. . . . teach the discipline of self-examination, taking a moral inventory, journal writing.

4. . . . build a "My Brother's Keeper Network" of people willing to cooperate in identifying early signs of problems in each other's children.

5. . . . send specific members to training programs for paraprofessionals, e.g., the Johnson Institute (alcohol and drugs), Compassionate Friends, Inc. (bereaved parents and their families), the Hospice Program (on death and dying).

"The fourth thing the Church needs to learn from AA is the necessity for a real change of heart, a true conversion."

1. We can ask members of various spiritual depths to preach once a month and help them to do so.

2. . . . teach an adult-education course on the ethical and moral problems of the day, on Bible, on Mission.

3. . . . take a talent/ability inventory of the congregation, to be used as a bank of parish resources or resource persons.

4. . . . enlist such people to offer their talents in the parish and in the community as lay ministers.

5. . . . establish witness groups, prayer groups, divorce/separated groups, parent-support groups, etc.

The suggestions in each of these four categories serve no purpose at all if they do not enable people to feel that they are members of a redemptive community, that they are ransomed, healed, restored, forgiven by God, and that they are witnesses of his grace. According to Samuel Shoemaker's tract, the greatest lesson we can learn from the AA model is that *the* fundamental principle of establishing a spiritual body is the promotion of spiritual health. It leads to the fulfillment of human potential and ultimately to a community in which there is mutual concern, interdependence, and social responsibility. When we stick to our goal of creating a spiritual fellowship, we are building a sound foundation from which to address the practical issues of chemical health.

We who are ministers, priests, and rabbis cannot tell people how to live, nor can we make them accept our ideas. We cannot communicate the love of God by being rigid, authoritarian dogmatists. If we hope to enable our congregations to discover the responsible use of chemicals, if we want to build a caring fellowship based on the model Samuel Shoemaker suggests, then we, the respected leaders, are going to have to be exemplary learners as well as catalysts. We must be examples for those we hope will themselves become models—models in the community, but more importantly, in the home. This does not mean we must be experts on alcohol and drug use, misuse, or abuse, in the hope our families will become experts. Rather, it means we must teach parishioners to be open to ideas that will change their attitudes and behavior by being open ourselves. It means discovering and exchanging ideas together.

All of us who have ever reflected on a favorite teacher know that our willingness to learn from him or her was directly related to the positive feelings and mutual respect in the learning environment. There was no perceived threat of censure, judgment, or rejection, only openness, interest and acceptance between the professor and the class and among members of the class. Not only did we learn but we loved learning, we integrated the ideas into our experience, we changed, we grew. It was both exciting and fun.

It is mutual concern, accurate information, openness, shared communication, and education in responsible decision making that will contribute most to an environment of chemical health. The extent to which this environment becomes a healthy lifestyle depends largely on how it is regarded by the community. Though we cannot be responsible for the attitudes of an entire town, we can make certain our religious institution is a nurturing environment. Its atmosphere will clearly be set by our example—by our process as well as content. Ultimately, one hopes, we will have an influence on societal attitudes, because society is made up of families and families are looking to their ministers for guidance.

DEALING WITH RESISTANCE

Patience is a key element in chemical education. *Patience*. It has taken years for parishioners to form their attitudes toward alcohol and drug use. They come to us with preconceived notions that are a part of their families' legacies. There are many whose parents lived through Prohibition, the most divisive movement in U.S. history, who still hold the belief that the most effective way to deal with any problem is the way of Prohibition—to draw up a list of "thou shalt nots" . . . rules, regulations, and commandments. Movies, TV, and magazines constantly normalize drug use. The pharmaceutical corporations and the beer, wine, and liquor companies have a vested interest in convincing people that the way to a pain-free and fun-filled life is by consuming their products. Better living through chemistry is a civil religion preached by the most powerful persuaders of all—the media—and our people are believers. Finally, there is the covert but powerful manipulation of the multi-billion-dollar illicit drug industry. Some of our parishioners are its consumers, too.

All these factors add up to one thing: The members of a congregation are as irrational in their attitudes about alcohol and drugs as they are in their prejudices on race, religion, or sex. And the issues they must face are laden with emotions, the most deep-seated being fear, fear of change, fear to change. It is called "denial."

"What's he preaching on alcoholism or drug abuse for? We don't have a problem in this synagogue!"

"How come we're setting up a chemical-education fellowship? That's not the Church's business."

"If we talk about chemical use in the church school, kids will want to try it."

"Instead of talking about responsible decisions, I want my priest to make my husband quit smoking."

"My pastor is a good preacher, but I would never come to him with a problem; he drinks."

"Peer counselors? I don't want my kid hanging around or counseling any druggies!"

"Our minister wants to let AA use the church. I'm against it, those drunks will damage our property."

Denial: The hesitancy to look at a problem for fear it will reveal something unpleasant, unacceptable, or troublesome. It's much easier to ignore it, to hide it, or to blame the problem on someone or something other than the cause. Denial is the number one symptom of alcoholism and drug dependency, and it is the number one symptom of a church or synagogue that resists learning about substance use. In the case of the person suffering from alcohol or drug dependency, denial exists because he cannot see the disease within him; his ability to assess his health is impaired. In the case of the church or synagogue, denial is the primary form of resistance because the members will not face the "disease" within themselves. People do not like to face distressing issues. Given a choice, they do not seek out perplexing problems. Their whole thrust is to escape pain or to anesthetize it—hence the popularity of chemicals. Why, then, would they be the least bit interested in going to a church, a hallowed place of serenity and peace, to discuss a disturbing or frightening problem? Suppose they heard something they did not want to hear? Suppose they learned facts that forced them to face home problems they had been ignoring? Confronting and resolving difficult issues is painful; it results in frustration or anger or anxiety or fear or sadness or regret or guilt; it is more comfortable to deny the difficult things.

Denial will wear many masks in any group asked to learn about chemical use and abuse. Like so-called reaction-formations, these masks are defenses that protect a person from pain and help him avoid problems. The most effective minister is the one who remembers that while change is taking place, these masks are legitimate and should not be torn away, for they can be transformed into new strengths. Some people will minimize the need for education. Others will ignore or pretend the problems do not exist. Some will try to skirt the issues rather than face them, and others will rationalize them away. Many will intellectualize and resist looking at the effect of misuse on the family, the church, or the synagogue. Still others will agressively blame alcohol and drug problems on other people or agencies. In all these cases, it is most important for us to remember not to take this resistance as a personal affront. Rather, it is in identifying these defenses that the priest, minister, or rabbi must know where to be most empathic and how best to plant the seeds for growth.

God asks us to be sowers of the seed; he does not demand that we be "growlights" forcing the plants to mature. Furthermore, he does not promise that the harvest belongs to us. Chemical education is not a matter of injecting a fearful congregation full of information in a one-shot presentation and then expecting or demanding that the quick fix is enough. If we are going to establish a caring relationship with a fifteen-, sixteen-, or seventeen-year-old so we can discuss the pros and cons of drug use, we must begin by expressing interest in him when he is five, six, and seven. It takes time for seeds to grow, for emotions to surface, for attitudes to change. If the clergyperson seeks to force a change of attitudes, behavior patterns, and lifestyles, his or her sense of urgency is construed by parishioners to mean disapproval. It makes them feel unaccepted and unacceptable. The impatience says to them, "You are not acceptable to me as a person until you change." This is hardly a reflection of the love of God. Patience, however, is; it communicates acceptance of a person where he is, not where we want him to be.

THE DISINTEGRATION OF THE FAMILY

When we create a fellowship that hopes to establish a chemical-education program to meet the expressed concerns of our people, not only is it useful to keep in mind the many masks of denial that will block individual change, it is helpful to appreciate why our parish families are resistant to change. Family educator H. Stephen Glenn, in his excellent booklet *Strengthening the Family*, acknowledges that the two essential roles of the family are: "First . . . the primary support system that individuals turn to in order to get their basic needs met. Second . . . the essential mechanism by which a child born with nothing but potential develops the capability to survive and function as an adequate person within his or her world."[3] He feels, however, that there has been a significant disintegration in the family over the last thirty years: the highest divorce rate ever; the highest rate of child abuse, spouse abuse, desertion, neglect, and sedativism; the highest rate of adolescent suicide, teenage pregnancy, and violent juvenile crimes; and the highest rate of alcoholism and drug dependency. The disintegration, he says, is clearly the inherent result of families in transition.[4]

Glenn illustrates the impact of this transition by pointing out that "in 1930 a child spent an average of three to four hours a day in interaction, actively involved in relevant experiences with various members of his immediate extended family."[5] In 1982, however, the average ten-year-old or older, from a two-parent family, spent only fourteen and a half minutes in interaction during a typical twenty-four-hour day. Of those fourteen and a half minutes, "12½ were spent with parents issuing warnings or correcting things that had gone wrong. There were about two minutes available for positive communication, assuming there was no lingering trauma from the previous 12½ minutes."[6]

Journalist Marie Winn, in her book *Children Without Childhood*, suggests that this disintegration has, in the last decade, robbed many middle-class American kids between ages six and twelve of their most precious birthright— childhood itself. Where once the typical fifth-grader was naive and ignorant of adult concerns, now he or she is aware not just of sex and violence, which are seen daily on TV, but of injustice, fear of death, adult frailty and cruelty, political corruption, and economic instability. Winn attributes this loss of innocence to the sexual revolution of the sixties, the soaring American divorce rate that has introduced children to parental self-centeredness, the parents' sexual freedom, the mass movement of women from the home into the workplace, and the "new-era child rearing" in which the child is asked to jump the generation gap and be an equal partner in his own parenting. The results are disastrous, Winn feels. Children do not grow, develop, and mature properly when they are treated as adults. Instead, what they need most is the safety of dependency, the security of their inherent inequality, and the opportunity for prolonged innocence in which they can devote their energies to learning, play, and skills that lead to creativity and achievement.[7]

When we look at the disintegration of the family in terms of lifestyles, the major transitions in the last half century make it obvious that the only constant in family life is change. Stephen Glenn provides a thought-provoking list:

MAJOR TRANSITIONS IN LIFESTYLE[8]

Norm, 1930	Norm, 1978
High family interaction	Low family interaction
Homogeneous value system	Heterogeneous value system
Consonant role model	Dissonant role model
Logical consequences experienced	Logical consequences avoided
Many informal associations with different generations	Few intergenerational associations
Less education	More education
Low level of information	High level of information
Low technology	High technology
Many non-negotiable tasks	Few non-negotiable tasks
Much family work	Little family work
Large families	Smaller families
Extended family dominant	Nuclear family dominant
Few broken homes (10–15%)	Many broken homes (38–42%)
Little anonymity	General anonymity

The value of these comparisons is that by looking back at the past we can find the principles that once nurtured individual and family health and apply them to the present. Listing seven significant steps in the development of strong, capable individuals, Glenn asserts we can provide or teach:

1. Identification with Viable Role Models: This refers to a person's reference group and self-concept.

2. Identification with and Responsibility for Family Process: In this context, "Family" is used in a broad sense: relationships with another person, in groups, mankind, God.

3. Faith in Personal Resources to Solve Problems: This refers to the skills and attitudes necessary to work through problems and the belief that they can be solved through the application of personal resources.

4. Adequate Development of Intra-Personal Skills: Those which a person uses to communicate with self; self-discipline, self-control, self-assessment.

5. Adequate Development of Inter-Personal Skills: Those which enable a person to relate to or build a relationship with another person.

6. Development of Systemic Skills: Learning responsibility, adaptability and flexibility.

7. Development of Judgmental Skills: The ability to recognize, understand and apply relationships.[9]

There is a change within and without. There is a loss of individual and family identity. There is a sense of hopelessness in the face of the forces that control a person's life. There are no longer the strong ties that bind and provide the security of belonging—not at home, not at work, not at worship. Generally, there is a lack of meaning and purpose in people's lives as a result of all this, a pervading sense of rootlessness. It isn't any wonder, therefore, that the Connecticut Mutual Life Insurance Company's survey found that the reason for the current religious revival is too much disruption and change. People are seeking to ground themselves in something firm and lasting. Religion, respondents told the survey, provides roots.

"In light of this, what do we seem to be heading for?" asks world-renowned therapist Virginia Satir in her book *People Making*:

> A more responsible human being who can make choices; who can plan according to his needs and not according to someone else's plan for him; someone who will recognize that there are differences concerning people, as well as predictable similarities.

> I think we are in the beginning of another evolution in the history of man. Probably never before have so many people been so discouraged and dissatisfied with the state of the human condition as now. Everywhere, there are huge pockets of people demanding change. The main cry seems to be for greater feelings of individual self-esteem and loving, nurturing contexts that go with it.[10]

Religious institutions are unique in that providing the loving, nurturing contexts for Glenn's seven steps of development to occur is one of the natural functions of a worshipping community. Samuel Shoemaker's tract outlines the model we can use. The clergy are already seen as role models. The key elements to support, to educate, to effect change, therefore, are already in existence as a natural part of the church's business; in fact, they *are* the Church's business.

FINDING A "SPARK PLUG," BUILDING A "CORE GROUP"

It is within the context of this church fellowship that we can initiate a program for chemical education and drug-abuse prevention. We can do so with one of the "companies" Shoemaker suggested. The goal is to establish a core group of knowledgeable parishioners, recovering alcoholics, recovering drug users, affected family members, and concerned people who will serve on the chemical-education committee and act as primary resources for dealing with problems in the parish and the community. Since we do not want to be responsible for the process itself, the extent of our involvement at this level is to select a "spark plug," a self-motivated starter, who will assemble this company. The success of an effective chemical-health program depends on who we ask to be that "spark plug." The person or persons will be, in effect, the lay equivalent of the minister. It would be helpful if he or she has some understanding of substance use, nonuse, misuse, and abuse, but that is not mandatory. What *is* vital is that this person be a facilitator of learning and growth more than an imparter of information. It is also important that his or her own personal values, attitudes, opinions, and decisions about alcohol or drug use not reflect judgments of right or wrong, superior or inferior, moral or immoral. The facilitator will find it much easier to build a group and establish rapport with the members if he has an attitude of acceptance that shows respect for, and understanding of, differing individuals and their lifestyles. To those ends the "spark plug" should be:

1. Respected—to give the committee and the concept immediate respectability and acceptability.

2. Tolerant—to help establish the tone of openness, honesty, and caring that eliminates judgment, fear, denial, and prejudice.

3. Charitable—to communicate a sense of warmth and acceptance that draws hesitant parishioners into the program.

4. Trustworthy—to be available as the recipient of confidential information.

5. Committed—to have the time, patience, and energy to move the idea out into the congregation.

One note of caution: If a recovering alcoholic or recovering drug abuser is selected to be the "spark plug," it must be made clear to him that he is to be a facilitator of people, not a teacher or an expert witness by virtue of his personal experience. One of the fundamental characteristics of many a recovering person is the need to be *in* control and the need *to* control, hence AA's slogan, "Let go and let God." Very often this need is incompatible with the aims of group process and is counterproductive to the open-ended communication and dialogue necessary for group maintenance. Therefore, if a recovering person is selected as the "spark plug," it is very important to appoint someone who has no chemical-dependency problem as chairperson of the core group. By the same token, selecting a parent whose child has been imparied by drug abuse may meet the requirements of enlisting a committed person, but in some cases the injury is such that it blocks the person's ability to tolerate others' attitudes, values, or lifestyles. Though it is hard for them to be facilitators, they are invaluable as members of the core group.

There is a ready-made core group in every church and synagogue. There are recovering alcoholics and recovering drug abusers, there are families who have been affected by chemical dependency, there are parents whose children are reaching the vulnerable age of ten, eleven, or twelve, or the driving age of sixteen. There are some youngsters who seek to resist temptation by learning how to say no, still others who want a basis for making responsible decisions about alcohol/drug use, and there are many adults who have a vested interest in being a part of a goal-oriented chemical-education/drug-abuse prevention program. Each person will have his or her own reasons for wanting to be involved in the group. For one it may be to obtain useful information; for another, to satisfy the need to be a part of a supportive family; for a parent it may be to establish communications with other parents who want to prevent problems; and for yet another, to learn whether he or she is suffering from misuse of chemicals. Whatever their reasons, these are people who are already primed to be members of a chemical-health committee. The minister usually knows who these people are and has only to ask them if he can give their names to the leader or chairperson of the core group. By seeking this permission, he signals to the church or synagogue his backing of this program. By announcing his search for people to help his "spark plug" develop a program of alcohol/drug education and drug-abuse prevention, he is the catalyst who promotes change.

EQUIPMENT FOR THE CLERGY

Some ministers, priests, and rabbis feel too inadequate or too uneducated to initiate a program of chemical health. They believe that to be equipped to meet their parishioners' questions about the specifics of substance use, misuse, and abuse it is necessary for them to know in detail about the psychological and physiological effects of the drugs most likely to be misused or abused. Not so; other professionals can provide that information, which the parishioners will acquire in their own search-and-discovery process. What we, the clergy, need is simply the information that will suit our own purposes, that is:

1. A theoretical basis for understanding the problems of alcoholism and drug abuse.

2. A pastoral yardstick for defining and determining chemical dependency.

3. A list of resources and resource persons to whom we can turn.

4. A theological perspective for understanding chemical use and for addressing chemical abuse.

Each of the above can be gained either from this book or by ordering the information listed below.

1. A theoretical basis for understanding the problems of alcoholism and drug abuse.

For further reading: The Reverend Joseph L. Kellerman's twenty-seven-page classic, "Alcoholism: A Guide for Ministers and Other Church Leaders," available from religious bookstores and the North Carolina Pastoral Care Council on Alcohol and Drug Abuse, Department of Human Resources, State of North Carolina, 325 North Salisbury Street, Raleigh, NC 27611, or Keller-man's "Alcoholism: A Guide for the Clergy," from the National Council on Alcoholism, 733 Third Avenue, New York, NY 10017 (ask also for the "Clergy Kit," $5.00). Two other helpful books are: *Seixes' Alcohol: What It Is, What It Does* and *Tobias's Pot: What It Is, What It Does,* available for $2.95 each from PRIDE, 100 Edgewood Avenue, Suite 1216, Atlanta, GA 30303; (800) 284-4241. The best text for clergy wanting to understand the overall effects of alcoholism on the victim and the family and the hope and health that is available is Sharon Wegscheider's 1981 book *Second Chance,* from Science and Behavior Books, Inc., 701 Welch Road, Palo Alto, CA 94306; $12.95.

2. A pastoral yardstick for defining and determining chemical dependency.

This yardstick is provided by this book. For more information, write to the Johnson Institute, 10700 Olson Memorial Highway, Minneapolis, MN 55441, (612) 544-4165, for the following tracts:

Chemical Dependency and Recovery Are a Family Affair (38 pages)	$1.95
Making Choices (24 pages)	1.75
Alcoholism: A Treatable Disease (19 pages)	.75
Some Perspectives on Alcoholism (16 pages)	.75
Medical Consequences of Alcoholism (15 pages)	.75
The Family Enablers (16 pages)	.75
Recovery of Chemically Dependent Families (9 pages)	.75
Dynamics of Addiction (see above; 11 pages)	.75
Intervention: A Professional's Guide (9 pages)	.75
	TOTAL $8.95

The clergy should also have a two-book lending library consisting of *I'll Quit Tomorrow* by Vernon Johnson (Harper & Row, $10.95) and *Marijuana Today* by George K. Russell (Myrin Institute for Adult Education, 521 Park Avenue, New York, NY 10021, $3.95).

3. *A list of knowledgeable parishioners, resources, helpful profession-als, referral services, and support groups we can use to help those interested or in need.*

To this end we must have a first-hand acquaintance with the professionals and leaders of the helping agencies. This means calling them or calling on them. Forms are provided in this manual.

4. *A theological perspective for understanding chemical use and for addressing chemical abuse.*

For further reading: T. Furman Hewitt's excellent 46-page booklet "A Biblical Perspective on the Use and Abuse of Alcohol and Other Drugs," available from most religious bookstores or the North Carolina Pastoral Care Council on Alcohol and Drug Abuse.

These are the tools of our trade. Though there are many more we might read and several are listed here as resources, it is not necessary for us to become practitioners in the field. The works mentioned above are sufficient to satisfy most pastoral interests and to enable us to support a program of chemical health. Unless we intend to become chemical-dependency specialists, we don't have the time, the training, or, as was shown in chapter 1, the interest or inclination to take on the responsibilities of being a parish or community expert. If we can build a spiritual fellowship, a "Greek family" in which growth can occur, if we can speak to the theological issues of chemical health, if we can identify the symptoms of alcoholism and drug abuse, if we can suggest resources and get resource persons or agencies to help us minister to those in need, then we are fulfilling our most useful, most enjoyable, most effective role—that of catalyst. Beyond that, the promotion of chemical health and the prevention of chemical dependency belongs to the parishioners, and the job of building such a program belongs to the "spark plug" and the core group.

CHAPTER 3

Prohibition or Prevention?

The church is beginning to see that there is much more to society's problems with alcohol than getting the problem drinker to A.A. There are some events and actions which show promise that the church is moving away from its old battle about drinking and not drinking to a much broader concern which sees that the chief issue is not just about a chemical, but a whole range of problems and attitudes, philosophies and values which affect and are affected by our use of alcohol.

One of the conclusions which can be drawn about the work of the churches in relation to alcohol problems over the last 35 years is that more and more of them are moving from concern primarily about the chemical, alcohol, to a comprehensive, holistic approach to the whole range of societal problems associated with its misuse; and then beyond that to help persons live their lives in such ways as to avoid trouble with alcohol in the first place.

David C. Hancock[1]

AVOIDING TROUBLE IN THE FIRST PLACE

Prevention! Prevention means stopping a problem before its starts.

We have all heard the saying, "An ounce of prevention is worth a pound of cure." Translated into the metric parlance of the chemical-dependency field, this would be, "A gram of prevention is worth a kilo of treatment." Just as the airline industry believes that all care and safety procedures are a matter of preventive maintenance, so it is the clergy's first priority to address the issues of substance use, misuse, and abuse from that standpoint. In the alcohol and drug field, efforts to keep a problem from developing before it begins is known as "primary prevention." It is usually accomplished through education. To interrupt or try to stop a problem that has already begun is known as "secondary prevention." The procedure is called "early intervention," and it requires special training. Finally, the treatment of a person who has become chemically dependent is known as "tertiary prevention," although the term "prevention" is a misnomer because the problem is already an acute illness. Treatment consists of a program prescribed for the chemically dependent person. For pastoral purposes, primary prevention is the most appropriate avenue to follow, for education is the one approach that has a beneficial effect on the greatest number of people. What's more, it is the only form of prevention our theological education has equipped us to initiate. We simply are not qualified to offer secondary or tertiary prevention, i.e., early intervention or treatment. Most clergy, however, have had some training in religious education, the purpose and principles of which are the same as those of primary prevention—the promotion of health and wholeness.

We ministers, priests, and rabbis are the only care-giving professionals who have daily or weekly access to the members of a congregation or parish. As Gallup's poll shows, we head the list of respected leaders and are looked to for guidance. It is clear our most useful and effective ministry will be in preventive maintenance. The goal, therefore, is to stop the problem before it starts, by enabling God's people to make responsible decisions about the use of his gifts—namely, chemicals. Prevention is primary! The question is, *prevention of what?*

PREVENTION OF WHAT?

Individual Use

Do we want to prevent the use of alcohol?

Do we want to prevent the use of alcohol and illicit drugs?

Do we want to prevent the use of licit drugs for illicit purposes?

Do we want to allow the use of alcohol but prevent the use of illicit drugs?

Do we want to prevent the use of alcohol and illicit drugs by specific age groups, e.g., adolescents?

Do we want to prevent potential harm to specific or vulnerable populations, e.g., children of alcoholics, pregnant women?

Do we want to prevent the use of alcohol or drugs in certain situations, e.g., drinking and driving, athletic contests, operating machines?

Do we want to prevent all use of alcohol until a certain age has been reached, e.g., eighteen, twenty, or twenty-one?

Since use is in fact abuse, do we want to prevent the use of any and all harmful drugs, e.g., marijuana and tobacco?

Do we want to prevent use from becoming abuse by restricting or limiting quantity or dosage?

Family Use

Do we want to prevent the use of alcohol by children at family celebrations?

Do we want to prevent the misuse of alcohol by parents?

Do we want to prevent the use of alcohol at family-sponsored teenage parties?

Do we want to prevent any use of illicit drugs (e.g., marijuana) in the home?

Do we want to prevent the abuse of licit drugs (e.g., tranquilizers, sleeping pills) by the adult members of the family?

Societal Use

Do we want to prevent the growth in our homes or communities of the notion that experimental drug use is a rite of passage?

Do we want to prevent the use of misleading and manipulative advertisements by the media?

Do we want to prevent the equation of alcohol or drug use with recognition, reward, relevance, or release?

When we read through these questions and think about what primary prevention means, opinions will vary greatly; what the phrase means to one person is not what it does to another. The fact is there are many facets to prevention, and some run counter to the interests and aims of other views of the same problem. Consequently, though the aim is to provide education that will stop the problem before it starts, the questions are so complex it is like trying to untangle a snarled fishing line; it is easier to cut out the bird's nest and leave it behind. The common response to such complex problems is inertia. If there is any approach at all, it seems it is to decide for oneself the question, "What does prevention mean to me and to my church?" In other words, the line of least resistance—personal preference. It must be remembered, however, that this default once led to a major schism in the Church and the U.S. from 1825 to 1933, one that still has not been closed. The issue was: Is drinking a sin? With the "wets," the drinkers, fighting the "drys," the abstainers, the temperance movement and Prohibition were born.

THE ROOTS OF DISPUTE AND PREJUDICE

We may not feel that temperance and Prohibition have any effect on us today or on our effort to prevent alcohol and drug abuse, but those major movements are the reason the above questions are still disputed in American churches. They are still the basis for the nation's inability to decide whether drinking is right or wrong. Furthermore, much of the present-day thinking about primary prevention is the result of America's long and controversial history of seeking to forestall alcohol problems. As the 1979 Gallup poll pointed out, one in five people would like to return to Prohibition, and nearly half the population basically disapproves of drinking. This conflict between thought, word, and deed is the direct result of reforms that began with a document published in 1785 by Dr. Benjamin Rush, an eminent Quaker physician from Philadelphia.

In 1784, it seemed to some in New England that their communities were deteriorating under the influence of alcohol. Benjamin Rush wrote a tract, based on medical evidence, against the use of distilled spirits. Entitled "An Enquiry into the Effects of Ardent Spirits Upon the Human Body and Mind," it was published by the War Department, circulated to the troops of the Continental Army, and was widely read and quoted.[2] Thus, the seeds for the temperance movement were planted; they would ultimately grow into the national movement of Prohibition. In their excellent story of alcoholism and the churches, *The Staggering Steeple*, Paul C. Conley and Andrew A. Sorensen present a very useful summary of this period:

THE TEMPERANCE MOVEMENT: 1825–1900

From the writing of Dr. Benjamin Rush and the preaching of Lyman Beecher on the increasing evils of drunkenness in American society during the first quarter of the nineteenth century, the American temperance movement grew to national proportions by the 1840's. Initiated by the New England Calvinist clergy and Federalist aristocracy, the temperancce movement rapidly changed to a self-help institution of the common man. Temperance was given considerable support by the revivalist movement in American Protestantism. With the rise of the common man and the increasing influence of the West in the temperance movement, the views of the extremists became dominant, and beer, wine, and cider were proscribed along with hard liquor as temperance became synonymous with total abstinence. . . . By the close of the century the foremost temperance group was the Women's Christian Temperance Union.

With the rise of the WCTU the temperance movement once again became a means whereby one class attempted to impose a reform on a lower class, rather than existing for the benefit of its members. By the end of the century temperance and abstinence were an integral part of the American middle class life-style, while drinking was equated with the immigrant urban working class. The original commitment of the temperance movement to moral suasion as the only acceptable means of obtainig its goal was abandoned in favor of prohibition legislation.[3]

The temperance movement sought to impose abstinence from all alcoholic beverages as a national norm. Early in the movement, however, the religious groups drew a distinction between dangerous spirits and harmless wine and beer, and that distinction is a part of our thinking today. A major effect of the movement still persists in the form of the division in the Church between those who believe alcohol is evil, drinking is sinful, and abstinence is the only acceptable religious posture, and those who believe alcohol is one of God's gifts and drinking it responsibly is acceptable. Finally, temperance caused primary prevention to take the form of educational public-school programs, the central message of which was to warn young people against the evils of alcohol. Abstention, the programs asserted, was the only answer. Therein lies the reason nearly half the U.S. still cannot decide if drinking is right or wrong.

THE PROHIBITION ERA: 1900–1933

By 1900 the leadership of the temperance movement was assumed by the Anti-Saloon League of America. The league, which often referred to itself as "the church in action," was dedicated to the single purpose of eradicating the saloon in American life. The league organized the mainstream Protestant leaders of America, particularly the Methodist and Baptist denominations, into the most effective political pressure group in the nation's history. Through this method the league achieved the passage of national Prohibition—the Eighteenth Amendment. . . . However, the utter failure of Prohibition to accomplish the end for which it was instituted and the wave of lawlessness that accompanied it led to its repeal in 1933—the Twenty-first Amendment.[4]

With the repeal of Prohibition, primary prevention became a set of local and state laws intended to regulate what Prohibition had failed to eliminate. Those regulations caused much controversy at the time, and they are still hotly debated today: the legal age at which a person may drink or purchase alcohol, the hours and days stores may be open, and the suitable distance a bar or a retail package store has to be from a church or school. The temperance movement's influence could still be recognized in the 1940s, the 1950s, and even the 1960s. Alcohol education (when it was taught) changed focus from promoting abstention to offering objective evidence that scientifically proved the dangers of all alcohol use by teenagers. In the late sixties and early seventies, owing to the dramatic increase in drug abuse, this approach was transformed into classroom programs designed to scare young people into staying away from nonalcoholic drugs. Facetiously described by the young as "reefer madness" (after the short film of the same name), the educational campaign backfired, and, like Prohibition, led to a popular counterculture that used alcohol and drugs as its primary sources of meaning, purpose, and fun. What was once an underground movement has turned into today's national pastime—getting high.

Few of us who are actively involved in the Church's ministry today remember many of the details of Prohibition, but all of us are deeply affected by the movment that ended only fifty years ago. The clergy who are now at mid-life were raised by parents who lived through that tumultuous period. Their memories, values, and attitudes were passed on to us, and they are part of our beliefs. If we, the clergy, are going to influence the lives of the people committed to our care, we need to remember that the issues of the temperance movement and Prohibition are still very much alive. The Church's and nation's division over abstinence still affects our theological position, and it affects our parishioners' receptivity to our position. We are dealing here with prejudices deeply rooted in ancestral history. Like racial prejudices, they are not altered by rational arguments because they are not the result of rational thought. Our aim may be prevention, but if prevention has even the slightest hint of Prohibition, then our efforts are doomed to the same fate the national movement suffered. A parishioner may be undecided whether drinking is right or wrong, moral or immoral, but to prohibit him from deciding for himself is to lose a member, possibly a life. Though our parishioners look to us for moral guidelines, we will cut off all communication with them if our approach to prevention equates use or nonuse with sin. As the man said when his pastor preached that drinking was a work of the devil, "That cuts it with me, pastor; you just went from preachin' to meddlin'."

Trying to solve a problem before it starts by imposing moral or legal regulations has not worked as far as alcohol and drug use are concerned. Trying to combat alcoholism, for instance, by restricting consumption has only added to the problem. As was pointed out in chapter 1, Harold Mulford's study found that the religious denominations with the highest number of problem drinkers were the abstainers—the Baptists and the other small Protestant denominations. Prohibition was the most zealously supported reform in U.S. history, and whether or not consumption of alcohol increased or decreased during that period is still argued. There is no debate, however, that Prohibition did not prohibit; as a legal preventive it failed. Regarding the drug-abuse epidemic of the 1960s, moralizing lectures on the dangerous and damaging effects of drugs served only to heighten curiosity about drug use and lessen the teachers' credibiltiy. Scare tactics as a deterrent were totally ineffective. Then, as now, it became clear that neither moralistic lectures nor law enforcement could prevent drug abuse before it started.

Finally, according to the 1983 issue of the *American Journal of Public Health* (73:163), when (between 1976 and 1981) Massachusetts raised its legal drinking age from eighteen to twenty, although bar and club attendance dropped among teenagers and liquor purchases dropped as well, the number of youngsters who had someone else buy alcohol for them nearly doubled. What's more, after the law was enacted, arrests of teenagers in Massachusetts for all other alcohol-related offenses—such as illegal purchases, possessions, and public intoxication—rose more than 150 percent. The average daily consumption of alcohol among sixteen- to nineteen-year-olds did not decline, nor did the incidence of fatal accidents among this group.[5]

When we focus on what we want to prevent and how we intend to prevent it, whether we are on the side of drinking or abstinence, use or nonuse, we need to remember that preaching prohibition is not only useless, it can and does add to the problem. As in Newtonian physics, "For every action there is an equal and opposite reaction." Primary prevention for us, therefore, must not be built on prohibition but on a foundation of caring, mutual regard, candor, and education. The hope of preventing problems before they begin is realized when parishioners are able to identify, examine, and evaluate their feelings about use, nonuse, and abuse of alcohol or drugs, without fear of religious condemnation. If they are to investigate constructive attitudes about chemical use, if they are to decide to behave in ways consistent with those attitudes, then they must have the opportunity to develop them without intimidation.

The development of effective decision-making skills is an individual learning process. It includes:

1. Learning how to recognize a problem.
2. Identifying alternative ways of dealing with it.
3. Gathering data that will lead to a solution.
4. Choosing an approach for resolving the issue.
5. Putting the decision into practice.
6. Evaluating the results and the effectiveness of the decision.

When individuals have the freedom to solve their own problems, make their own decisions, and formulate their own guidelines in the face of contrasting attitudes, then they are open to selecting new patterns likely to help them avoid problems before they begin.

MAINTAINING FREEDOM OF CHOICE

The most expedient philosophy in alcohol- and drug-abuse prevention is: *The freedom of choice to drink or not, to use or not, must be maintained.* This statement is frightening, espcially when one realizes that *any* use of illicit mood-altering drugs by young people disrupts their growth and development, but it reflects the only approach that respects the rights of the individual and places the responsibility on him or her. In the case of adolescents and, especially, children between ages six and twelve who are too young to make well-informed choices, it is the parent who has the responsibility for their behavior. The "freedom of choice" rests with them. After all is said and done, it is the person or parent who decides, *not* the minister. This doesn't mean we need refrain from involvement. The most effective thing we as ministers can do is what we do best—that is, preach God's will to his people. As Billy Sunday, who in 1920 joyously heralded the death of John Barleycorn, said in 1933, "I can't continue to preach Prohibition and preach the Gospel. I'm not as strong as I used to be and the load is too heavy. So, I'm returning to my first love— preaching the Gospel."[6]

The most useful approach we can use to prevent problems is to establish a relationship with our congregations wherein we can investigate responsible decisions about the use of alcohol and drugs. That is preaching the Gospel. Continuing to argue over the issues of Prohibition is to be a part of the problem. Ten years ago, in 1973, a task force set up by the National Council of Churches saw this as one of the urgent priorities vis-à-vis alcohol:

> At this time American society is virtually without any guideline dis-
> tinguishing between responsible and irresponsible drinking. Little or
> no opportunity is given for persons to clarify their own feelings about
> alcohol use through open discussion, largely because of the excessive
> emotionalism and controversy associated with the alcohol use-non-use
> debate. In order that guidelines for responsible and irresponsible
> drinking and abstaining can be established, the church must reopen
> the discussion on a level which deals with the more basic human
> issues. It is essential to maintain and continue this concern in the
> center of the American religious community to insure that the
> churches engage in the effort to develop these guildelines.[7]

In today's chemical-consuming society it is an even more urgent priority. We are witnessing the waste of too many lives to continue fighting over who is right or wrong. Like Billy Sunday, instead of pointing out what we are against, we need to proclaim what we are for. We represent the fact that God cares for his people, and we can best demonstrate that care by treating people as God does, as human beings who have received life as a gift and are free to live and grow into the persons he intended. It is as the National Council of Churches' report suggests:

> Until a person has the capacity to shape his own life within the

possibilities open to him, he is not free. True freedom is the possibility of accepting the responsibility for realizing one's own God-given potential and the consequences of his own decisions. Until a person takes responsibility for his own choices he is not free. Thus, the goal of the church involvement is to offer the possibility of freedom to choose one's own path to fulfillment. . . . [8]

When an individual lives any way he pleases, without regard for self or others, he is not making responsible choices on behalf of himself or the community. Narcissism is another form of addiction. If we are going to help that person lead a more fully expressive and fulfilling life, we need to show we care and are concerned about him. Problems of life are complex. Social, economic, and cultural pressures are overpowering. Ancestral and historical prejudices are disruptive. As ministers, however, we can alter the influence of all these forces, we can change the direction of peoples' lives. The proven method is the simplest of all; it is by offering a genuine , honest-to-God measure of concern. It is, as the Hallmark motto suggests, "when you care enough to send the very best." The very best, in this case, is offering what psychologist Carl R. Rogers calls a "therapeutic attitude": congruence, empathetic understanding, and unconditional positive regard. Congruence means genuineness as a person, knowing and owning one's feelings, not being a phony. Empathetic understanding means tuning into the feelings of another. Unconditional positive regard means warm, human regard for the individual as a person of unconditional worth, acceptance of him or her as is. [9]

In the realm of preventive education and promoting responsible decisions, candor, above all else, is the best policy. No matter what we think or where we stand, as long as we are truthful about our feelings and share them, our parishioners will respect us and value our opinions. If we think alcoholics are weak and drinking a sin, then it is most helpful and healthful to be authentic and say so. It is no use trying to camouflage loaded attitudes, because they are obvious to anyone sensitive to the problems. It is not only legitimate but an expression of empathy and positive regard to say, "My friends, I was brought up in a family that believed drinking is a sin and alcoholics are weak. That still is my opinion, even though there is evidence to refute it. Please don't hold it against me. Thank God we are forgiven our sins. If you know of someone who has the problem or if you need help, I can refer you to resource people, the best available. My prejudices may affect the way I feel, but as your minister I can promise you they will not affect what I can do to be useful to you. What's more, if you think I'm wrong, come in and help me understand your opinions. We can afford to disagree with each other, but we cannot afford to disregard one another."

FAITH VERSUS PRACTICE

Everyone has attitudes when it comes to the subject of alcohol and drugs, and ministers are no different. What we proclaim about chemicals is our professional view, but what we do with them is our personal attitude—how we use them; what we take; the ones we offer our children and those we forbid; the circumstances that make their use acceptable; the hazards that make us feel some are not appropriate. All these factors define our prejudices about chemical use. Unaware of the contradictions, we may get into a "wet"-versus-"dry" argument and condemn our neighbor's use of alcohol, yet at the same time suggest tranquilizers for a parishioner's anxiety. We may condemn our son's college friends for drinking purposely to get drunk, and then think nothing of suggesting that sleeping pills might be in order for a man who has just lost his wife. We may preach on the hazards of air pollution but pollute our lungs with cigar, cigarette, or pipe smoke. We say our beliefs about the use and abuse of alcohol and drugs are rooted in the firm ground of biblical theology, but our theology frequently is inconsistent with our personal practices. What we believe from our religious perspective is very different from the practical application of those beliefs to our daily lives. We sometimes appear sanctimonious. There is no congruity between faith and practice. No sooner do we condemn the athlete for pumping himself up with steroids than we are condemned by our own use of diet pills to deflate ourselves. As soon as we say swallowing, sniffing, or shooting drugs is right or wrong, we are challenged by a habit in our personal life that proclaims the opposite view. That habit represents not only our personal attitude but our professional stand. Congruence is measured by what we do as well as what we say.

More often than not we will find it difficult to match our theology of chemical use and our personal practices, and vice versa. It is important to understand this point, because it explains why many ministers are unwilling to venture an opinion on the use of alcohol or drugs. Who wants to be accused by his own uncertainty? Who wants to be condemned by his own inconsistency? Who wants to look at himself and agree with nearly half the country's population that he does not know whether drinking is good or bad, right or wrong? Who wants to admit that in fact he has no viable basis for an opinion on the right or wrong use of most chemicals? What religious leader wants to say, "I have no consistent guidelines or rules for my or my parishioners' use of any and all chemicals"?

Most of us have no problem with the use of chemicals for their proper, legitimate, or prescribed purpose. We know that in our drug-oriented society we are fortunate to have the many medicines that keep us healthy. Our confusion begins in seemingly harmless problems, such as, "My wife's prescription medication for her strep throat has run out. I'll let her finish my prescription; it's apparently the same." Or, "I'm going to need a good night's sleep. Think I'll borrow a sleeping pill from my friend." Or, "This minor ear infection feels like the same thing I had last year at this time. I'll get started using the medicine from that one." From innocuous situations such as these, we must decide more difficult questions: "Hey, I hear these sleeping pills act as an aphrodisiac. I'm going to ask my doctor for a prescription." Or, "I'm under a lot of pressure, Doctor, will you give me some tranquilizers to relieve the stress?" Or, "I need at least three amphetamines before I can get going in the morning."

Then there are the clear-cut misuses: "I saw my lawyer sniff a line of cocaine in the locker room last week. . . . Forget it, I didn't see anything." Or, "It's harmful to abuse analgesics, but Bill's professional football career would be over without them." Or, "I've got a migraine, a whole ward to cover, and four more hours on my shift. I'm going to shoot some of Mrs. Smith's Demerol. She doesn't need all of it, and I need a lift."

How we decide such questions as these determines where our professional beliefs confront our private behavior. Just as abstinence from alcohol is basically a theological posture, so are the answers to these questions. But it is not as though there is a monolithic religion by which we can gauge each and every situation with certainty and positive effects. The fact is, we can take many stances depending on our needs, we express contrasting beliefs depending on who and what is involved. Often we are like people trying to apply situation ethics when we are confused about the situation and have never studied basic theology. Consequently, many of us do what feels most comfortable—we take the line of least resistance, we beg the issue. How can we provide meaningful answers for others when we do not have theoretical answers or workable beliefs for ourselves? How can we be responsible to act for others when we have no clear-cut guidelines for our private responsibility?

"Congruence" is the answer to these problems. Openness and honesty. Open honesty is the essence of redemptive love. It speaks to young and old alike. Our parishioners don't expect us to be experts on alcohol and drug use or misuse; they want us to be preachers and pastors. They want to know what we think even if they hold the contrary point of view. Because they are more interested in being cared *about* than cared *for*, we can offer our beliefs, we can challenge their ideas, we can even be in conflict with them and still remain a primary pastoral resource. As George Bach says in his book *The Intimate Enemy*, conflict is a function of caring. If one doesn't care about the other person or what he is doing, one will not be motivated to fight with him.[10]

Realizing this, there will be times when we say, "I disagree with you, but I care about you; therefore, I'm going to fight you for you."

Beyond differences of opinion, there are times when our prejudices, our lack of training, or our insufficient knowledge prevents us from being as useful as we might be. In that case it is most beneficial to say so and refer to another or call in an expert. The North Conway Institute of Boston, for instance, is basically a one-man operation that directs people to the appropriate source of help for alcohol or drug problems. It runs on a budget twice that of most small churches, and nearly all of it is donated by appreciative people. Too often we want the glory of being the one to provide the service. We forget that a parishioner referred to the appropriate helping agency is just as grateful as a counselee.

When people are in trouble, sorrow, need, sickness, or adversity, they want help. If we can provide it, even if it is by referral, we are being empathetic and concerned pastors. When people are confused, they want guidelines. We may feel drinking is a sin, but if we invite someone to preach about making responsible decisions on alcohol use we are manifesting positive regard and are being effective preachers. The net result of this open honesty is mutual appreciation and acceptance and the building of a loving relationship that makes it possible for us to prevent problems in families.

An open, honest, therapeutic attitude also means we must consider our own use or misuse of chemicals. We must answer for ourselves questions such as:

Is it acceptable for us to use alcohol?

Is it acceptable to get high on marijuana or cocaine?

Is it all right to get intoxicated?

Is it all right to get high or intoxicated whenever we want, as long as it is in the privacy of our own homes?

Is it appropriate to consume drink for drink with a parishioner who has had an emotional setback?

Is it acceptable to drink in public?

Is it acceptable to smoke pot or snort cocaine with friends?

Is it okay to get high with everyone else at a party?

Is it okay to become intoxicated at a party?

It is clear we are regarded as examples and models; the polls and studies verify this impression. We, more than any other helping professionals, are in a position to communicate by thought, word, and deed a responsible, healthy lifestyle or an irresponsible, unhealthy one. Whether we are comfortable with the fact or not, we preach health and wholeness by what we do as well as by what we say; it is the price we pay for the space God allows us to occupy. Each of us has the same freedom a parishioner has to drink or abstain, to smoke or not, to use or refuse. There is no double standard or biblical injunction about clerical consumption. If, however, we are going to take advantage of our unique calling and select position, if we are going to interpret the issues that nurture wholeness and those that destroy, if we are going to be a channel of God's love, his redeeming grace, and his forgiving compassion, then we need to consider our own use in light of how he is trying to use us.

THE AUTHORITY IS OURS

On most of the issues of life, public attitudes determine the guidelines for public behavior. Avoidance is the predominant public attitude toward alcoholism and drug abuse, and disregard is the standard way of dealing with them. *Acedia!* On the other hand, the media purposely mold the public to believe that chemicals are the magic keys to a pleasurable or a pain-free life and that consumption of large quantities of alcohol or drugs is acceptable, normal, and fun. Prevention, therefore, is a subject loaded with controversy and emotion, emotions that have their prejudicial roots in temperance, Prohibition, and repeal. What possible hope does a clergyperson have of changing public attitudes in the face of such conflicting and powerful forces?

Public attitudes are simply common ideas held by a body of individuals, people in families. Changing them may seem like an impossible task, but influencing the ideas of *one* family, then another, *is* possible.

We have both immediate and unlimited access to the family. We, the clergy, have an influence on half the families of America. Since families across the nation see alcohol and drug problems as today's number one concern, we have a vitally interested, receptive audience. As the Gallup poll pointed out, of all public leaders the clergy is held in highest trust. Finally, as the Connecticut Mutual Life Insurance Company study revealed, religious commitment has a greater impact on determining values than age, race, sex, income, or political viewpoint; attitudes toward all aspects of life change according to the level of religious commitment. In the face of the challenges and threats posed by constant change and too many choices, the Connecticut study found, religion provided people with roots. In response to the above question—"What possible hope does a clergyperson have of changing public attitudes?"—the answer is clear: We are in a prime position to change attitudes. We deal on a daily or weekly basis with the individuals and families that shape public opinions, and we embody the religious "roots" and teachings that affect those opinions. In the idiom of today, "We are where it's at." The power to influence and change is already ours. We accept such power as a force ordained in us by God, and we have only to realize it has been entrusted to us by his people as well. We are called to use it; the authority is ours.

Prevention of problems before they begin does not mean preaching against or prohibiting specific acts. Similarly, focusing on alcohol or drug problems alone does not stem the rising tide of abuse. What we are dealing with here, among the families of the congregation, is a "people problem." How these families live and relate, what their values and attitudes are, what they do to meet the problems, how they seek pleasure, when, where, and to what extent they use alcohol or drugs—these are the underlying issues that either prevent or create problems. All reflect people's decisions. By the same token, people are the greatest resource for addressing these issues, and we have access to that resource. The place to begin, therefore, is with our people, and the most effective plan is the promotion of a healthy, responsible, and mutually responsive way of life. The recent movement to stop smoking is a good example. It began as a ground-swell movement of health promotion and continues as a public wave of physical fitness. Those who joined the movement and stopped smoking feel good about themselves and each other.

When we seek to prevent rather than prohibit, when we promote the freedom and opportunity to make responsible choices, when we ground those choices in a practical theology of individual and corporate wholeness, then we are promoting health—personal and societal. That is what God intends for his people.

Robert L. DuPont, M.D., president of the American Council on Marijuana, in the paper "Learning from the Past to Cope with the Future," has this to say about the need for preventive efforts that promote personal and societal health:

> Lifestyle issues are the future for dealing with the health of our country. Drug abuse prevention is now, and will become increasingly in the forefront of those new efforts. It is easy to caricature the new attitude, the "no-saying" attitude about drug use, and say that it becomes a matter of what we do *to* each other, particularly what adults do *to* kids. That would be a terrible mis-reading of what the problem is and what we can do about it. My point is this: in thinking about drug abuse prevention we need to care a lot more about each other. The question becomes not what we do to each other, but what we do for each other. That is the way toward the future. . . . [11]

CHAPTER 4

Alcoholism—Sin or Sickness?

> But the much deeper issue is that America must wake up to
> the fact that alcohol and drug addiction is not a moral issue,
> not a question of right or wrong. People don't talk about
> diabetes in terms of its being someone's fault. They shouldn't
> with addiction. It's a biochemical, genetic disease.
>
> Dr. G. Douglas Talbott
> Director, Disabled Doctor's Program
> Ridgeview Institute, Smyrna, Georgia[1]

DISORDER OR DISEASE?

Alcoholism is a biochemical, genetic disease. It is an illness. To quote
physician LeClair Bissell, a renowned expert in the field of alcoholism:

> In the current way of thinking, alcoholism is seen to be a primary
> illness, a legitimate disease. It is not seen as willful misbehavior, as a
> learned set of bad habits or as poor communication skills, as a symp-
> tom of some other problem or as something that can be explained
> simply by exposure to alcohol.[2]

In describing the Johnson Institute's beliefs about alcoholism and drug
abuse, Vernon E. Johnson, founder of the famous training and consultation
institute in Minneapolis, writes:

Nature of the Disease

We believe that alcoholism and related chemical dependencies are primary, progressive, chronic and fatal diseases which, by their nature, and
particularly in their later stages, render the victims incapable of the
spontaneous insight required to offer themselves remedial care. . . .

Family

We believe that those living with harmfully dependent persons, on the
job, but more particularly in the home, become emotionally involved

and distressed to the point where they display similar symptoms, and need remedial care as well, as they become progressively immobilized by their distress. . . .

Society

Likewise, we believe that the misunderstanding of the nature of harmful chemical dependency by the general public is contributing not only to the incidence of the disease, but is consistently enabling the disease to progress to its later and more dangerous stages even before it is recognized. . . .

Intervention

We believe that the progressive nature of the disease requires that intervention be applied at the earliest possible time for two reasons, namely (1) the suffering is limited to both time and degree; and (2) the likelihood of successful recovery is enhanced. . . .

Finally, we believe that the illness is treatable.[3]

The National Council on Alcoholism describes alcoholism as "a complex, progressive disease in which the use of alcohol interferes with health, social and economic functioning. Untreated, alcoholism results in physical incapacity, permanent mental damage and/or premature death. The onset of the disease varies widely and may appear at the first drink or may take years to develop."[4]

These statements from leading authorities make it clear that alcoholism is defined as a medical illness. It is every bit as much an illness as diabetes or an allergy to bee stings. It is now known to rank with heart disease and cancer as one of America's three major health problems. It is also known that alcoholism in *not* the result of a sinful nature, a moral weakness, or a character flaw, nor is it caused by a miserable childhood, a lack of self-control, or self-centeredness. To the contrary, the research data verify that it is a physiological illness and that it can be predetermined by the genes.

James R. Milam, Ph.D., and Katherine Ketchum, in their 1981 book *Under the Influence*, challenge and refute the myths, distortions, and prejudices that hold alcoholism to be a moral or psychological problem. They offer sound evidence that the factors that cause alcoholism are physiological. In their summation of the research evidence, they state:

In other words, while psychology, cultural, and social factors definitely influence the alcoholic's drinking patterns and behavior, they have no effect on whether or not he becomes alcoholic in the first place. Physiology, not psychology, determines whether one drinker will become addicted to alcohol and another will not. The alcoholic's enzymes, hormones, genes and brain chemistry work together to create his abnormal and unfortunate reaction to alcohol.

The scientific evidence clearly indicates an interplay of various hereditary, physiological factors—metabolic, hormonal, and neurological—which work together and in tandem to determine the individual's susceptibility to alcoholism. . . . While additional predisposing factors to alcoholism will undoubtedly be discovered, abundant knowledge already exists to confirm that alcoholism is a hereditary, physiological disease and to account fully for its onset and progression.[5]

In 1983, a Harvard psychiatrist (one of the most respected researchers in adult development), Dr. George Vaillant, completed a landmark sixteen-year study entitled *The Natural History of Alcoholism: Causes, Patterns, and Paths to Recovery*. In his investigation Vaillant was able to define a connection between the alcoholic and an inherited predisposition for alcoholism. What made his study so valuable was that it was the first long-term scrutiny of alcoholism as it develops in the victim's life. Usually the alcoholic is asked how his sickness evolved. Vaillant followed his subjects from the beginning of their adult lives. Using two hundred Harvard graduates and four hundred inner-city, working-class men as subjects, he chronicled and analyzed their lives from 1940 on. In the case of 136 of these men who became alcoholics, he matched 26 from the Harvard group and 110 from the inner-city group as they progressed along their separate paths to alcoholism. Noting that one out of three victims had a close family member or relative who was alcoholic, he was able to substantiate cause and effect, a genetic contribution to the disease of alcoholism. The extraordinary fact about Vaillant's achievement is that his book, instead of causing more argument on a much-disputed subject, was and is hailed by the leaders in the field as a major breakthrough.[6]

Dr. George A. Mann, in his paper (written for the Johnson Institute) *The Dynamics of Addiction*, says the major factors contributing to chemical addiction are stress, heredity, the autonomic learning process of rewards and punishments, and the cellular changes in the body. As to how much a person's predisposition to alcohol addiction is related to heredity, he writes:

Whether an individual has to have a genetic factor like this to become addicted is unknown. We do know, however, that if you take a careful family history of an alcoholic, you will usually find an alcoholic in the background, even though it might look at first as though the patient is the first ever to occur in that family. The lone alcoholic is rare. You will generally find a history of the disease. This may be in the immediate family, among the siblings, parents, and grandparents; or it may be harder to trace, but you can generally find a history of it.[7]

Though there is now ample empirical evidence proving alcoholism is an illness caused by hereditary and physiological factors, though there are statistics showing that as one of America's three major health problems alcoholism is costing the nation $54.1 billion annually in lost time, health and welfare benefits, property damage, divorce, medical expenses, insurance payments or prison expenses . . . *nevertheless*, both as a nation and as a society, we are still denying it is a disease, and we still minimize its effects on the health of individuals, families, and the community. As was noted in chapter 1, it is a national crisis, and yet we refuse to believe it is an illness.

In spite of the hard scientific evidence and national studies to the contrary, a 1979 survey sponsored by General Mills revealed that 67 percent (or two out of three) of 2,181 respondents felt that alcoholism is a sign of "personal emotional weakness."[8] That the disease's impact on the health of United States citizens is forcibly denied or minimized can be seen in that, in 1977, the federal government spent twice as much on dental research as it did on alcoholism research.[9] Disregard for the toll the disease takes on human life is illustrated by the fact that in the ten years of the Viet Nam war (1961–1971), though 45,000 U.S. soldiers were killed by the enemy, 274,000 U.S. citizens died in automobile crashes involving alcohol.[10] That is 27,400 per year, or 75 citizens a day. The fatal accident rate has not decreased. There is not now, nor has there been, a nationwide governmental program to combat drunk driving. Despite that in 1984 the College of American Pathologists reported its documented figures showing alcohol is involved in up to 90 percent of all fatal motor-vehicle accidents, the national Highway Traffic Safety Administration in Washington still maintains that drunk driving is involved in only 50 percent of all fatal accidents. Consider the government's response to this death toll compared to what it might be if a commercial airliner crashed every day for ten days, killing seventy-five citizens each time.

The tragedy of the biochemical, genetic disease of alcoholism is that it does not show up on an X-ray, a CAT scan, or an electroencephalogram. It is every bit as much a physical illness as those that can be measured by diagnostic instruments, but because its psychological consequences make it appear otherwise, it is still considered the result of a weak will, a character disorder, or selfishness. Coauthors Milam and Ketchum provide insight into this common misconception:

> Today, the alcoholic is generally considered to be a moral degenerate who chooses a life of abasement and through lack of will power and maturity, allows himself to lose his job, his family, his self-respect. The typical alcoholic, the myth informs us, is a person who would rather be drunk than sober, who lacks confidence and maturity, who is riddled with guilt and shame over past sins and misdeeds, yet lacks the

strength of character to change his ways, and who has no guiding purpose or motivation in life. This myth is only one of many which rule the way we think about the disease and its victims.[11]

That alcoholism is a disease was accepted by the American Medical Association (AMA) as long ago as 1956. Even then, however, the illness model was compromised, for the treatment of the disorder was relegated to the Association's psychiatric branch, where it still remains. As far as the Church's attitude is concerned, even though the United Presbyterian Church formally declared alcoholism a disease in 1946—thus establishing a theological definition for all Churches—the century-old conflict over whether drinking is a sin and alcoholism a moral disorder still divides the institutional Church into the "wets" versus the "drys." The breach caused by the temperance movement of 1825 and Prohibition which followed in 1900, still exists. The result: Half of America's population cannot decide if drinking is right or wrong

MORAL PROBLEM OR MEDICAL PROBLEM?

Among religious leaders there is no agreement or even consensus of opinion on the question, "Is alcoholism a sin or a sickness?" Howard J. Clinebell, Jr., in his book *Understanding and Counseling the Alcoholic*, points out that not only is there a wide variety of beliefs among ministers but there is much confusion over how the sin, if any, is related to the sickness, if any. Citing results from 146 questionnaires returned by ministers who attended the first seven years of the Yale School of Alcohol Studies, Clinebell shows that the survey of these trained Church leaders falls into as many as seven theological positions. He offers his evaluation of each.

1. *Alcoholism is a sin and not a sickness from start to finish.* The minority (about 5 percent) opinion. According to this view, alcoholism begins as the sin of drinking and ends as a sinful habit. The "all-sin" view errs in oversimplifying the causes of alcoholism.

2. *Alcoholism begins as a personal sin and ends as a sickness.* One who drinks exposes himself to the dangers of becoming an alcoholic. Once the drinking has passed a certain point and is out of volitional control, it becomes a sickness. This view is limited by oversimplifying the causes, although it recognizes that in its advanced stages alcoholism is a sickness.

3. *Alcoholism is a sickness that involves the sin of abuse.* This, the Roman Catholic view, says it is the abuse and not the use of alcohol that constitutes the sin. It is the sin of excess. This concept does not establish responsibility in

relation to the compulsion to drink, nor does it define a line beyond which a person is not responsible.

4. *Alcoholism is a sickness caused by a combination of factors involving both sin and sickness.* This represents those ministers who see drinking as wrong but recognize the existence of etiological factors beyond the control of the individual. It holds that one is responsible for the factors that produce the "mental obsession" to drink, even though one is not responsible for having an atypical physical response to alcohol.

5. *Alcoholism involves sin in the sense that it has destructive consequences.* The first of three nonjudgmental concepts. Here, if sin is defined as anything that harms personality, then alcoholism is certainly a sin. It is not a moral sin. If this definition of sin is accepted as legitimate, there can be no quarrel with its application.

6. *Alcoholism is a social sin.* This view suggests that it is a sin only in the sense that it can be attributed to society, a symptom or evidence of the sinful condition of society. Whatever one's view of the alcoholic's responsibility, one can accept that "society greases the slope down which he slides."

7. *Alcoholism involves original sin.* Alcoholism is the result of certain etiological factors, which include Man's egocentricity. There is a selfishness at the very center of Man's nature that keeps him from doing that which he knows to be good. This selfishness is evident in the alcoholic as a symptom of inner conflict and insecurity.

Though Howard Clinebell himself suggests that an adequate view must include recognition of factors in concepts 5, 6, and 7 and that many ministers would also include number 4, he points out there is no easy or complete answer on which all the clergy can agree. "It seems probable," he says, "that failure on the part of many ministers to find adequate answers to this question is one important reason why organized religion has not made a larger contribution to the solution of the problem."[12]

In Chapter 1 it was shown that one of the primary reasons the clergy rightfully resist dealing with alcohol problems is that they are ministers, not chemical-dependency specialists. The Yale survey and Howard Clinebell's evaluation make it clear that trying to address alcoholism by importing concepts from ethical and moral theology is futile. As Father John C. Ford, a moral theologian and one of the leading Roman Catholic authorities in the field of alcoholism, says, "One must never approach an alcoholic on the basis of what is called 'morality'."[13] To moralize with an alcoholic or to try and prevent alcoholism by moralizing is, as anyone who has ever tried knows, an exercise in futility.

Recalling the United Presbyterian poll that showed the clergy's uninvolvement and especially the one question that was never asked, "What is God saying in this mass resistance by his chosen leaders?" all the evidence points to the fact that clergy are called to manage ordinary pastoral problems, but most are not called to handle alcoholism and its related complexities. They have not been equipped to do so, and, in fact, they are not qualified. Their resistance indicates that they themselves realize this inadequacy. Alcoholism is not simply a pastoral problem, nor is it a spiritual one, nor a moral or ethical one; it is a biochemical, genetic disease, a primary illness. It demands the knowledge of a practitioner or the skill of a specialist or the personal insight born of recovery. Religious knowledge, pastoral counseling skills, and moral answers are inadequate to deal with the illness. It is for these compelling reasons that an expedient approach designed specifically for parish ministers is provided in chapter 8, "The Cry for Help." With this field-tested, effective technique, the clergyperson can very usefully deal with alcohol problems without having to be proficient at it.

The medical facts are irrefutable: Alcoholism is an illness, "not a moral issue, not a question of right or wrong," as Dr. G. Douglas Talbot says. To see it in any other way is the equivalent of ignoring a diagnosis of coronary heart disease in a parishioner hospitalized with a heart attack and describing the patient's illness in terms of total collapse from immoral behavior. If we, the clergy, want to communicate God's message of hope to a society that puts its hope in chemicals, if we want to be useful as catalysts who initiate programs of chemical health in our parishes, if we want to be a resource for those one in four parish families affected by chemical dependency, then we had best subscribe to the disease concept of alcoholism, a medically accepted definition that carries no moral judgments. To that end, we can be most effective if we understand alcoholism to be a primary, progressive, chronic, and fatal disease. Though the disease may progress owing to the sufferer's physiological susceptibility or the conditioning rewards of the mood-changing chemical, the psychological symptoms are secondary to the physiological disease; they are not the primary factors leading to its onset. In short, *alcoholism is not a symptom of a more serious problem.*

The "disease concept" of alcoholism is very difficult for most care-giving professionals to accept. It flies in the face of the more easily observed psychological problems and seems to be an excuse for aberrant behavior. The reason the AMA placed treatment of alcoholism under its psychiatric wing, the reason clergy have regarded the sickness as willful, the reason a 1972 study (conducted by *Human Behavior* magazine) of public attitudes toward various disabilities found alcoholism—along with mental illness—at the bottom of the list rated "least acceptable" is because most people consider the alcoholic to be the cause of his own sickness, *not* the victim of an illness. *Human Behavior's* survey revealed that ex-convicts, hunchbacks, dwarfs, diabetics, amputees, heart patients, paraplegics, and epileptics all are rated more "acceptable than alco-holics." With the exception of the ex-convict, who has served his time and paid for his misdeeds, all others are the victims of circumstances beyond their control. Not so the alcoholic; he is believed to have chosen his own fate.[14]

Because the term "alcoholism" elicits such prejudicial myths, misconceptions, and misunderstandings, Kathleen Whalen Fitzgerald, an author, writer for *Newsweek*, and recovering alcoholic, feels strongly it should be called "Jellinek's disease," after Dr. E.M. Jellinek (1890–1963), who, at Yale, was the first to define the term medically and to chart the progression of the fatal disease through its various stages. The Church could be very instrumental in erasing the stigma attached to the illness if it accepted Fitzgerald's suggestion and substituted the term "Jellinek's disease." Though the word "disease" often connotes bacterial infection, its use, as in the case of Parkinson's disease (named after James Parkinson, the English physician who first described it), would help make alcoholism understood as a sickness instead of a self-induced degeneracy. Henceforth, with the sole exception of quotations, this will be the case here. And, the alcoholic person will be described as the "dependent."

DEFINITIVE CHARACTERISTICS

If Jellinek's disease is considered a medical illness, then it must have an accepted definition and known characteristics. The nature of the disease is very succinctly outlined by the Johnson Institute; it is the basis of the medical definition:

THE NATURE OF CHEMICAL DEPENDENCY

I. Chemical dependency is a primary disease.
   1. It has its own symptomatology which is identifiable across the population of its victims.
   2. It is not a symptom of more serious problems.

II. Chemical dependency is a progressive disease.
   1. A long-term plateau of observable symptoms is not possible.
   2. The physical, emotional, and spiritual symptoms become worse when chemical use continues.
   3. The symptoms of the disease can be corrected.
   4. The victim must abstain from mood-altering chemicals in order to recover.

III. Chemical dependency is a chronic disease.
   1. There is no known cure.

2. The victim is always susceptible to pathological chemical use.
3. The symptoms of the disease can be arrested.
4. The victim must abstain from using mood-altering chemicals in order to recover.

IV. Chemical dependency is a fatal disease.
1. It is a terminal illness unless the chemical use is permanently stopped.
2. Chemical dependency deaths are often misrepresented on death certificates.
   a. Physical deterioration.
   b. Accidents while under the influence of chemicals.
   c. Suicide.
3. The disease can only be arrested.[15]

As to the identity by which the illness is most clearly recognized, a world-famous treatment and educational center, the Hazelden Foundation in Center City, Minnesota, describes eight characteristics commonly used to diagnose Jellinek's disease:

1. *Preoccupation with alcohol use.* When social relationships and activities become secondary to drinking, which serves increasingly to structure the drinker's existence.

2. *Protecting the supply.* A person makes certain not to become obligated to participate in nondrinking social situations, and stockpiling or assuring ready acccess to alcohol becomes paramount.

3. *Use of alcohol as a medicine.* When drinking alcohol is used to make a person functional by steadying the hand or affecting the psychological state, it may be said to be a self-prescribed and administered medicine.

4. *Solitary use of alcohol.* Alcohol use becomes an autonomous objective, preempting other life goals and social interaction. It evolves as a central life focus.

5. *Rapid intake of alcohol for effect.* There is no interest in group conviviality; the user is seeking the effect of the alcohol.

6. *Increased tolerance.* Due to adaptive cell metabolism, increased tolerance results in a greater quantity of alcohol consumed.

7. *Blackouts or memory holes.* A chemically induced period of amnesia or loss of memory, not to be confused with "passing out."

8. *Episodes of unplanned excessive drinking.* An inability consistently to regulate or control alcohol use.

It is Hazelden's opinion that evidence of four or more of these characteristics suffices for a positive diagnosis. *The bottom line, however, in the definition of Jellinek's disease is that the person's drinking results in harmful consequences for the drinker and others close to the drinker.*[16]

From a theological perspective, the disease concept makes it clear that the dependent's primary relationship is with the chemical, not with God, not with his own body, mind, and spirit, and not with family and friends. Neither personal and social obligations nor work responsibilities take priority over his dependence on alcohol. It is the insidious illness that separates the victim from every aspect of his personhood and potential. As man is created in the image of God, with an opportunity to actualize that image in the fulfillment of his God-given potential, it is the nature of Jellinek's disease that such an opportunity is undermined by the use of alcohol. Though the dependent may try to exercise control over whether or not he drinks, he has no control over the harmful effects that separate him from God, self, and others. It is as Milam and Ketchum say, "The alcoholic's enzymes, hormones, genes and brain chemistry work together to create his abnormal and unfortuante reaction to alcohol."

WHAT IS THE CAUSE, WHO IS RESPONSIBLE?

"Well, if it is a sickness, how does it get started and why does the alcoholic continue to drink?"

These are the first questions most of us in the ministry ask when confronted with the fact that Jellinek's disease is an illness. The unspoken thought, of course, is: "The alcoholic has a choice whether he gets sick or not; he doesn't have to drink!" The question is important; theologically, it has to do with the exercise of free will.

As to the etiology of the illness, the question, unfortunately, cannot be answered. There is no single cause. Dr. George Vaillant's study verifies that the causes are as complex as people, themselves, but that somehow and at some level the social drinker becomes both physiologically and psychologically addicted to alcohol. Vaillant doubts researchers will ever isolate a biochemical marker to predict Jellinek's disease, but that one out of three dependent people has a relative who has (or has had) the illness is evidence enough that there is a genetic connection. The best analogy, he feels, is with coronary heart disease, in which there is a genetic factor and the rest is due to maladaptive lifestyle.

Any addiction is the result of both physiological and psychological factors. Alcohol addiction involves a physical predisposition to the illness that includes tissue adaptation, cellular changes, autonomic processes, tolerance changes, and withdrawal reactions. It involves psychological factors as well: response to stress, conditioning by reward and punishment, compulsive behavior, habit formation, sociocultural conditioning, and denial. All these factors contribute to the illness's unique pathology. Jellinek's disease can result from a family predisposition, from habitual use, or from a combination of these forces. No matter what the cause, it is, like diabetes or an allergy to bee stings, a physiological illness. Furthermore, it is a fact that the addiction creates its own progression; that is, it becomes its own cause for drinking. Therefore, it is a primary illness, not the symptom of a more serious sickness. This raises the question of choice, of free will.

There are those in the Church who believe that the only choice is abstinence. Since alcohol is a toxic chemical, its nature is to destroy cells and disrupt physical health. It is destructive and evil. In response to this view, it can be argued that alcohol, too, is part of God's creation. The evil lies not in the agent but in its use. Although drunkenness is condemned in both the Old and New Testaments, nowhere is the use of alcohol as a beverage denounced. As to its sacred use, there is no scriptural differentiation between grape juice and wine as the symbol of God's holy union with His people. Jesus, a Jewish rabbi, blessed wine when he instituted the sacrament that would become Holy Communion. As far as abstinence is concerned, the Jewish and the Christian traditions hold that it is a matter of religious choice rather than biblical injunction.

There are some who believe that Jellinek's disease is caused by the sick person because the latter chooses to drink. Therefore, drinking is wrong, sinful! There is some moral justification for this view, because it is destructive to misuse and abuse alcohol. But no one sets out to drink with the intention of becoming chemically dependent. "Alcoholics do not choose to be alcoholics," as the saying goes. Drinking for the explicit purpose of getting drunk—the reason so many of today's youngsters give for drinking—is morally wrong. If it is not a willful act to destroy personhood, it is an intentional effort to diminish selfhood. And, in most instances, it is premeditated.

Free will and choice are a matter of the ability to consider all sides of the question and to choose among alternatives. Up to a point the chemically dependent person does have a choice—he or she needn't ever start to drink. Certainly this is so for children of alcoholics, for it is known that if one parent is chemically dependent, there is a 50 percent chance one of the offsprings will have difficulties with alcohol; if both parents are dependent, the chances are 85 to 90 percent that all children will have problems as a result of drinking. Alcohol, however, does not have the same chemical and physiological effects on everyone who drinks it. Alcohol is not addictive for everyone. Most people who drink, many who drink daily and many who drink heavily, do so without becoming dependent. Jellinek's disease is insidious because it is selective. There is no way of being certain who it will strike. A person who exercises free will and chooses to drink socially can be a responsible drinker one minute and the next, an irresponsible one. Since it is the nature of the disease to create its own cause for drinking, as it does so the opportunity to exercise free will and consider alternatives is diminished. Because it is a progressive illness, the freedom to make responsible decisions and to act in a responsible way is progressively eroded.

An individual is responsible for his behavior only to the degree that he can make rational, informed choices, understand the consequences of his actions, and maintain control over himself. For the chemically dependent person those options are removed. He cannot be responsible even if he wanted to be; he is no longer in control—a chemical is. Responsibility, therefore, is excused and forgiveness is in order. That he is sick, however, does not free the person from responsibility for the consequences of his actions. Sick or not, he is both morally and legally liable. Just as a drunk driver who causes an accident must answer for his wrongdoing, so too is the chemically dependent person answerable for the damage caused by his illness. If he hopes to arrest his dependency, ultimately he must admit to the injurious effects of his sickness and make amends for the results. This is a critical step in physical, emotional, and spiritual recovery.

Whether we are on the side of abstinence or drinking, it is not our purpose to focus on the consequences of the dependent person's behavior and hold him liable for his actions. To become self-righteous and judgmental is to take sides; it is to remove ourselves from the pastoral task for which we are liable—the creation of an understanding and accepting environment in which forgiveness for the dependent's irresponsibility is available.

Responsibility is removed by Jellinek's disease and so, too, is the responsibility for seeking help. The victims are rendered, as Vernon Johnson says, "incapable of the spontaneous insight required to offer themselves remedial care." Consequently, unless the chronic illness is confronted by someone who is aware that it can be dealt with and arrested, it takes its progressive toll on all aspects of the individual's life and everyone in his family.

CONSEQUENCES OF THE ILLNESS

Sharon Wegscheider, a certified chemical-dependency specialist, family therapist, member of Virginia Satir's AVANTA network, former staff member at the Johnson Institute, and now president of Onsite Training and Consulting, Incorporated, Palm Desert, California, wrote the book that offers the most insight into the hope and health available to the alcoholic family: *Another Chance*. What makes her book so helpful to clergy is that it explains Jellinek's disease as an illness that infects the *whole person*. The disease damages what Wegscheider calls six distinct "personal potentials": physical, emotional, social, mental, spiritual, and volitional.[17] To the extent that it does so, it affects those around the dependent until other family members begin to display many of the same symptoms. Just how the dependent's potential is diminshed and how it affects family members is information vital to the pastor's appreciation of the complex problems caused by the disease.

Sharon Wegscheider depicts a person as a circle—a figure long recognized as a symbol of wholeness. In her model the circle is divided into six equal and equally important segments, each representing a "personal potential." The segments, like slices of a pie, all join at the center. Likening the circle to a wheel, Wegscheider points out that each potential, though distinct, affects and is affected by the others, much as a deformity in one part of the wheel will have an effect on the functioning of the whole. Ordinarily these potentials are in operation all at once and in many combinations, but a look at the effects of alcoholism on each explains how the whole person is imparied.

The physical potential: Each of us is born with a body. The one we have is uniquely our own, a set of possibilities that no other human being shares. . . . It is our first line of contact with the world around us. It holds all our receptors for perceiving what is out there and all our equipment for responding to what we find. It is the foundation of health. . . .

Deterioration of all aspects of the physical potential is rarely seen as dramatically as in the victims of alcoholism. . . . The body once offered the alcoholic a number of avenues for enjoying his life and wholeness. One by one they are destroyed: physical skills, personal appearance, sexual desire and satisfaction, health.

The emotional potential: Developing the emotional potential unlike the physical calls for no nurturing or practice. The whole range of emotions springs naturally in each of us, giving life zest and flavor. Emotion is just another word for feelings—an inner response to both inner and outer events. . . .

Feelings honestly felt give life its pulse and color. They allow that part of ourselves that we experience as human to reach out and relate dynamically to the material world and the humanity of those around us.

Whatever the personal pain that first made social drinking attractive to him, the chances are the alcoholic once felt good about himself and his life at least part of the time. . . . But as social drinking slipped into harmful dependency, the good feelings became fewer, and there were onslaughts of uncomfortable feelings that made his original discomfort, for which he started using alcohol in the first place, seem mild indeed. In time he experiences the whole catalogue of painful human emotions: anger, hostility, resentment, fear, anxiety, tension, shame, guilt, feelings of worthlessness, remorse and depression.

When the burden of painful emotions reaches a point he can no longer tolerate, he begins to repress them—to turn them off . . . he is left with no feelings at all—numb, "turned off," no longer able to relate to other people or events as a human, feeling being.

The social potential: None of us lives alone. . . . We draw on the social potential in even our most superficial relationships. If it is functioning well, it can make all those contacts more pleasant and effective. . . .

Qualities like honesty, opennesss, intimacy, compassion, or coop- eration . . . are the aspects of the social potential that are absolutely essential to forming and deepening the more important relationships in our lives, relationships with spouses and children and parents, with friends and lovers, with all those who truly matter to us.

As the alcoholic begins to drink more heavily and frequently than the others in his social group, the friendly connections become strained. . . . As the disease begins to transform his personality and the hale fellow becomes increasingly hostile, all but his close friends learn to avoid him.

At home his relationship with wife and children is cold, stormy, tearful or intermittently all three. Those close to an alcoholic must endure watching this person they love turn into a series of different and difficult strangers as the disease advances through its progressive stages.

His marriage and home remain intact, if they do, through his wife's sense of duty, her ability to make changes—or most often—her own participation in all symptoms of his disease except the phar- macology.

The mental potential: It has often been exalted as the single gift that separates us from other animals. . . . The most lavish rewards are bestowed on those with the greatest mental potential. . . . The mind has immense internal value in helping the individual become a whole person.

The mental power has three aspects; one is in the past, in the memory, [one] focuses on the present through ideas, the third is in the future, in fantasy and imagination.

At first glance, the incipient alcoholic seems to have his mental powers honed to a fine edge. He alibis, "cons," charms, bluffs, covers all the bases. . . . But his cleverness is an illusion . . . the defenses that he has called into action to protect him from criticism and from his own painful feelings end up giving him a distorted picture of reality. Rationalization and denial keep him from seeing the truth about any person or situation. . . .

Blackouts are a profound insult to the mental potential, in effect destroying it for limited but growing periods of time.

The spiritual potential: In a fully developed person the spiritual potential can find expression in a wide variety of both inner and outer activities: meditation, prayer, discipline, organized religion, development of the higher Self, humanitarian service. . . .

The possibilities for joy and satisfaction in such pursuits transcend anything else that the human potentials can offer.

But the spiritual potential does not forever drift among the clouds. It is also a very practical matter, for it is the source of our values. When the [value] system is illumined by a lively spiritual awareness it can give even the most mundane aspects of our lives meaning, beauty and nobility.

When the spiritual potential is not activated the person sees little reason to exist.

A person who finds relief in social drinking sees alcohol as a resource with value. But if he becomes dependent on it, the chemical moves from something that HAS value to something that IS value in itself—in time, the central value of his life. All else begins to revolve around it, and preserving his relationship with it is his first priority.

If the dependent has formerly belonged to an organized religious group his ties to it are likely to be one of the early social connections broken. . . . If he had an inner personal relationship with a Higher Power, he has probably turned away from it in his growing sense of unworthiness.

The volitional potential: The volitional potential is the capacity for making choices. . . . Centered in the will, it mobilizes the data, experiences, values, and energy generated by all the other potentials and puts them to work in the service of the whole person.

The healthy will effectively sets goals, ranks priorities, makes decisions, perseveres in the face of difficulty, and sustains effort until its goals are reached or changed.

The alcoholic loses his power of choice by slow increments. . . . As dependency sets in, loss of control literally deprives the drinker of choice over one very important thing in his life, how much he will drink and when he will stop. Later when the dependency has evolved into total physical addiction there is no choice at all; continuing to drink is a matter of life and death. Indeed, the life-style of the chronic alcoholic . . . offers few choices about anything.

Wholeness: The root of self-worth: Each of the personal potentials, then, as it is developed, brings its own rewards in both inner satisfaction and effective behavior. But that is not all. When all six are healthily developed the individual not only is whole he feels whole . . . he enjoys strong feelings of self-worth. Self-worth is an essential ingredient—perhaps THE essential ingredient in personal well-being and interpersonal harmony.

> When some of a person's potentials are damaged or under-
> developed, he cannot find within himself much justification for feel-
> ings of self-worth. It is very hard for such a person to experience honest
> intimate relationships with others.
>
> The situation of the chemically dependent person and eventually
> the members of his family as well is even worse. They feel so vulnera-
> ble that honest interchange is almost completely closed off. . . . [18]

When we develop a true understanding of Jellinek's disease as an illness
that diminishes the whole person, we can stop arguing over whether it is a sin
or a sickness. As theologians, we, more than any other caregiving professionals,
can appreciate that the real moral issue is not whether drinking is right or
wrong but that the substance, when consumed in large quantities, separates
man from himself, from others, and from God. It can and does lead to chemical
dependency, and when it is misused or abused it results in untold damage to
person, family, community, and society.

Ministers are in a unique position to witness the damage wrought by
Jellinek's disease. As the only professionals who have regular contact with
parishioners, it is painfully apparent to us that some of the cruelest effects of the
illness are those on the families. No member escapes unscathed, and to the
pastor who has a "front row seat," it is clear the whole family is sickened. This
family disease is vividly described in a tract published in 1973 by Al-Anon
Family Group Headquarters, New York, the organization founded solely to
help and support families that include a dependent member. The tract,
entitled "Understanding Ourselves and Alcoholism" offers a disturbing
vignette:

> Alcoholism is a "family " disease. Compulsive drinking affects that
> drinker and it affects the drinker's relationships, friendships, employ-
> ment, childhood, parenthood, love affairs, marriage—all suffer from
> the effects of alcoholism. Those special relationships in which a person
> is really close to an alcoholic are affected most, and the people who
> care are the most caught up in the behavior of another person. They
> react to an alcoholic's behavior. They see that the drinking is out of
> bounds and they try to control it. They are ashamed of the public
> scenes, but in private they try to handle it. It isn't long before they feel
> they are to blame and take on the hurts, the fears, the quilt of an
> alcoholic. They become sick, too.
>
> These well-meaning people begin to count the number of drinks
> another person is having. They pour expensive liquor down drains,
> search the house for hidden bottles, listen for the sound of opening
> cans. All their thinking is directed on what the alcoholic is doing or not
> doing and how to get him/her to stop drinking. This is their OBSESSION.

Watching other human beings slowly kill themselves with alcohol is painful. While the alcoholic doesn't seem to worry about the bills, the job, the children, the condition of his/her health, people around begin to worry.

They make the mistake of covering up. They fix everything, make excuses, tell little lies to mend damaged relationships and they worry some more. This is their ANXIETY.

Sooner or later the alcoholic's behavior makes those around him/her angry. They realize that the alcoholic is not taking care of responsibilities, is telling lies, using them. They have begun to feel that the alcoholic doesn't love them and they want to strike back, make the alcoholic pay for the hurt and frustration caused by uncontrolled drinking. This is their ANGER.

Those who are close to the alcoholic begin to pretend. They accept promises, they believe, they want to believe the problem has gone away each time there is a sober period. When every good sense tells them there is something wrong with the alcoholic's drinking and thinking, they still hide how they feel and what they know. This is their DENIAL.

Perhaps the most severe damage to those who have shared some part of life with an alcoholic comes in the form of the nagging belief that they are somehow at fault, they were not up to it all, not attractive enough, not clever enough to have solved this problem for the one they love. They think it was something they did or did not do. These are their FEELINGS OF GUILT.

It is clear the family is just as much at the mercy of the chemical as is the dependent. The disturbances throughout the family system produce actions and reactions that diminish each person's six "personal potentials." The dependent lives in relation to his chemical, the codependent family to the signs and symptoms of the sickness. Consequently, the family is controlled by a set of unspoken rules that grow out of the chemical dependency. Each member, whether he likes it or not, is forced to subjugate his freedom and limit his potential in order to abide by these rigid regulations. Sharon Wegscheider lists them:

Rule: *The dependent person's use of alcohol is the most important thing in the family's life.* The family's behavior, schedule, social life, etc., all revolve around the dependent's drinking. His alcohol consumption is the overriding concern of the family; everyone acts or reacts in response to it.

Rule: *Alcohol is not the cause of the family's problem.* Denial. At first they deny that alcohol is the problem, then they deny there is a dependency, and finally they deny it is what caused them to need help. This denial is both conscious and unconscious.

Rule: *Someone or something else caused the alcoholic's dependency; he is not responsible.* Because the dependent is so adamant in blaming something or someone other than himself for his drinking, members of the family accept the delusion, take on themselves responsibility for his drinking, and suffer feelings of inadequacy, guilt, and worthlessness.

Rule: *The status quo must be maintained at all costs.* The dependent cannot allow anything that might change his lifestyle. The family enables him to maintain his habit by keeping peace, harmony, and equilibrium, and by denying his dependency.

Rule: *Everyone in the family must be an enabler.* By protecting the dependent, covering for him, supplying him, apologizing for him, taking over his responsibilities, accepting his demands, each person in the family enables the dependent to maintain the status quo and stay dependent.

Rule: *No one may discuss what is really going on in the family, either with one another or with outsiders.* This unwritten rule is required by the dependent, who does not want family affairs—specifically the degree of his dependency and the magnitude of its impact on his wife and children—discussed inside or outside the house.

Rule: *No one may say what he is really feeling.* The alcoholic cannot handle painful feelings, his own or his family's. So he requires that everyone's true feelings be hidden. As a result, communication among family members is severely hampered.[19]

The damage to a family so governed is tragic. Contrariwise, in a healthy family each person has the following:

1. The opportunity to have an equal, open, and honest relationship with every other member of the family and to enjoy each other's trust.

2. The understanding and assurance that each individual is ultimately responsible for his actions.

3. The security of stable relationships in which a person can negotiate with another without being rejected and can agree or disagree without fear of reprisal.

4. The chance to ask for the satisfaction of needs, wants, desires for oneself, as well as to be asked to meet those of others.

5. The freedom to discuss one's views outside and inside the family and to express them in the home without fear of criticism.

6. The opportunity to express all manner of feelings freely in a family environment of mutual honesty and empathy.

An analogy Sharon Wegscheider finds very useful is that of a mobile consisting of five or six beautiful butterflies of various shapes, sizes, and colors, each butterfly representing a member of the family. Suspended by strings from three sticks, the mobile is in equilibrium until a puff of wind hits it and the butterflies move and sway each in relation to the other. If one of the butterflies is jarred, all the others move erratically. Such is the case in a family affected by chemical dependency; everyone acts in erratic patterns equal to the impact of the illness on the dependent.

NUMBER ONE SYMPTOM—DENIAL

For anyone trying to help a chemically dependent person or the family members and friends of the dependent, it is imperative to understand that the number one symptom of the illness is *denial*. The term "denial" is here used clinically. It applies to the dependent and those in any way related to him who, consciously or unconsciously, avoid insight into the severity of the illness. By pretending that the harmful situation experienced by them or described to them by a caring person is reasonable or exaggerated or nonexistent, they effectively blind themselves to the possibility of help. In the dependent person, the chemical's toxic effects disrupt the brain's chemical and electrical balances, causing intellectual and emotional disturbances that render him incapable of perceiving his own deterioration. In the family and friends, the dependent's behavior causes such painful feelings—anxiety, worry, fear, embarrassment, resentment, anger, guilt, shame—that psychological reaction-formations set in. They lead to protective "fight or flight" responses that render the victimized person unable to address the factors causing his distress and incapable of accepting the diagnosis of the dependent's distress.

It is the overpowering force of *denial* that so often frustrates efforts to help the chemically dependent person or members of the family. Not that those who are sick *won't* face the problem; it is that they *cannot*. They simply are unable to internalize the reasons for their distress. The dependent person is totally controlled by alcohol, and the family is totally controlled by the behavior of the dependent. The self-delusion of the dependent is both physiological and psychological; denial is his *only* way of life. The family, in its efforts first to care for, then to protect, and finally to control the dependent, becomes so mired in the guilt and shame of continual failure that it has no alternative other than to deny the disease's impact.

When a clergyperson is called in to be of service to this impaired family, he must realize he is in the midst of a delusional system of denial caused by a medical illness. Otherwise, he will follow his pastoral propensity to be useful by empathizing with the family's emotional pain. No matter who comes to him first, he will listen to the complaints and then, drawing on his pastoral counseling skills, identify the hurt, describe what the person is feeling, and define the pain in terms of the stated cause. What he does not realize is that he is focusing on the family's delusion—on the symptoms, not the illness. Because of denial, the family members, dependent and codependents, will describe their discomfort as marital problems, teenage troubles, lack of money, or in-law difficulty. If drinking is ever mentioned as a factor, it is as an appropriate and understandable response to these difficulties.

In his efforts to help, the minister often seeks to minimize, control, and reduce the distress by making allowances for the family's reactive behavior and by offering suggestions to resolve the problems. If and when he does so, he becomes what Sharon Wegscheider calls a "Professional Enabler": "Any counselor or other helping professional who engages in the same kinds of dysfunctional behavior as the family Enabler—denial, avoidance, covering up, protecting, taking responsibility for someone else, either the dependent or another family member—is acting as Professional Enabler."[20] Ordinarily, when seeking to resolve other types of pastoral problems, there is nothing wrong with being an enabler; seminaries teach that the role is an effective way to express empathy, to affirm a person's distress, and to help the sufferer mobilize his resources to endure the pain and resolve the problem. In ministering to a family distressed by chemical dependency, however, being an enabler makes the clergyperson party to the family's delusional system. He validates the symptoms, not the disease, as the cause of its problems. As the family reacts to the dependent's behavior, the minister reacts to the family's denial and becomes just as codependent as the others in the household. By seeking to assuage their pain, he comes between the individuals and their crises. Pain is the only thing that will ultimately motivate them to address the real issue—chemical dependency—and to accept appropriate professional help. By soothing the pain he enables the family sickness to continue. Then, as his answers to their problems are ignored, as his suggestions are disregarded, as his counseling is obviously ineffectual, as his efforts to contain and control the situation fail, he, too, becomes exasperated, rigid, frustrated, angry, and finally guilty. His guilt causes him to react as codependents do, with a "fight or flight" response, and he signals that he is not available for further assistance. In so doing, he, along with the others, is swallowed in the delusional system and turns his back on the family problem.

Denial! Therein lies the reason many professionals and (especially) ministers do not enjoy dealing with dependents and their families' problems, therein lies the reason many clergy describe Jellinek's disease as a moral problem and a character weakness. It is because the minister's very best efforts to help, to comfort, to heal, and to restore seem to be willfully disregarded by those who sought help in the first place. They simply do not respond to his loving, pastoral care. But then, they *cannot*. They are powerless over this family illness.

LEADING PEOPLE TO WHOLENESS

If a minister has had appropriate training or has an understanding of the skills needed to intervene in the life of an impaired family, he can be a primary resource for helping the one in four families affected by Jellinek's disease. But if he does not have the requisite knowledge, if he has to rely on his pastoral counseling expertise only, he can be most useful by referring the family to an alcohol or a drug specialist. *Referral is the secret to success for ministers who are called on to resolve alcohol/drug problems.* No apologies are necessary. The complexities of chemical dependency are such that unless the minister refers, one sick family may consume all his counseling time, most often to no avail. On the other hand, with the numerous resources now available (e.g., professional counselors, agencies, treatment facilities, members of the parish who are in Alcoholics Anonymous, Al-Anon, or Al-teen), he can put a distressed family in touch with the most appropriate source of help and lead them to make their own appointment. Though at first it may feel heartless to refer a dependent or a codependent family member, it is far more effective to do so than it is to respond to the family's problems disguised by denial and end up a "professional enabler" who is as codependent as everyone else affected by the dependent's sickness. Acting as a referral resource is the minister's most helpful pastoral role. The technique discussed in chapter 8 provides the tools necessary.

Jellinek's disease is a family sickness. It is a biochemical, genetic disease that is primary, progressive, chronic, and terminal. As it destroys the God-given potential of the individual, it also diminishes the God-given potential of all those affected by the illness. By proclaiming Jellinek's disease as a sickness, we can do much to refute the myths and misconceptions that condemn the dependent to the realms of moral degeneracy. By understanding the causes of the disease, we can promote the education needed to prevent its onset. By knowing the effects of the sickness on the individual and family members, we can guide the latter to the source of hope and the resources for help. Though we do not have the time or training to be alcohol counselors, as guides we can express our concern by leading these sick family members toward health. Our role is beautifully described by Sharon Wegscheider in her prayer:

A Prayer for Guides

Help me to create a setting for risk,
As each new person comes to visit me,

Help me to recognize and accept
The fear and pain they bring with them.
Let me show them that I am not afraid,
Let me use my sensitivity and courage
    To mirror back to them all that I see and hear
    That keeps them in their bondage
    Of pain and loneliness
Give me the care and perception
    To show them their gifts and their power.
Let me reach out and touch—
    Then let me leave them alone.
Let me trust in their strength and courage.
Let me let them make their own decisions and
    choices.
Help me to lead people to wholeness
    By being whole.[21]

CHAPTER 5

The Misuse and Abuse of Licit Drugs

> Drug abuse means the use of any drug to the point that it
> damages the user's health, job, education, personal rela-
> tionships, judgments, or ability to cope with daily life.[1]

Strictly speaking, it is incorrect to differentiate between Jellinek's disease
(alcoholism) and drug abuse. Alcohol is a drug, and if regular consumption of it
damages the user's health, education, and welfare, it is considered drug abuse
by professionals in the field of chemical dependency. Similarly, if the taking of a
licit or illicit drug diminishes any of the user's six "personal potentials"—
physical, emotional, social, mental, spiritual, or volitional—that, too is drug
abuse. The importance of understanding this definition is that today, more than
ever before, the numbers of men and women mixing alcohol and drugs (such as
sleeping pills and tranquilizers) to the point of abusing themselves has reached
unprecedented levels. The National Institute on Drug Abuse estimates that in
the months from May 1976 to April 1977, forty-seven thousand persons suffering from the effects of mixing alcohol and drugs were admitted to emergency
rooms. That's 130 people a day. There were twenty-five hundred deaths.[2]

POLYDRUG ABUSE AMONG WOMEN

When we think of drug abuse we often imagine a teenager sitting with a group
of friends, smoking a joint of marijuana or dropping a hit of acid. Clearly, that is
drug abuse, because any use of illicit drugs by anyone at all is in fact abuse.
Most of us, however, do not realize that polydrug abuse is just as rampant
among the US. adult population as drug abuse is among teenagers, but the
drugs the grownups are abusing are legally prescribed by doctors. This critical
problem was brought to light in April 1978, when former First Lady Betty Ford
was hospitalized for a medical problem—dual addiction to Valium and alcohol.
Because we live in a society in which it is normal and acceptable to enjoy a drug
(alcohol) for social purposes and to use a prescription drug for emotional or

73

physical problems, we never consider that the combination of the two might be addictive. In the U.S., however, where there are 120 million consumers of alcohol (one in eight of whom suffers from Jellinek's disease), where doctors, each year, write out an estimated 100 million prescriptions for minor tranquilizers such as Valium and Librium, chemical dependency that involves not just alcohol but other drugs is skyrocketing. As Dr. Jack H. Mendelson, director of Harvard Medical School's alcohol and drug abuse research center in McLean's Hospital, Belmont, Massachusetts, says: "What comes at you is that people who abuse alcohol are also abusing a variety of other things. They're not drug gourmets, they're gourmands."[3] The alarming fact is that it does not make any difference whether the drug is used for social or psychological purposes; all sedatives do the same things to the brain. Ironically, tranquilizers like Valium and Librium are often prescribed for the dependent person, to help with the withdrawal from alcohol. The danger is that alcohol interacts in various (sometimes lethal) ways with various drugs.

When alcohol is used in conjunction with another drug it produces either of two basic reactions: It may reduce the overall effects of both drugs, producing an antagonistic interaction, or it may result in a synergistic or potentiating interaction (i.e., one plus one equals ten or fifty) in which the total effect of the drugs is far greater than the effect of either. The latter is known as "supra-additive interaction" and is, from a health standpoint, the most dangerous. For instance, a person can take much less than a lethal dose of alcohol and much less than a lethal dose of phenobarbital—the former a common social drug, the later a common sedative and antispasmodic—and together they will kill him. Tragically, the public and even many health-care professionals (including physicians one would trust to know) are not aware of the potential hazards of combining drugs with alcohol.

Among the drugs most often used with alcohol are those classified as the minor tranquilizers: Valium and Librium. Since both are central-nervous-system depressants, the serious effects they have when mixed with alcohol—also a central-nervous-system depressant—are: slowed reaction time, marked diminution of judgment, coordination deficits, mental *and* motor impairment, and increased intoxication at low levels of blood-alcohol content. Regarding the use of alcohol with stimulants such as amphetamines, 50 to 80 percent of which are reportedly used by women, the effects include gastrointestinal upset and heart palpitations. The combination can produce hyperexcitability or antagonize the alcohol's depressant effect. When combined with the common antidepressants, 70 percent of which are used by women, the effects include reduced motor responses and impaired reaction times, greater alcoholic intoxication than expected, and, in some instances, hypertensive reactions of nausea and severe headaches. Then there are the major tranquilizers (i.e., Thorozine,

Mellaril, and Serpasil), 50 percent of which are used by women. When these nervous-system depressants, commonly prescribed for serious emotional disturbances, are used with alcohol, the mixture can cause severe, possibly fatal, respiratory and liver dysfunctions. At the very least, they can produce a radical reduction in the user's ability to drive a car (without the user realizing it).

Though we clergy are not called to be diagnosticians of medical problems, often we are in a position to hear of parishioners who use medications and also drink. Therefore, it is helpful to know about the dangerous mixes.

1. Alcohol + Antihistamines (including many cold remedies and allergy medicines) = Increased central-nervous-system depression, e.g., drowsiness.

2. Alcohol + Aspirin = Stomach and intestinal bleeding.

3. Alcohol + Narcotics (e.g., codeine, heroin) = Increased central-nervous-system depression with acute intoxication; possible respiratory arrest.

4. Alcohol + Nonnarcotic Painkillers (e.g., Tylenol) = Stomach and intestinal irritation and, possibly, bleeding.

5. Alcohol + Antebuse (an alcoholism medication) = Flushing, hyperventilation, vomiting, drowsiness.

6. Alcohol + High-Blood-Pressure Medications = Increased effect; in some cases blood pressure can be lowered to dangerous levels.

7. Alcohol + Oral Anticoagulants = Increased anticoagulant effect initially, decreased effect in chronic drinkers.

8. Alcohol + Oral Antidiabetic Drugs = A reaction similar to the interaction of Antebuse and alcohol; decreased antidiabetic effect.

9. Alcohol + Antibiotics = A reaction similar to the interaction of Antebuse and alcohol.

10. Alcohol + Sedatives and Tranquilizers (e.g., Valium, Librium, Milltowns) = Increased central-nervous-system depression. WARNING: The effects listed here can be altered dramatically by such factors as past drinking habits, amount of alcohol already consumed, and chronic ailments.[4]

The population most vulnerable to dual addiction or polydrug abuse is women. Dr. Stanley Gitlow, a high-blood-pressure specialist and psychotherapist at Mt. Sinai School of Medicine, has treated the chemically dependent and dually addicted for twenty-five years. He believes physicians are overprescribing tranquilizers, sedatives, and other psychotherapeutic drugs— 69 percent of which are for women. This is being done partly out of ignorance and partly out of the common attitude that psychological and social problems have medical causes and chemical solutions. Dr. Gitlow says:

> When I started out 25 years ago, about a third of my patients who were alcoholic had at one time or another mixed it with solid sedatives. Now

that's up to 50 percent. It's progressing, particularly in the female section.

The physician is sometimes unaware of the true relationship among the soporific drugs. He might be prevailed upon to replace alcohol with solid sedatives thinking he's doing the patient a favor. Usually all he's doing is helping the patient out of the frying pan and into the fire.

We live in a society where, when things get tough, you take a drink, if you're uncomfortable, turn to some chemical magic. No one says, "Hey, tolerate the stress and learn to cope." So doctors are constantly pressured to provide instant relief.[5]

The National Institute on Drug Abuse estimates that there are 32 million women as opposed to 19 million men using tranquilizers prescribed by doctors, and more women than men use sedatives and stimulants prescribed by doctors. There is a double standard in our society that suggests it is acceptable for a man to use and even to abuse alcohol, but if a woman uses it to the point of abuse she is considered a "lush," a promiscuous person, or an unfit mother. Consequently, a woman is more likely at first to turn to a prescription drug for relief from the crises in her life.

The treatment of all emotional discomfort in the U.S. female population has become a vast enterprise. As a result of mental-health professionals' medicalization of life's common problems, as a result of the pharmaceutical industry's advertisements for chemical relief from life's ailments, as a result of physicians' attitudes toward appropriate drug use reflecting these accepted societal values, women are prescribed drugs for such "medical problems" as sleeplessness, financial difficulties, general feelings of unhappiness, marital discord, headache, disobedient children, loneliness, fatigue, inability to concentrate, anxiety, apathy, depression, conflict, and tension. What's more, it is for these same reasons that four million women in the U.S. quietly become early and consistent drinkers. When the isolated, bored and lonely housewife covertly turns to the bottle and the drug her doctor prescribed, the result can be polydrug abuse and dual addiction. Tragically, at no point in her quest for relief is she assured that she has within her the God-given abilities and strength not only to cope but to prevail.

We who minister to families where drinking is clearly a problem need to remember that the problem may be caused by more than one chemical. In the case of a grandmother or a wife or a mother or a daughter, the sickness more often than not is the result of polydrug abuse. It is very uncommon to find a woman who is abusing alcohol only. Should we be called to a home where a woman appears to be in a stupor as a result of drinking, it is vital to bear this finding in mind. Chances are her imbalance, slurred speech, and lack of coordination are due to some sedative she has taken in conjunction with the alcohol. Rather than trying to learn from her or from the caller if this is the case, it is much safer to assume it is so and call immediately for emergency medical assistance. It is better to be safe than sorry. Calling for a doctor, the local police, or an emergency ambulance instead of trying to protect the woman's reputation or the family's social image is the only way to be sure she gets the medical attention needed to treat her potentially lethal problem. What's more, calling immediately for help is a very useful way to break through a family's denial system and force them to face the fact that one of its members is suffering from chemical dependency. The family may be incensed at making it a medical emergency, but an illness that requires an ambulance to come to the front door is very difficult to deny.

CHEMICAL DEPENDENCY IN THE OLDER GENERATION

Another population in the U.S. is often disregarded but is very vulnerable to drug abuse—the older generation. Although information about the numbers of the elderly involved in chemical misuse is limited, it is a fair estimate, according to the Johnson Institute, that 2 to 10 percent in any community will have chemical-dependency problems.

In the sixty or over age group, the percentage of women using stimulants, minor tranquilizers, sedatives, and hypnotics is larger than the percentage of men. In the use of minor tranquilizers (Valium or Librium, for example) 5 percent of the men and 10 percent of the women report usage during the past year. This suggests that the problems from mixing different drugs are more likely to occur among women than among men and that this difference holds up throughout life. Older men, however, are not without problems. One community survey shows that of the people who have alcohol problems, men outnumber women five to one.[6]

As with most other people, it is not unusual for elderly people to trust that when their doctors order prescriptions for them, it is unlikely the medications will cause any problems. What's more, like their younger counterparts, they have been socialized to believe that chemicals relieve life's problems. Faced with inactivity, feelings of worthlessness owing to retirement, isolation, loss of friends, loneliness, living without families, it is understandable that one of the minor tranquilizers might be taken to overcome the depression or that alcohol be used to combat it. It never occurs to the elderly or their doctors that the full, long-term effect of these sedatives, used separately or in conjunction with alcohol, will produce dependency. The fact is, however, that for any person whose physical condition is limited or debilitated, the combined effects of tranquilizers and alcohol can be harmful.[7]

When Grandpa gets quietly intoxicated every evening and falls asleep without bothering anyone, it is very easy for his family to make allowances by suggesting it is the only fun and comfort he has and he isn't hurting anyone. Unless we address the fact that he is hurting himself by reducing his potential for living a creative life and that he is hurting the family by being more in relation to his chemical than to his children and grandchildren, then very often the drug abuse is allowed to continue until he dies. Helping families see that the value of life is life itself and that Grandpa's life can be enjoyed by him as well as the family often is the incentive children need to seek help for the chemically dependent parent. There are many cases of older people who, at the age of sixty or seventy, have overcome drug abuse and led enthusiastic, joy-filled lives.

But a note of warning: Once Grandpa's problem is pointed out to the children, the most appropriate thing for them to do is to have him examined by his doctor. It is at this point that efforts to resolve his chemical dependency can fail. The doctor very often does not ask Grandpa or the family about Grandpa's drinking or drug use. In some cases the doctor is not even aware of the addictive effect of mixing alcohol with other drugs. Consequently, he misses the chemical dependency and gives Grandpa a clean bill of health. The children are assured there is not really a problem and Grandpa is allowed to waste his remaining evenings by quietly drinking and passing out. As Dr. Edith Lisansky Gomberg says in her pamphlet *Sober Days, Golden Years*:

> Older problem drinkers (as well as the older pill taker) are not beyond helping themselves or receiving help from others. They deserve to live full, rewarding lives whether they have six more months or thirty more years before they die. Taking responsibility for one's life means not allowing chemicals to replace creative consciousness with drugged acceptance.[8]

ADOLESCENCE AND ALCOHOL

Again, when one thinks of drug abuse the first image one usually has is of an adolescent smoking a joint of marijuana or getting high from a pill. When addressing the problem of teenage drug abuse, that image is only partly correct; it omits the number one drug of choice among adolescents, the drug most commonly abused—alcohol (the most popular is beer). Because the public and parents have focused so much attention on the use of illicit drugs (e.g., marijuana, LSD, cocaine), the illegal abuse of alcohol among teenagers has been ignored and the rise in teenage alcoholism denied. (Note that an adolescent under the legal drinking age who drinks alcoholic beverages is, by definition, using an illicit drug.) The statistics cited in chapter 1 make the extent of the problem self-evident; they bear repeating. According to the National Council on Alcoholism, 31 percent of high-school students are considered alcohol misusers—drunk at least six times a year; 15 percent of students in the tenth to twelfth grades are heavy or problem drinkers—consuming five cans of beer or mixed drinks at least once a week. The average age kids begin to drink is thirteen. The younger a person is when he starts drinking, the quicker and easier he becomes an alcoholic. "The action of the alcohol is channeled directly toward the adolescent's imbalanced hypothalamus and autonomic nervous system, thereby obstructing his emotional maturation on both psychological and physiological levels," according to Dr. Jorge Valles, director of alcoholism therapy, U.S. Veterans Hospital, Houston, Texas. This explains why an estimated 3.3 million drinking teenagers aged fourteen to seventeen are showing signs they may develop serious alcohol problems.[9] Drunk driving is the leading cause of death among fifteen- to twenty-four-year olds, and in 1980 close to nine thousand teenagers (ages 15 to 19) were killed in motor vehicle crashes. Considering the College of American Pathologists' research statistics suggesting that 90 percent of all fatal auto accidents are alcohol related, that is 8,100 teenagers killed in accidents involving alcohol, or 22 children a day.

Because of society's acceptance of drinking, parents too often forget that alcohol—beer, wine, sherry, rum, gin, whiskey—is a drug; it is toxic chemical described as ethyl alcohol or ethanol C_2H_5OH. Though most people regard it as a stimulant (owing to the energizing effect of its high sugar content), it is in fact a central-nervous-system depressant. The more alcohol is consumed, the less stimulating it is and the more depressing, dulling, anesthetizing it is. Pure alcohol, a colorless liquid that has a very harsh, burning taste, gets its various flavors, tastes, and smells by combination with other chemicals called congeners. It becomes beer, wine, sherry, whiskey, gin, or vodka by the inclusion of various congeners and the use of various processing methods, i.e., brewing, fermenting, distilling.

The most common hazard of teenage drinking is that very often youngsters have a tendency to underestimate the potency of alcoholic beverages and to overestimate their ability to drive. They will differentiate between hard liquor, beer, and wine without realizing that, though these beverages differ in percentage of alcohol (called "proof"), the amount of alcohol consumed per standard drink is nearly equal no matter which drink it is. One-half the proof printed on the label is the alcohol content. Therefore, scotch, bourbon, and rye, listed at 86 proof, contain 43 percent alcohol; table wines—burgundies, sauternes, etc.—contain 12 to 14 percent alcohol; port and sherry, 18 to 20 percent; and most beer, 5 percent. When a 150-pound teenager drinks five cans of beer or five five-ounce glasses of wine or five highballs (rum and coke, for instance) in one sitting, he is consuming the same amount of alcohol in each instance.

A beer, a five-ounce glass of wine, and an ounce and a half of liquor all contain equal amounts of alcohol. Its accumulation in the body is described as Blood Alcohol Content (BAC), and in each case, one drink per hour will result in a BAC of 2 percent. When a teenager drinks five in an hour's time, his BAC will reach 10 percent. In *all* states a person with this level BAC is considered legally drunk. The age-old remedies for drunkenness, such as cold showers, black coffee, fresh air, or exercise, have no effect in reducing BAC; the body burns up (oxidizes) alcohol at a rate of one ounce per hour. If no more drinks are consumed, the BAC drops approximately 2 percent per hour, and it would take about four hours before it would be safe for the 150-pound young man to drive. Tragically, the young man does not consider this fact, and because he underestimates the effect of beer compared to that of hard liquor, he believes he can drive. With a BAC of 5 percent his chances of an accident double; at 10 percent they increase seven times. What the young person does not realize is that by drinking slightly more than two beers, though he barely feels the effects, his BAC will be 5 percent and his ability to drive will be seriously impaired by the loss of depth perception and peripheral vision. The time it takes him to reach a BAC level of 10 percent will vary according to whether he is gulping or chugging his drinks, whether his stomach is full or empty, whether he is drinking beer or straight shots undiluted by a mix, his mental and physical condition, his body size, his purpose in drinking, and whether he has been using any other drugs—but, all these things considered, if he has had five drinks in an hour's time, his reaction time, coordination, and vision will be reduced to the point at which he cannot drive without being a serious danger to himself and others. Over half the drivers killed in auto accidents have a BAC over 8 percent.

The vast majority of Americans who drink enjoy alcohol as a beverage with meals, at social gatherings, celebrations, and religious ceremonies, and occasionally for medicinal purposes. Whiskey, in particular, is part of American tradition. In Andrew Jackson's day, over 150 years ago, because the water tasted foul, tea was too expensive, wine cost more than whiskey, and beer was unprofitable to brew, people had whiskey with lunch and dinner (some even had it with breakfast). In the first fifty years of U.S. history, people drank more alcoholic beverages than at any other time since.

Today most of the 120 million people who drink do so without abusing themselves. Among young people, however, the drug culture's message—"GET HIGH"—has influenced their reason for drinking and has drastically increased the numbers abusing themselves. Like adults, teenagers drink to have a good time and, sometimes, to escape from problems or the stress of school. Unlike most adults who drink socially, however, teenagers very often drink for the sole purpose of getting high. It is considered a macho thing now, for both young men *and* young women, to get drunk. "Let's have a party" no longer means staging a social function for conviviality and fun; it means gathering to "get wasted," "smashed," "wiped out." If asked, most youngsters are at a loss to offer any reason for drinking other than "getting high" or "getting drunk." The danger of this abusive drinking is that it separates the young person from the social interaction necessary for his psychological growth and development. The more he counts on alcohol to make him feel good, the less he is able to define his sense of self and develop his innate strengths and social skills.

Basically, there are five reasons why alcohol has a greater effect on young people than on adults. First, youngsters usually weigh less than adults, and the less the body weight, the greater the effect. Second, because teenagers are inexperienced at drinking, they have not yet learned to compensate for alcohol's effects. This ability to compensate is called "psychological tolerance." Learning to allow for the loss of control over the five senses, to make judgments that conterbalance it, requires years of experience as a social drinker. Even then, many adults are never able to do so. Hence the novice can be a real hazard to himself and others. Third, young people are in the process of acquiring new skills and practicing newly established habits. When these skills are blunted by alcohol (i.e., by drinking and driving), they are difficult to employ successfully or safely. Furthermore, the learning, not a result of the teenager's natural abilities but a consequence of chemically influenced behavior, does not establish confidence and a positive self-image. Fourth, the teenage years are emotionally tumultuous. When adolescents regularly use alcohol to enhance or blunt their feelings or alter their moods, they do not get a chance to become familiar with the vast range of their natural emotions. Finally, alcohol has a great effect on youngsters because they want it to, they expect it to; they drink to get high. There is, therefore, a predisposition to psychological intoxication whether or not enough alcohol has been consumed to produce physiological intoxication. This continual quest for euphoria can lead to psychological addiction and, ultimately, chemical dependency.

It is now known that the more the chemical is consumed, the greater the chances of the user becoming addicted. As Dr. George Mann states in his pamphlet *The Dynamics of Addiction*:

> The mood changers vary a great deal in their potential to addict. We are much more vulnerable to some drugs than to others. . . . Over and above any mood changes that might be involved there must be cellular

changes occurring from the use of these [addictive] chemicals. We know that almost any person can become addicted to or dependent on almost any of these chemicals if that person is exposed to a high enough dose for a long enough period of time.[10]

According to the National Council on Alcoholism, "Evidence suggests that problem drinkers started drinking at a younger age than others. Earlier use of alcohol among teenagers may increase the potential for developing alcoholism later."[11] Weekly drinking to get high will assuredly result in problems of some kind, at the time as well as later.

While the young person is abusing illicit drugs like marijuana, cocaine, LSD, and others, and developing a reliance on them, he is also developing a dependency on liquor, beer, and wine without even consuming them. The use of the illicit drugs brings about cellular changes that will make the abuser, if and when he drinks, unable to control his use of alcohol. Since dependency can result when a "person is exposed to a high enough dose for a long enough period of time," as Dr. Mann suggests, as the youngster exposes himself to one of the addictive illicit chemicals, he is making himself vulnerable to the licit ones as well. In short, he is ruining his chances to be a social drinker. Usually, when he does turn to alcoholic beverages, he immediately becomes a problem drinker.

Inevitably, when we begin promoting chemical health in our parishes we will be asked to define responsible drinking habits for adolescents, or we will be asked to suggest the responsible decision a teenager can make about drinking alcohol. The answer to these questions must be decided by the parents in conjunction with their youngsters, *not* by the pastor. The freedom of choice is theirs because living with the ramifications of those choices is theirs. Today, coming to terms with the use of alcohol or drugs is a developmental task adolescents face as a part of growing up in the U.S.; their experience with these chemicals is now statistically normative. Parents, in the face of this fact, are asking us for guidelines. In response we can ask them what example they are setting. Do they come home from a hard day and announce they need a drink? Do they ever press a party guest to take a drink, as opposed to accepting the refusal and offering a soft drink? Do they ever, as a good host or hostess, "load" people's drinks with more than a measured ounce and half of liquor? Do they serve enough to get a guest intoxicated? Do they allow party guests to drive home after five or six drinks? Do they make drinking, as opposed to food and fellowship, the focal point of the party?

Beyond such questioning we can be helpful by pointing out that a "responsible drinking habit" is not responsible behavior for a youngster. A habit by definition means habitual use, and habitual drinking is harmful to the maturing adolescent. Parents who do all in their power to help their children grow up need to know that that help does not have to include providing alcohol for teenage parties, offering them an alcoholic drink at adult parties, or rewarding them with a drink on a birthday or other special occasion to signify adulthood. Although seemingly unrealistic today, it is useful for parents and teenagers to understand that a responsible decision about adolescent alcohol use is to say, "No, thank you. At my age it is not beneficial to my personal growth and development. Furthermore, at my age, I'm under age." Too often we forget that abstinence or refusal is a valid and responsible choice. It is not popular to suggest that it is the most responsible decision for young people to make because it flies in the face of already established patterns. Though it is true that teenagers strongly influence each other's dress and personal appearance, hobbies, fads, interests, leisure activities, language, and use of alcohol and drugs, it is also true that parents have the most influence over their children's moral and social values, vocational choices, and educational plans. Parents need to be reminded, therefore, that it is okay to say no and that discussing the reasons for their stand is both a means of communicating parental values and of teaching responsible decision making. Making decisions is never easy, but a parent can teach a child to develop a step-by-step procedure by which the child:

1. Defines the problem clearly
2. Sets his own goal
3. Lists the alternatives
4. Considers the consequences of each
5. Makes his decision based on the above

In so doing, the youngster will learn to hold onto his values in the face of societal pressure because they are his own. He will be able to accept responsibility for his actions, understanding that what he does affects not only his life but the lives of those around him. When it comes to drinking, he will have prepared his own guidelines for responsible behavior.

"There is no such thing as 'responsible decision making' and/or 'responsibile drinking' among young people," asserts Dr. William Mayer of the National Institute on Alcohol Abuse and Alcoholism. "It cannot be responsible decision-making to drink when it is illegal to drink and if someone is too young to drink legally he or she cannot drink responsibly."[12] This stand makes observance of the law the only criterion for responsible behavior. It also rules out the use of alcohol as a beverage with meals, a common practice in many families. Still, it does raise the question whether alcohol use by teenagers is responsible or irresponsible. It is a question that needs to be raised. It will provoke much-needed discussion and challenge parental attitudes, especially those that condone illegal drinking but condemn illicit drug use. Though we may not agree wtih Dr. Mayer's position, the one stand we can all unite on is that drinking and driving is hazardous for adults and totally irresponsible and unacceptable for teenagers. There is only one guideline in the case of teenage drinking and driving: "NO! ABSOLUTELY NOT!"

Where alcohol is served to teenagers or where teenage parties include drinking, some parents have contracts with their children whereby they will come and pick up the kids rather than have them drive home while under the influence or ride home with a driver who is. Though the object is to prevent drinking and driving and to provide safe transportation home, it is a contract that authorizes the irresponsible use of liquor, beer, wine, by teenagers and endorses their drug abuse—drinking to get high or intoxicated. It is a parent's answer to a realistic concern, but there is a prior question that needs to be answered: Whose responsibility is it to see that teenagers do not abuse themselves with alcohol and drugs in the first place?

Responsible drinking is the use of alcohol in a way that does not harm the person or have a negative effect on others. If parents are going to allow their children to drink, it is important they teach their children from an early age that drinking is an activity that improves social relationships, it does not impair or harm them. Drinking is responsible when it is an adjunct to some other activity, as opposed to being an end in itself or the sole purpose of a party. Of course, the most effective way of teaching this attitude is for the parents to be models of it.

Many parents want to help their youngsters develop guidelines about drinking. We can help them by suggesting they read *Kids and Booze* by Wilbur Cross. It is excellent because it offers practical ways of discussing teenage drinking without lecturing the youngster. We must remember, however, that when we suggest material to be read, some parishioners may equate the content of the material with our personal theological positions unless we say otherwise. We have an obligation to make it clear that using alcohol to get high is in fact drug abuse, that it can and does result in dependency that undermines the person's potential, that it not only disrupts the life of the user but that of every member of his family. We also have an obligation to point out that alcohol abuse by adolescents is a step on the way to illicit highs.

OTHER LEGAL "HIGHS" AND "LOWS"

Approved use of alcohol by teenagers is one aspect of drug abuse in our culture that is widely accepted, but there is another cultural value that encourages use of licit/legal drugs; it comes from the medical world. Owing to society's belief that no one should experience any physical or psychological pain, doctors routinely not only prescribe medication for the cause of the pain, but often a painkiller as well. They become not only practitioners who fill out prescriptions, but the pushers who fulfill society's demands and expectations. To young people, however, this pervasive use of drugs to kill both physical and psychological pain suggests that all pain is bad and the purpose of life is to feel good or be high. The way to avoid the pain, and, more importantly, to maintain the pleasure, therefore, is to use drugs—licit as well as illicit ones. Teenagers are influenced by the pharmaceutical companies' suggesting there is "better living through chemistry." Since licit drugs are available in so many parents' medicine cabinets, the ones they experiment with and learn to abuse are primarily the two groups most commonly used by adults—stimulants, which speed up the central nervous system, and depressants, which slow it down.

Two of the most common stimulants not controlled by law are nicotine and caffeine. Young people smoke to look cool or feel grown up, but it results in both physical and psychological dependence, and long-term use can result in shortness of breath, emphysema, lung damage, heart and respiratory disease, and death. Caffeine is most often consumed in the form of coffee, tea, cola, or chocolate. It raises blood pressure, stimulates mental capacity, increases heartbeat and reaction time, and provides some feeling of energy. It can cause stomach disorders, restlessness, nervousness, insomnia, and irritability. One form of caffeine, No-Doz, is used by many youngsters as a means of staying awake while studying. It results in mental dullness, blocks memory storage, and retards memory retrieval the following morning.

It is not as important for us to know all the trade names of the stimulants as it is to know that the legal ones are classified as amphetamines. Generally, they are prescribed to control weight, combat fatigue, or treat mild depression. Called "speed" or "Bennies" (Benzedrine), or "Dex" (Dexedrine), or "Meth" (Methedrine), they are used by the young to feel confident, uplift the spirits, feel strong, and improve physical stamina and performance. For the youngster feeling uncertain or incompetent or insecure, these "uppers" provide instant confidence, certainty, and strength. The physical hazards are headaches, stomach distress, chills, fever, and chest pains. Tolerance develops rapidly, and psychological dependence and preoccupation with the drug are usual. This dependence leads to the psychological hazards of paranoia, anxiety, irritability, and fear. Withdrawal symptoms include fatigue, hunger, long periods of sleep, disorientation, and, most frightening of all, severe depression. In terms of a young person's personal development, the use of "uppers" interferes with his ability to gain confidence in his own gifts. Because he never gives himself the chance to discover that he can cope, that he can manage, that he can determine his own rewards, he does not acquire that indelible positive self-image which is the basis of all mental health. The result is that he becomes dependent on external stimuli, primarily chemicals, for his ongoing sense of self-worth. The problem is that chemical reinforcement is self-perpetuating.

Turning to the legal depressants, those most commonly used among teenagers are classified as barbiturates and methaqualones. Because they slow down the central nervous system, their medical use is to treat high blood pressure, epilepsy, and insomnia, to relieve tension, and to sedate patients before surgery. Barbiturates, described as "Blues" (Amytal) or "Yellow Jackets" (Nembutal), or "Goof Balls" (Phenobarbital), are used by teenagers to produce mild intoxication, relaxation, and a pleasurable "buzz." Methaqualones and Quaaludes, called "Ludes," a sleeping medication, are used as an aphrodisiac to lessen inhibition, produce sexual stimulation, and enhance aggressiveness. "Downers" are popular because they act like alcohol without the bulk needed to achieve the same effect. They can be easily used in school. The hazards are that tolerance to the sedative effect increases, but tolerance to lethal effect does not. A user may kill himself with a fatal dose while trying to regain a former high. Beyond that, these "downers" can produce slurred speech, shallow and slow respiration, slowed heart rate, clammy skin, and a hangover. Because of the potentiating effect, they are *very* dangerous to use with alcohol. Withdrawal symptoms include anxiety, insomnia, tremors, delirium, and even convulsions. Both barbiturates and methqualones are highly addictive, physically and psychologically. To young people they are pleasure-producing pills that combine an inner peacefulness with a sense of being "laid back." The problem is, the young person (as in alcohol abuse) conditions himself physically and psychologically to need these chemicals in order to feel good. They become his primary means of pleasure, and they become more important than his relationships with others and, ultimately, more important than his relationship with himself. That is chemical dependency.

Whether we are discussing prescription-drug addiction, teenage alcohol abuse, or polydrug dependency, we need to remember that the use of licit chemicals becomes abuse the moment the chemical damages the user's health, work, education, personal relationships, judgment, or ability to cope with daily life. If a person's potential is consistently diminished, if the use of a chemical is making him less or different than what God would have him to be, or if the chemical is not contributing to his health and welfare, that is drug abuse. More often than not, the problem is overlooked, ignored, or avoided, but that does not change the fact that abuse of licit drugs is just as damaging to the person as the deliberate abuse of illicit drugs.

CHAPTER 6

Illegal Drug Abuse

There is no responsible use of marijuana, cocaine, LSD, heroin, PCP, hashish, mescaline, or STP. Any use of these substances is drug abuse.

There is no responsible use of amphetamines, barbiturates, tranquilizers, or narcotics when taken solely for the purpose of getting "high." That , too, is drug abuse.

Unless a drug is used for its prescribed purpose or to enhance God's gift of life and human fellowship, any other self-gratifying reason for using a drug is either misuse or abuse.

We are losing too many lives to drugs. Drug abuse has reached epidemic proportions in the U.S. today, and unless we begin taking a stand on what is abuse and what is not, our families will continue to be irreparably damaged. This national crisis is not limited to the young, as many people believe. The use of illegal drugs has become an American pastime. Not a day goes by without a story about drug abuse appearing in the local, state, or national media. It is everywhere, it affects every community, every church or synagogue and every family. In short, illicit drug abuse not only affects every home, it is within each house; it starts in each house.

Drug abuse consists of saying yes to the use of illicit drugs. This can take the form of condoning society's "Do Drugs" messages, ignoring a friend's use of cocaine, or disregarding a parishioner's drug-dependent child. Whenever and wherever any of us accepts the use of illicit drugs, turns a blind eye to it or denies it, therein is the fertile ground that allows drug abuse to flourish. That is drug abuse. It is just as sinful to allow the sin as it is to commit the sinful act, as it were. By the same token, unless we speak out on drug abuse, unless we help people realize what it is and what it means, we cannot hope to defuse the continuing crisis.

An earlier chapter has described the many changes that have battered the family over the last quarter century. Perhaps the change most responsible for the drug-abuse epidemic has been the erosion of the parents' authority and ability to control their children's introduction to, and intitiation into, the drug culture. Where once they could influence their children's behavior and guard them against temptations, today no one's child is immune to an introduction, no child escapes it. Our own child may never use drugs, but his friend will, and the effects on the friend affect the abstainer. Consequently, parents' ability to maintain the behavioral standards of the family has been undermined by this "accomplice" mentality and the popular notion that "everyone is doing it— therefore it's OK."

Helping professionals have been little help to the bewildered family. For at least ten years they have publicly debated the hazards of one of the most popular illicit drugs, marijuana, and in this psychologically oriented society they have suggested that the youngster should be treated like an adult and given the right and freedom to make his own choices. Parents have acquiesced! The parenting role has been reduced from that of authoritative shepherd to merely that of friend of the flock. The 1980s opened with irrefutable evidence that America is hooked on drugs. As a result, our teenagers are the only population in the nation with deteriorating health. Families, however, have been lulled into believing there is no problem, that to experiment with illicit drugs is harmless. Consequently, drug abuse is accepted as normal behavior, it is allowed—that is, until one's own child is discovered using drugs.

The first question a parent asks when he learns his child has been using an illicit drug is: "How much are you using?" It is as though the quantity will determine whether or not the drug is being abused. The fact that *any* use of illicit chemicals is drug abuse is not even considered. This, then, is followed by the next logical question, "How'd you get caught?" It suggests that the use of marijuana, cocaine, heroin, LSD, and other illegal psychoactive substances is not considered abuse until the child has been caught by an outside authority, suspended from school, or harmed. So complete is the influence of the drug culture that when parents do learn there is a problem, they are angry at their child not because he is hurting himself but because his use has been dis-covered. When the problem surfaces, it is considered abuse because it has disturbed the equilibrium of the family. Finally the parents ask the most perplexing question of all, "How did this start?" Here the intent seems to be to focus the blame on some other person, place , or thing. If they can fix blame, it seems, they can explain away the abuse in terms of enticements and absolve themselves of any responsibility. Blame is irrelevant, but the question "How did it start?" *is* important.

REASONS FOR DRUG USE, MISUSE, AND ABUSE

In two follow-up surveys of 5,468 New York State high-school students in the fall of 1971 and the spring of 1972, and 985 seniors five months after graduation, it was found that students start by using legal drugs—beer and wine—and go on to smoke cigarettes and drink hard liquor. Of the students who smoke or drink, 27 percent progress to marijuana within a five-or six-month period. Only 2 percent, however, of those who did not drink or smoke progress to marijuana. Marijuana, in turn, is a critical bridge to other illicit drugs. Though 26 percent of the marijuana users will experiment with LSD, amphetamines, and opiates, only 1 percent of the drug nonusers and 4 percent of the legal-drug users do. A 1980 study confirmed the statistical progression of marijuana to cocaine and heroin use. The following diagram illustrates the successive stages in adolescent drug use:

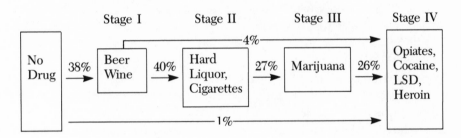

With regard to those who do not use alcohol or drugs: In 1981 an organization in Springfield, Illinois, "Research and Education on Alcohol and Drugs," published an information sheet called *Teenager's Drug Scoreboard*. Its research showed that by a nearly two-to-one margin, youths who have not used alcohol or other drugs described themselves as having strong religious values and said they had found religion to be helpful in solving their problems.

The reasons adults give for abusing drugs are many and varied: to control pain, to alter feelings, to overcome boredom and loneliness, to socialize, to satisfy medical needs, to expand the mind, to avoid responsibilities, to obtain instant gratification, to express themselves. By and large, most reasons involve efforts to escape—escape self, escape someone or somthing else. The reasons most teenagers give for abusing drugs are: to get high, to feel good, to get off the world, for the fun of it, to relax. Though their reasons also include escape, they focus far more on pleasure. In the face of pressures from the family, friends,

school, a technologically changing world, a competitive society, personal afflu-
ence or the lack of it, television, and dehumanizing institutions, drugs help
them feel good. Aware of it or not, they are in revolt, and their strategy is to seek
pleasure. Today's youngster has little control over his own life, that is, unless he
seeks a world where he cannot be reached or manipulated. The only such world
is the safe haven in his head. Drugs provide not only an escape to that safe haven
but the avenue to a self-created and pleasurable heaven. It is fun. It is all-
consuming. It is a high.

Parents and professionals try to understand and explain teenage drug
abuse as: (1) a desire to escape, (2) peer pressure, (3) an unstable family life,
perhaps a broken home, (4) a way of coping with stress, (5) the means of
overcoming loneliness (6) due to low self-esteem, (7) a form of antisocial
behavior, or (8) all of the above. All these explanations have some validity, but
the primary reason a youngster uses drugs is: *It is fun! It feels good! The more
the good feeling, the more the fun!*

Pleasing oneself is the major objective. Drugs are the most effective means
of gaining pleasure. In light of this knowledge, what do we have to offer the
youngster that is as gratifying? We need to explain this point when we are trying
to help parents who wonder how their child's drug abuse started. We need to be
sensitive to it when we are talking about abstention with the young. We need to
remember it when our hope is to help a teenager get off drugs. We are trying to
persuade or pressure him into giving up the only control he has of his life. We are
suggesting he trade in the pleasure he creates for himself for the pressures his
world creates for him. Unless we can help him prepare to function independently
in a world of instability, change, and pressure, he is going to continue to turn first to
alcohol, then to marijuana, and then to other illicit drugs—for it is *fun*!

MARIJUANA—A SERIOUS PROBLEM

According to a University of Michigan report, *Student Drug Use: Attitudes
and Beliefs, National Trends 1975–1982* (funded by the National Institute on
Drug Abuse), American young people exhibit truly alarming levels of substance
use and abuse, whether gauged by historical standards or by comparison with
other countries. In fact, they probably reflect the highest levels of illicit drug
use in any nation in the industrialized world. Though a dramatic drop in
marijuana use among high-school students occurred between 1981 and 1982,
fully 59 percent still used marijuana and 27 percent reported some use in the
past month.[2] Seven percent of the 1981 graduating class—one out of every
fourteen seniors—used marijuana daily. About a third of this group smoked
four or more joints a day.[3] The decrease in the early eighties is encouraging, but

one out of every fourteen seniors using pot each day is yet ample reason to be alarmed. Knowing that the average marijuana cigarette is eight to ten times more potent today than it was a few years ago, it is clear the abuse of this illicit drug is a major health hazard to the teenage generation. In the opinion of "the man who knows more about marijuana than anyone else in the world," Dr. Carlton Turner, former director of a government-sponsored marijuana research project at the University of Mississippi and now director of the White House Drug Policy office:

> There is no other drug used or abused by man which stays on in the body as long as cannabis (marijuana) does. And there is no other drug—legal or illegal—which affects every major organ of the body. And every system of the body. And every single cell in the body. . . .

> I am concerned that marijuana will prove to be one of our most dangerous drugs. The inescapable fact is, that unless our current pot smoking habits are reversed sharply, marijuana will have drastic long-term biological and psychological health effects on our young people and, therefore, on the future of our families and our nation.[4]

According to Dr. Robert DuPont, founding director of the National Institute on Drug Abuse (NIDA) and now chairman of the Drug Dependency Section of the World Psychiatric Association and president of the American Council on Marijuana:

> Today, my opinion has changed completely. Marijuana combines the worst effects of alcohol and tobacco. It has the intoxicating, cancer-causing effects of tobacco plus many other effects that neither of them have. I now consider marijuana to be the single biggest new health problem in our nation.

> For today's youngsters kicking the marijuana habit, individually and as a group, is going to be a life and death struggle.[5]

Though the drop in marijuana use reflects young people's growing awareness of the health hazards, one in fourteen of America's high-school seniors lost to this drug is a national disaster. We cannot remedy the damage to a population of adolescents by focusing on the decrease in use; we must sound the alarm about the damage marijuana use *is* causing. The evidence is clear: *Any* use of marijuana is harmful; *all* use of it is drug abuse.

To proclaim that smoking pot is drug abuse will not be popular in our parishes, especially not with the youngsters. Teenagers do not consider it abuse; illegal, yes, but not hazardous. To them it is a savior, the perfect pleasure. First, from outward appearances it is almost impossible to detect that one is high. Second, it can't be smelled on the breath. Third, it is quick acting.

Fourth, there is never a hangover. Fifth, it is reliable and consistent. Sixth, it guarantees the maximum relief from pressure or pain by providing the maximum amount of gratification.

The psychoactive effect, the high, distorts the five senses; it makes them seem more acute. Colors seem more brilliant, music sounds brighter, odors smell stronger, food tastes better, and tactile sensations feel more overpowering. Since the high elevates each sense to the pinnacle of sensitivity, colors seem to have sound, sound seems to contain color and sensation. The brain's suppressive and discriminative functions are nullified, and all internal and external stimuli are rendered equally intense. Awareness is an ongoing orgasm of sensations.

Marijuana is not ordinarily described as a physically additive drug; rather, it is thought of as a psychologically addictive one. The psychological need starts because the drug heightens the senses, making normal, everyday stimuli seem more acute. When the two-hour high is gone, however, those same stimuli seem routine, dull, and boring; they have completely lost their stimulating effect. The user's life feels routine, dull, and boring, and those things that were once the natural highs of life are no longer fulfilling or gratifying; they have lost their pleasurable appeal.

To counteract these feelings of ennui, the youngster returns to the one thing he knows will give him certain pleasure—marijuana—and the cycle of psychological dependence is established. Once there has been a long enough period of exposure, there develops (1) a growing preoccupation with, and anticipation of, use, (2) an increasingly rigid lifestyle, in terms of using the drug at particular times, maintaining a supply, and resenting attempts to limit use, (3) a growing tolerance to the drug, and (4) a loss of control over use and its effects on emotional, physical, mental, social, volitional, and spiritual behavior. It now is a chemical dependency, a progressive, primary illness—and it gets worse. It is chronic and now can only be arrested. It is terminal in the sense that it kills potential and can be a bridge to more dangerous drugs.

At a time when a young person must have the external stimuli of social interaction to foster cognitive and emotional development, pot turns him inward and makes him self-absorbed. At a time when his personality strengths and social skills usually grow from exchanges of self-expression, pot imprisons him in self-centeredness. At a time when the youngster usually receives an indelible impression of his God-given resources by learning to cope with the daily storms of adolescence, pot fastens all his attention on self-gratification. The overall result is regression, a stunting of intellectual and emotional growth, and nearly irreversible immaturity.

When a youngster decides to experiment with pot (and it *is* a premeditated decision, because, like alcohol, it takes five or six tries to get the pleasurable sensation), he is in effect not just experimenting; he is abusing himself. Trying anything once (perhaps twice) is an experiment, but beyond that, smoking "dope" is a deliberate choice, a matter of volition. The adolescent seeking the "high" is saying yes to drugs. But in his pursuit of pleasure he is unknowingly promoting his own destruction. Too often this cause-and-effect relationship is ignored by parent and teenager alike, and it is overlooked by most helping professionals. The teenager is allowed to seek his own pleasure without ever being taught that he is responsible for the consequences of his self-gratification. No one helps him understand that the only person who can be the guardian of his health is the one who is his constant companion—himself. With no understanding of the damage caused by marijuana and no feeling of personal responsibility for his physical and psychological health, the teenager is lulled by his indomitable spirit into believing he is immune to the hazards. Even occasional use results in inner changes, but because they are so similar to the growing pains of normal adolescence, they often go unnoticed. Recognizing those changes therefore is vital.

SIGNS AND SYMPTOMS OF DRUG USE

1. Unexplained periods or reactions of moodiness, depression, anxiety, irritability, oversensitivity, or hostility.
2. Strangely inappropriate overreactions to mild criticism or simple requests.
3. Lessening of accustomed warmth toward family—avoids interaction and communication with parents, withdraws from family activities.
4. Preoccupation with "self," less concern for the feelings of others.
5. Loss of interest in previously important activities such as hobbies or sports.
6. Loss of motivation and enthusiasm (so-called amotivational syndrome).
7. Lethargy, lack of energy and vitality.
8. Loss of self-discipline and sense of responsibility.
9. Need for instant gratification.
10. Change in ideas, values, beliefs.
11. Change in friends, unwillingness to introduce friends.
12. Secretive phone calls—callers refuse to identify themselves or hang up when parents answer.
13. Unexplained absences from the home.
14. Disappearance of money or items of value from house, becomes secretive about handling money.
15. Increased desire for sensory stimuli.
The most commonly observed school changes are:

1. Decline in academic performance—drop in grades.
2. Reduced short-term memory, concentration, attention span.
3. Loss of motivation, interest, participation in school activities, energy.
4. Frequent tardiness and absenteeism.
5. Diminished interest in participation in class.
6. Sleeping in class.
7. Untidy appearance, dress, personal hygiene.
8. More frequent discipline, behavioral problems.
10. Change in peer group.[6]

It is obvious marijuana produces a wide spectrum of symptoms, not all of which are evident in every user; some teenagers manifest some of the effects, some show others. One blatant symptom, however, is evident in every chronic marijuana smoker—youngster or adult—and it is the greatest obstruction to help and treatment: denial, the extraordinary refusal to accept the hard scientific evidence about the drug's harmful effects, and the complete inability to see the damage to personal potential it is causing. Very seldom does a marijuana user seek help on his own; he simply *cannot* see any reason for it. Yet being aware of this need is critical! It is useless for parents to point out the signs, symptoms, or ramifications in hopes of convincing their child to seek help. The user will scoff at the evidence, deny his impairment, ignore the parents' pleas, criticize their intrusiveness, and withdraw into a chemical haven. His ability to conceptualize his behavior in terms of personal responsibility or to visualize the consequences of it in terms of present irresponsibility is obliterated by the chemicals in the marijuana. The parent's only alternative is to take the youngster to qualified help, for he is suffering from a medical illness—chemical dependence.

THE EFFECTS OF MARIJUANA

Marijuana—also called pot, grass, reefer, weed, or herb—is a very complex substance derived from a plant named *Cannabis sativa*. There are 421 chemicals in marijuana, of which 61 are classified as cannabinoids found only in the marijuana plant. The psychoactive or mind-altering cannabinoid is delta-9-tetrahydrocannabinol, or THC. It is the THC content, varying according to its concentration in various parts of the plant, that determines potency. Where once the foreign-grown marijuana rolled in a joint contained 4 percent THC, today supplies of a California-grown variety, Sinsemilla, are as high as 10 to 12 percent. The greater the THC content, the greater the intoxicating effect and the greater the personal injury. Most important to understand is that long after the two-to-three-hour high has ended, the remainder of the cannabinoids are having by far the most damaging effect.

Marijuana is fat soluble. Unlike alcohol, which is water soluble and fully metabolized in twelve to eighteen hours, the cannabinoids cling to, and are stored in, the fat-laden centers of the body—the brain, the lungs, and the sex organs. Because the THC is eliminated into the blood stream in "half-lives," it takes nearly a month to metabolize fully. That it stays in the system so long is the reason it causes such damage. The dramatic growth and hormonal changes of adolescence are regulated by the brain. These processes, however, are impeded by the THC, which collects in and surrounds each brain cell. The cells become insulated one from the other. This insulation interferes with the production of DNA, RNA, and proteins in each cell, causing decreased cellular activity, eventual stoppage, and frequently cell mortality. The result is impairment of every function in the body. The person who smokes as few as three joints a weekend, therefore, winds up becoming a THC bank. It takes approximately twenty-one to twenty-nine days for the THC from one marijuana cigarette to be excreted from the body. By the time the chemicals from a joint smoked on the first of the month are totally metabolized, the user has accumulated the residue of twelve more joints. The following diagram depicts this accumulation:

Three Joints a Week for One Month

Relative Accumulation					Relative Cumulative Total
Fri (day 1)					1
Sat					2
Sun					3
	Fri (day 8)				4
	Sat				5
	Sun				6
		Fri (day 15)			7
		Sat			8
		Sun			9
			Fri (day 22)		10
			Sat		11
			Sun		12
				Fri (day 29)	13

It is obvious the effects of the joints smoked on the first of the month diminish as others are added, nevertheless, the illustration clearly shows that the weekend user is never free of the damaging effect. Usually the early signs of marijuana use are gradual: diminshed drive, loss of ambition, decreased motivation, apathy, disaffection, forgetfulness, disinterest, shortened attention span, poor judgment, and an inability to complete sequential steps or carry out complex plans. Occasional use will also cause an inability to connect present behavior with future ramifications or rewards. The capacity to anticipate consequences and to choose or assess present conduct in relation to them—the basis of conscience—is lost. This is why the user appears to be so amoral. It also accounts for his total disregard for others and explains why he is so difficult to help.

The question young people often ask is, "How many joints can I smoke without being harmed?" The graph makes the answer obvious: None! Each joint depresses the entire system for nearly a month, and the greater the accumulation, the greater the damage. The THC build-up distorts normal perception, interferes with the individual's ability to store information into long-term memory, diminishes the ability to make computations and do sequential functions, blunts focus and attention, and retards maturation.

In the reproductive system, THC interferes with the pituitary gland's production of hormones in both males and females—a function crucial to the maturing adolescent going through puberty. This is the time when a youngster's body, particularly its reproductive system, is developing. In males THC can interfere with the production of the male hormone, testosterone, resulting in arrested pubertal development, lack of muscle growth, and undeveloped secondary sex characteristics. Marijuana smoking also causes a decrease in sperm concentration and motility and a marked increase in the production of abnormal sperms. In females it affects the ovulation cycle. More frightening is that the THC accumulation around each ovum has the potential of injuring that precious cell, possibly destroying it. Consider the possible harm to the offspring of a young married couple, if both parents were habitual marijuana users.

Because marijuana tar contains 50 to 100 percent more carcinogens than tobacco, smoking marijuana is far more injurious to the lungs than smoking cigarettes. One joint is equivalent to sixteen to twenty standard cigarettes. In the body's immune system, marijuana undermines the production of the white blood cells that fight off infection and illness.[7]

Like alcohol, marijuana impairs depth perception and peripheral vision; it also slows reaction time and confuses tracking behavior. These effects impair driving performance five to six hours after intake of a strong social dose. With 60 to 80 percent of the regular marijuana users admitting to the National Institute on Drug Abuse that they sometimes drive while high, it is not surprising that the increasing numbers of stoned drivers (as well as drunk drivers) are fast becoming a public menace.

When its effects are considered as a whole, it is no wonder Dr. Carlton Turner considers marijuana "one of our most dangerous drugs." The use of pot is so common, however, that parents will say they would rather have their child smoking a joint now and then than out getting drunk. They believe it is less harmful. Nothing could be further from the truth! Smoking three joints a weekend is more damaging than being intoxicated every day for a week (though that, too, is extremely hazardous to a young person's health). If a parent at all doubts that marijuana use is in fact dangerous drug abuse, we might recommend he or she read *Pot Safari*, by Peggy Mann, the woman who in her *Reader's Digest* articles brought the matter to public attention. Her book is frightening, and ought to be. Parents who want to know what to do about the problem can get (free of charge) one copy each of three excellent booklets, *Parents, Peers and Pot, For Parents Only: What You Need to Know about Marijuana*, and *For Kids Only: What You Should Know about Marijuana*, from the National Institute on Drug Abuse (NIDA), Rockville, Maryland. For parents who would like to join forces with other concerned parents, kits that explain how to form a "families-in-action" program are available. They contain the most up-to-date drug information available. Write PRIDE, Atlanta, Georgia, for its information kit, or write the National Federation of Parents for Drug-Free Youth, Silver Springs, Maryland, for its educational kit.

COCAINE ABUSE

Marijuana is the most commonly abused, illegal, mind-altering drug among teenagers today. Hashish, a more highly concentrated derivative of the *Cannabis sativa* plant, is equally popular but more difficult to obtain. There is, however, another stimulant competing for the "drug of choice"—cocaine. Commonly called "coke," it is a white crystalline powder extracted from the leaves of the coca bush. Once used medically as a local anesthetic, coke is now widely snorted or sniffed through the nostrils to achieve an instant rush of intense feeling. Like a shot of adrenalin, coke causes an immediate feeling of euphoria that results from increased heartbeat, raised blood pressure and body temperature, and heightened perception.

Since the drug is very expensive, costing between $100 and $125 a gram, it is often distilled and the base is smoked or injected. Because "C" is so costly it was first popular among the well-to-do, specifically, entertainers, young lawyers, doctors, and business executives. No longer, however, is it the exotic pleasure of those select groups; today it is the all-American drug. Because it is seen as the status symbol of the wealthy and the elite, coke is the drug of choice of millions of otherwise conventional people. When rampant use of it was revealed in professional sports and reached crisis proportions in the National Football League, youngsters seeking to emulate their sports heroes turned on to it and have now made this socially prestigious drug an "in" high among their peers. Its high cost keeps it from becoming a fad, but that does not deter enterprising teenagers who pool their money to snort "a line" with each other.

The short-term effects of using a large amount of cocaine are similar to those of amphetamines: irritability, agitation, initially rapid pulse turning to slow and weak, rapid breathing becoming shallow and slow. The long-term effects are more dangerous. Where once cocaine was considered mildly physically addictive but highly psychologically addictive, now it is known that it carries a high risk of chemical dependency—physically as well as psychologically. Because of the intensely pleasurable sensations and the energy lift the drug produces, the user centers his life around acquiring and maintaining his supply. The money needed to do so results in borrowing, stealing, bartering, and often dealing the drug to others. Cocaine generates more illicit income than any other drug sold in the United States; it is estimated that street sales in 1980 reached $30 billion (marijuana sales amounted to about $23 billion). Some researchers estimate that ten million Americans now use coke regularly, another five million have experimented with it, and about 28 percent of young adults eighteeen to twenty-five years old have used the drug.[8] These figures suggest there are a large number of Americans pushing drugs to satisfy their need for coke's pleasure. Unlike marijuana, the supply of which is provided by peers and friends, cocaine use many times leads to associations with professional dope dealers and criminals. Wherever cocaine use is popular—in school, a business, a hospital, a legal profession, pro sports, etc.—professional criminals are waiting like predators on the sidelines.

The most common symptom of cocaine withdrawal is the frenzied urge to continue using it, for withdrawal produces intense depression and paranoia. To forestall suicidal feelings, the user requires ever more of the drug, and the dependency progresses. In short, cocaine is a very dangerous drug because it quickly promotes a high degree of dependency, a dependency that must often be financed by ulterior and illegal methods, including dealing with and for criminals. Regarding use by teenagers: Once the youngster's focus is on recreating that synthetic euphoria, little else matters to him—not family, not friends, not personal values. All his potentials are used to maintain a relationship with the drug. Because the pleasure is so strongly reinforcing, it often results in dependency.

HALLUCINOGENIC DRUGS

Many of us remember the campus revolts of the 1960s, the flower children, the runaways, and the communes. Those were the days when Harvard professor Timothy Leary inspired a generation of adolescents to believe that hallucinogens were the doors to higher consciousness, religious insight, philosophical truth, and uncharted worlds in the expanse of the mind. Drugs with the street names LSD (lysergic acid diethylamide), STP or DOM (2,5-dimethoxy-4-methyl amphetamine), DMT (dimethyltryptamine), "Cactus" (mescaline), "Buttons" (peyote), and "Shrooms" (Psilocybin mushrooms) were the psychedelic mind benders used to change perception and consciousness. Today their use has decreased, but that does not mean they are entirely bypassed for the highs of pot and coke. Among teenagers psychedelic drugs are still popular, because sounds reportedly can be "seen" and sights "heard." When used while one is listening to hard rock music, the sensation is akin to swimming in a surf of sound waves. The altered state can last from a half-hour to sixteen hours, depending on which drug is consumed. Though not considered physically addictive, there is evidence that psychological dependency develops. Users often are known to make rash or unsound decisions while under the influence, and they exhibit unpredictable or bizarre forms of behavior. When bad trips occur, they can produce profound depression, panic, paranoia, and may even lead to suicide.

Of all the hallucinogenic drugs, LSD or "acid" is the most popular. Produced in makeshift laboratories, the colorless, odorless, tasteless liquid is dispensed, drop by drop, onto small sheets of blotter paper. Because some of these sheets have designs on them (unicorns, dragons, Mickey Mouse) similar to those of "lick-and-stick tatoos" or Easter egg designs, they frequently fall into the hands of younger children. Parents need to be alerted to this hazard so they can in turn warn their children about it.

HEROIN

Most people equate "hard drugs" with narcotics, the best known of which is heroin. Heroin has no medical use in the U.S. Few people realize, however, that other, legal forms of the drug include morphine, an analgesic; opium (in paragoric); codeine, an analgesic cough suppressant; and Demerol, Dilaudid, Methadone, Meperidine, and Percodan, all analgesics. The sole function of these drugs is to mask pain by creating a mental haze, a drowsiness, and, in some people (depending on dosage), a mild to extreme euphoria. Effects of misusing these drugs may include lethargy, heaviness of limbs, apathy, loss of ability to concentrate, loss of judgment and self-control. Often found in home medicine cabinets, these are among the medical drugs so tempting to young experimenters.

Heroin used to be thought of as the drug of the inner city, but we now find it being used elsewhere by the same adults who are getting high on cocaine. Instead of shooting it, however, these people are smoking or snorting it, erroneously believing they will not become addicted. Not so; it is highly addictive no matter how it is internalized. Because of the dramatic increase in the availability and purity of the heroin, there is a high risk of dependency or overdose among unsuspecting users who believe they are indulging in a relatively harmless drug. That heroin produces a dreamlike high, a euphoria comparable to sexual orgasm, accounts for its popularity. The body becomes accustomed to it, however, and it soon takes more and more to produce the same effect. Withdrawal nearly always requires some form of hospitalization. Without treatment, the symptoms are extremely unpleasant—anxiety, restlessness, irritability, tremors, loss of appetite, panic, chills, cramps, watery eyes, runny nose, nausea, vomiting, and muscle spasms. For a dramatic presentation of the effects of heroin and an addict's withdrawal pains, rent and show the movie *The Man with the Golden Arm*, starring Frank Sinatra. It is very powerful.

ANGEL DUST

In recent years another drug has gained popularity among the young, a drug commonly sprinkled on tobacco or marijuana to produce an overpowering hallucinogenic high. It is an animal tranquilizer, Phencyclidine, more commonly called PCP or "Angel Dust." Because it affects the user as a stimulant, an anesthethic, and a hallucinogen all at the same time, it can turn a normally passive person into an extremely aggressive and violent one. Taken as a powder, a tablet, or a liquid, PCP affects the central nervous system, causing perceptual distortion and drastically altering the user's mood. Though not physically addictive, PCP is considered extremely dangerous because of these unpredictable behavioral changes, which include disorientation, rambling speech, anxiety, panic, and violent outbursts. It has been known to produce comas, convulsions, and even death. It is ironic that adults are frightened about teenage PCP use because of the immediate damage it does, but they do not fear other drugs that take longer to destroy the user.

A THEOLOGICAL POSITION ON ILLEGAL DRUG ABUSE

Focusing attention on drug abuse in specific populations (e.g., professionals, women, the elderly, or teenagers) can make us forget that the use of illegal drugs has become an accepted way of life that costs the American economy nearly $26 billion annually, $16.6 billion in lost productivity. This way of life has become so acute a crisis for business that some experts suggest it is one of the reasons the U.S. is losing its industrial leadership to Japan: America's workforce is stoned. Employees who use drugs regularly are one-third less productive than those who don't, are injured three times more often, and are absent far more frequently. No business, no profession is immune to the problem. It is rampant in the high-tech industries, securities businesses, auto industry, airlines industry (both manufacturing and commercial), the mass media, the textile and steel mills, among secretarial employees, construction workers, electrical contractors, the legal and medical professions, the United States military, and, of course, the entertainment profession and professional sports. The reason is clear: The drug-epidemic generation of the sixties and early seventies has grown up and become a solid part of the workforce, and it has taken its drug-abuse habit into the business world. These workers are using illegal drugs like marijuana, cocaine, and heroin; they are abusing prescription drugs like Percodan, Dilaudid, and Quaaludes; and they are combining amphetamines and barbiturates with alcohol. Alcohol is still the most abused drug; its cost to the economy is $23 billion annually.

What "in heaven's name" can we do about this? We can be clear about our theological position on drug abuse, and we can make that position clear to the people we serve. Regarding the use of illegal drugs and the abuse of legal drugs, there is no such thing as "responsible use"; each is clearly drug abuse. (Lest we forget, the use of illegal drugs is illegal.) When drugs are taken for a specific purpose that contributes to an individual's health, welfare, growth, stability, or strength so that he can fulfill his God-given potential, that is appropriate use of one of God's gifts. But, when drug use contributes directly or indirectly to the blocking of an individual's fulfillment, when it damages his personality or his relationship with himself, his family, or his friends, that is abuse. For youngsters experiencing the growth spurt by which they become the adults God intends them to be, *any* use of *any* chemical that impairs physical, emotional, social, mental, spiritual, and volitional development is drug abuse. No amount of rationalization or understanding or liberalism can alter this fact: It is abuse!

One of the best books we can recommend to parents on this subject is *Steering Clear*, by Dorothy Cretcher. It is a short, sensitive, easily read guide to help children through the high-risk drug years. As movie actress Joanne Woodward, who lost her son to drugs, says, it is "must reading for parents."

All drugs, licit or illicit, are potentially harmful. Drug abuse means the use of any drug to the point that it damages the user's health, work, education, personal relationships, judgment, or ability to cope with life. The frustration of dealing with drug abuse is that there are no clear distinctions between use, misuse, and abuse. When asked for our opinion, we are often at a loss to know whether a person is a "real alcoholic" or a "true drug addict." We have good reason: It is difficult to define the differences, and even more difficult to tell. Consequently we refrain from intruding into a troubled family for fear of violating its privacy or rights. To help resolve this uncertainty, a set of questions that can be used to establish chemical dependency is included in the following chapter. A simple rule of thumb to apply is the following: *Is the use of this chemical enhancing the individual's life, or is it detracting from it?*

In most cases, it is chemical abuse when the individual is limiting his personal potential, when he is cutting himself off from his sense of self, his relationships with his family and friends, and when he is relying on the mind-altering substance to help him escape reality or make him feel happy and well. If this is the case, he is suffering from chemical dependency. He is sick. He needs help.

Though we in the Church have not agreed on the appropriate use of alcohol, we all can unite on the position that chemical abuse is one of the major illnesses in America today, for it affects every aspect of our society, every member of our community and parish. In the face of this disease, we need to proclaim that life is a gift and trust, to be lived to its fullest, that each of us is a person of worth who has an opportunity to realize his God-given potential, and that we all live in a community guided by rules of interdependence, mutual respect, and love. Damaging one's body, mind, and spirit to the extent that it diminishes one's celebration of life in the family and the community is contrary to God's intentions. When chemical use turns into misuse and abuse, therefore, we need to help our parishioners realize that drug abuse is treatable and recovery possible, that the sick persons and members of the family can be healed, restored, and redeemed. But someone has to cry for help. We are our brothers' and sisters' keepers.

CHAPTER 7

The Cry for Help

In most situations calling for pastoral care, the way in which the personal or familial trouble is presented to the minister determines the way the latter responds to it. Depending on what the situation requires, the pastor will wear the hat of spiritual guide, personal counselor, family therapist, crisis mediator, confessor, Dutch uncle, ally, teacher, advisor, director, strengthener, sex educator, marriage counselor, or child psychologist. By and large, as a result of his seminary training in pastoral counseling, he is equipped to deal with most conventional problems. The approach in each circumstance is the same—to focus on the individuals involved and to help them understand the depth of their distress in relation to the magnitude of their problem. The goal is to enable them to mobilize their God-given resources, to find a way of healing their inner hurt, and to implement it. The solution can mean anything from living with the pain and persevering to alleviating the pain and all precipitating factors. No matter what the solution is, however, the pastor's most supportive approach is to empathize with the pain of the people involved. In most situations requiring pastoral care, this approach is helpful. For problems related to chemical dependency, however, it is not.

THE MINISTER'S MOST EFFECTIVE APPROACH

When the cry for help reaches the minister, or if the minister has any reason at all to suspect that its basis is chemical abuse, the most efficient and effective pastoral technique is that of a *problem-solving therapist*. Here the therapeutic emphasis is *not* on the individual or individuals involved, nor on their personal pain; it is on the social situation. The cardinal rule in dealing with chemical dependency is: *Focus on solving the problem. Do nothing to alleviate the pain.* This does not mean, of course, to ignore the plight of the individuals or to disregard their pain. The function of this rule is to make the pastor's tasks clear:

1. To ascertain that the problem is related to alcohol or drug abuse.

2. To explain that the emotional distress is a symptom of a chemical problem and is a beneficial warning that all is not well.

3. To establish a goal that includes help or treatment for those affected by the problem.

4. To refer the sufferer(s) immediately to the most appropriate treatment.

Seeking to assuage the pain only addresses the symptoms of the disease; it prolongs the underlying problem of chemical dependency by nullifying the only motivating force in the distressful situation—*pain.* The minister should do nothing about the chemically dependent person's pain, and he should allow the family to hurt, too. The goal is to use the suffering as leverage to prod, pry, or push the individuals into seeking professional care. This technique is contrary to ordinary pastoral-counseling practices, but then the biochemical, genetic disease of chemical dependency is different from any other problem a pastor may face. It requires extraordinary measures. Of chief importance among those measures is to offer warmth and concern, not so much as an expression of empathy as an expression of interest in resolving the problem.

Jay Haley, in his book *Problem Solving Therapy*, defines a problem as:

> ... a type of behavior that is a part of a sequence of acts between several people. The repeating sequence of behavior is the focus of therapy. . . . [1]

With regard to the professional's helping approach, Haley says:

> Shifting one's thinking from the individual unit to a social unit of two or more people has certain consequences for a therapist. Not only must the therapist think in different ways about human dilemmas, but he or she must consider himself or herself as a member of the social unit that contains the problem . . . since he (or she) helps define the problem. . . . [2]

Finally, concerning the minister's attempt to solve the problem:

> The task for the therapist has no easy solution. Whatever radical position he takes as a citizen, his obligation as a therapist is to define the social unit that he can change to solve the presenting problem of a client. . . . The effectiveness of the therapist is evaluated in terms of the outcome of his therapy, not his justifiable indignation at the society that is contributing to the problems he is trying to solve. The most

useful point of view for the therapist is the idea that there is sufficient variety in any situation so that some better arrangement can be made.[3]

Using Haley's methodology to solve chemical-dependency difficulties requires that the minister focus on the sickness of the entire family and not solely on the symptoms of the dependent person, that he point out the actions and reactions in the social unit that reveal the family illness, and that no matter how he feels about the situation or social circumstances, he must explore all possible solutions until an appropriate one is evident. *At no time is the minister responsible for solving the problem!* His primary concern is to define the problem and then refer the dependent person or members of the family to appropriate treatment. The minister offers hope, but that hope is not grounded in his being the one to fix everything and make it right; it is in his ability to bring reason and confidence to a chaotic situation.

It is well known that alcohol and drug problems generate a centripetal force that can, like a whirlpool, suck in everyone involved. Allowing this to happen by taking responsibility for the problem to its resolution is to fall into a codependent pattern. The minister's natural response is to try to be helpful. With the best intentions, he seeks to resolve the problem by taking control and, like the director of a play, designing and staging the most beneficial procedures for everyone involved to follow. The first sign of codependency is when he becomes impatient and angry with the denial symptomatic of all chemical dependency. Anger is the telltale sign of having been drawn in. If the minister feels exasperated it is because he has taken on himself the duty of getting the social unit to do what he wants it to do (or thinks it ought to do). When it isn't done, frustration sets in! Because of this inability to control the situation, many ministers shun alcohol or drug problems. If they only realized that the most successful approach is to identify the sequence of acts that characterize the illness, identify the most useful form of help, and then not only refer but defer, they would not feel the anger that comes with owning another person's problem.

Treatment is not the minister's responsibility. Once he has acted as problem-solving therapist and articulated the troubling behavior as a chemical-dependency problem, the responsibility to accept professional help or follow through on treatment recommendations rests squarely with those involved. The aim of seeking help is groundless if it comes from the wants or expectations of the minister. Because the recovery process must take place in the family, the reasons for it must be theirs as well. To become angry and frustrated over a family's denial only adds to the chaos. The individual will seek help not when the problem is pointed out, or as treatment is recommended, but when his pain motivates him to act.

This approach, which allows crisis to force a decision, rests on the facts that it is impossible for one person to change another, that the minister does not want to be responsible for changing another in the first place, and that it is in the process of changing themselves that drug-dependent people develop their potentials, realize their strengths, and come to appreciate their self-worth. From a purely practical point of view, this approach confronts the individuals with the special help they require without requiring the minister to be the chemical-dependency specialist who provides it. It allows the minister to be a pastoral "problem solver," not a practitioner.

EXHIBITING HOPEFUL ATTITUDES

Since the minister represents stability to those who come to him for help, his attitude must reflect hope. Professional counselors Lena DiCicco, Hilma Unterberger, and John Mack, of the Alcoholism Program at Cambridge-Somerville (Mass.) Mental Health and Retardation Center, argue that to inspire hope care-givers need to develop hopeful attitudes. They suggest the following:

1. Recognize that chemical dependency is a chronic, relapsing illness.

2. Recognize that chemical dependency is a treatable disease, that a sick person does not have to "hit bottom" before he is ready for help.

3. Realize that chemical dependency has definite signs and stages of progression.

4. Understand that the treatment of chemical dependency is often successful.

5. Know that help is readily available in most communities and that referral is the minister's main function.

6. Understand that chemical dependency could happen to anyone.

7. Understand that the dependent's recognition of his self-loathing, isolation, depression, and guilt feelings while he is abusing himself is essential to successful treatment.

8. Recognize that AA, Al-Anon, Adult Children of Alcoholics, Alateen, and NarcAnon can be effective in treating chemical dependency.

9. Realize that standard psychiatric methods are generally ineffective in treating chemical dependency *per se*; in fact, the dependent can use them to avoid dealing with his dependency.

10. Recognize that the dependent's spouse cannot cause his/her problem, although he or she may aggravate it.

11. Recognize that the members of the dependent's family need treatment as much as the dependent person.

12. Acknowledge that to all practical purposes a dependent cannot return to normal, controlled drinking or drug use.

13. Understand that, to the dependent person, following through on a referral presents an extreme life-crisis, a decision not to drink or use. In the sick person's view, alcohol or drugs are the only means of survival. Most often, therefore, seeking treatment is the result of a series of confrontations, not of a one-time suggestion.

14. Understand that, to the dependent's family, following through on a referral presents an equally extreme life-crisis; it is a commitment to engage in a process that will reveal not only the family problem but the problems of each member of the family. It is unrealistic to expect the family to seek help at once.

15. Understand that the recovery process is a frightening, difficult, lifelong task for all affected by the disease. It requires a complete reordering of the social aspects of the dependent person's life, major adjustments by the family, and lifelong support for everyone.[4]

The greatest value of these attitudes is that they allow for the most successful interaction between the minister and the social unit, while guarding the minister against being drawn into a coalition with one party versus another. Taking sides is a natural response, especially when it is usually what the crisis caller will request. "I think my wife has a drinking problem. Will you help get her into treatment?" . . . "My son is on drugs. Will you talk with him?" . . . "My father is an alcoholic. Will you make my mother do something?" In each of these requests there is: (1) the tacit invitation to join in an alliance, and (2) the expectation that the minister will straighten out the offending person and make things right. Seldom, if ever, will the cry for help be: "My husband is drinking too much and the whole family is sick. Will you help us?" Consequently, the minister needs a safeguard that prevents him from becoming the agent of one person or the other. The best safeguard is not only to understand one's role as problem solver but to make that position perfectly clear to those asking for help.

EXAMINING THE PROBLEM

The need for help usually comes to the minister's attention in one of four ways: (1) via a third party who has some vested interest, (2) from a member of the immediate family, (3) from the sick person himself, or (4) from the minister's observations. When the call comes from an interested third party, the temptation is to take charge and begin gathering facts about the nature of the alcohol or drug problem. Instead, a great deal of time and effort can be saved if the minister suggests that the concerned friend act as a shepherd and bring those in need of help in for an interview. If the third party does not want to do this (or cannot), the minister's stance should be to do nothing until he is invited to participate by those immediately involved. Again, the minister is not "Mr. Fix-it" for those who want him to "do somthing!" Unless he is trained in leading an "intervention" (described later), he should wait for those involved to call. In most cases, when he insists to the concerned third party that he can do nothing until invited by the impaired person or a member of the family, it isn't long before those who are suffering call for a meeting. At this point the minister becomes the problem-solving therapist.

"If successful therapy is defined as solving the problems of a client, the therapist must know how to formulate a problem and how to solve it," says Jay Haley. "The act of therapy begins with the way the problem is examined. The act of intervening brings out problems and the relationship patterns that are to be changed."[5] Ordinarily the minister would begin by seeing the one person whose symptoms most clearly reveal an inability to adjust, adapt, or cope, but in problem solving it is understood that to begin with one person is to begin with a handicap. It is widely accepted that people cannot objectively describe their actions, nor can they accurately report their social situation. Therefore, if at all possible, it is better to interview as many directly involved people as possible. Bringing together the members of the family is the surest way to avoid an unspoken coalition and to identify the whole family's illness. It must be remembered that this is not a typical individual-counseling or family-therapy session in which one hopes to change the person or his relationships by talking about feelings and relationships. Nor is it a meeting to join forces for the sole purpose of getting the sick person into some kind of treatment where he will be healed. Though the ultimate goal is to help the chemically dependent person abstain, it must also include help for the codependent family. At the Johnson Institute, for instance, when family members ask for help with someone who is abusing alcohol or drugs, the counselors do not turn their attention to the sickness of the "identified patient" until the family members have had six counseling sessions in which to reflect on how the sickness has sickened them as well. The minister's objective is to identify the family illness so it can be used as leverage to bring about the needed change in the individual and his family. Jay Haley's model outlines the four stages in the first interview:

1. A social stage, in which the family is greeted and made comfortable.

2. A problem stage, in which one inquires about the present problem.

3. An interaction stage, in which the family members are asked to talk with each other.

4. A goal-setting stage, in which the family is asked to specify just what changes they seek.

Whether or not one sees several members of the family, the problem will usually be described as one person's fault, and his alcoholism or drug abuse will be the subject of discussion. To enable the counselee(s) to appreciate the need for change, the minister needs to think of the problem in terms of more than one person. His perspective will be different than that of those who are presenting the problem, but it is not necessary that he persuade them to think about it in his way; to do so would only disturb the family interaction. As Haley says:

> As the therapist listens, he or she should do certain things and not do others.
>
> First, the therapist should not make any interpretation or comment to help the person see the problem differently. He should accept what is said. If something is not clear it can be asked about. If the therapist needs to rephrase something to see if he understands it, he should do so—but he should not rephrase anything to help the other person "discover" something.
>
> Second, the therapist should not offer advice even if asked for it. He should use a phrase such as: "I need to know more about the situation before I can say what might be done."
>
> Third, he should not ask how someone feels about something, but should gather facts and opinions.
>
> Fourth, the therapist's attitude should be one of helpful interest. He should not be diverted from what is really outside the question of why the family is there.[6]

At no point should the minister offer any interpretation or equate the problem with emotional pain. The data he gathers will, for the most part, be expressions of pain in terms of *blame*—blame directed at the problem person, at every member of the family, and at self. Each person is so filled with hurt and resentment that the only way to deny responsibility for the distress and disruption is to say someone else caused or permitted it. It is important for the minister, therefore, to guard against being pulled into affirming or refuting these expressions of blame, for to do so is to be an instrument for fixing guilt. This portion of the problem-solving procedure is solely for data gathering.

Following the initial inquiry, the next step is to get the members of the family to discuss their problem with each other. Here it is paramount that the people involved interact with each other and that the minister withdraw from the roles of inquisitor and fact-gatherer. It is only by family interaction that the issues in the family illness can be clarified. It is only by understanding their own issues that the members can discover in themselves a need for change. Therefore, once the members have had the chance to talk with each other, the minister needs to obtain from them a statement of what changes they would like to make as a result of help.

The problem the minister identifies and articulates and the changes desired by the family must be stated in solvable form. It is not enough to define the family illness as "distress caused by another's chemical dependency" or the desired changes as "relief from personal anxiety and worry." Psychological jargon is not useful in identifying the problem or formulating its solution. What is needed is specific information on observable behavior, clear statements about the family's reactions to behavior, and agreement on the practical changes needed to resolve the family's problem. The minister needs to make it very clear that his own role will be to articulate the problem in such a way that something can be done about it. To accomplish this goal, the problem-solving therapy must be as brief as possible. In many cases, because the minister already knows the family, it will not take more than one interview to identify the problem as alcohol or drugs.

After the desired changes are specified, the pastor should immediately initiate the referral stage, at which he helps the family understand that those changes are attainable by calling a specific professional office, center, group, or treatment program. To help them make the difficult first contact, the minister offers to place the call while the family is with him. "I'll phone the counseling center to let them know you will be calling for an appointment," he might say. Once the minister's phone call to the appropriate helping agency is made, his role as problem-solving therapist is terminated. The entire social unit knows what the family's next step must be. The minister can make it clear that he is not the source of counseling or treatment, and at the same time he can offer the family helpful concern by saying he will see them to the first meeting. For example, he might say, "Make your appointment as soon as you get home. They are expecting your call. When you have, call me and tell me when it is. I'll meet you there and introduce you." Once the referral has been made, the minister does not hold any further responsibility for the family's treatment; he has satisifed his pastoral duty.

MINISTER'S ASSESSMENT OF CHEMICAL DEPENDENCY

There are times when it is impossible to see members of a family as a social unit, when only one person (other than the dependent) is available or when only one person is willing to come in for an interview. If this is the case, as it often is, it is helpful for the minister to cull data from a set of prepared questions. A structured set of questions reduces the chances of a coalition forming during the interview and helps identify the problem in terms of specific symptoms. The principal question to be answered (to the minister's satisfaction) is: "Is there an alcohol or drug problem, or not?" Once he is certain it is a chemical-dependency problem, he can help the troubled person by getting him to formulate the behavioral changes he wants for himself as well as those he wants for the dependent person.

To establish if there is an alcohol or a drug problem, the minister must judge if there is sufficient loss of control to warrant the need for help. The focus here is on the sick person. A set of field-tested questions, compiled specifically for the minister's purpose, is offered below to facilitate this task. Called "Minister's Assessment of Chemical Dependency," it is arranged into categories according to Sharon Wegscheider's six "personal potentials": physical, emotional, social, mental, spiritual, and volitional. As Wegscheider says, "In any given real-life situation our feelings and behavior are the result of several or even all six, of the potentials interacting in various proportions. Altogether, they offer their possessor a rich variety of possibilities for relating to himself, other persons, his environment and the universe. . . ."[7]

When an individual uses chemicals to the extent of misuse or abuse, these personal potentials begin to erode. The loss becomes apparent in some areas earlier than in others. The following "Assessment" is arranged in the order in which one's personal potentials are diminished. As a diagnostic tool, it is the surest way to determine if professional help is needed.

MINISTER'S ASSESSMENT OF CHEMICAL DEPENDENCY

A tool to assist clergy in clarifying whether or not a chemical-dependency problem exists. To be used for determining if there is a need for professional help or treatment. Make a check (√) for each question answered "Yes." IMPORTANT: Make no editorial comments while administering the assessment.

Loss of Emotional Potential

_____1. Has she/he ever sought professional help for emotional problems? Was chemical use involved?

_____2. Does she/he become upset if a supply of alcohol or drugs is not readily available?

_____3. Does she/he use the chemical when frustrated, anxious, angry, or worried?

_____4. When using the chemical, does she/he regularly have enough to become high?

_____5. Is she/he using more now than before?

_____6. Has her/his moods been affected by alcohol or drug use?

_____7. Is she/he harder to get along with as a result of alcohol or drug use?

_____8. Does she/he ever show confusion or memory losses because of chemical use?

Loss of Physical Potential

_____1. Does chemical use have an effect on his/her sleeping habits?

_____2. Does she/he ever use the chemical the following morning?

_____3. Does she/he usually want to drink or use drugs at a particular time?

_____4. Has the use of chemicals had an effect of her/his energy level?

_____5. Has she/he ever gone to a doctor or hospital for physical problems related to chemical use?

_____6. Does she/he ever express a need for alcohol or drugs?

_____7. Has her/his eating habits changed as a result of using alcohol or drugs?

_____8. Is use of the chemical affecting her/his physical health or physical appearance?

Loss of Mental Potential

_____1. Has she/he ever suffered a blackout as a result of chemical use?

_____2. Does she/he occasionally forget what she/he said or did as a result of drinking or drug use?

_____3. Does chemical use affect her/his ability to meet obligations or follow through on responsibilities?

_____4. Is chemical use affecting her/his job or school performance?

_____5. Has she/he ever lost time from work or school because of chemical use?

_____6. Does she/he drink or do drugs alone?

_____7. Has she/he ever had financial problems as a result of use of alcohol or drugs?

_____8. Have her/his intellectual capacities been impaired by chemical use?

Loss of Social Potential

_____1. When with others, does she/he ever sneak drinks or make it a point to get a satisfying amount of drugs for her/himself?

_____2. Does she/he accept or refuse invitations depending on whether alcohol or drugs will be available?

_____3. Is use of chemicals affecting her/his reputation?

_____4. Has her/his chemical use resulted in seeking other friends or social environments?

_____5. Has her/his chemical use caused problems with friends or members of the immediate family?

_____6. Has she/he ever been stopped by the police for driving under the influence?

_____7. Is there a noticeable personality change because of the use of alcohol or drugs?

_____8. Does she/he usually have a reason for the occasions when she/he drinks too much?

Loss of Volitional Potential

_____1. Does she/he lack perseverance in pursuing goals as a result of chemical use?

_____2. Has she/he attempted to control her/his use of alcohol or drugs and failed?

_____3. Has she/he ever jeopardized her/his safety or the safety of a family member as a result of chemical use?

_____4. Has her/his ability to keep dates, appointments, or promises been affected by chemical use?

_____5. Does she/he drink or use drugs alone rather than seek group conviviality?

_____6. Has her/his ambition been affected by the use of alcohol or drugs?

_____7. Does she/he use chemicals with the expressed intention of getting drunk or wasted?

_____8. Does it annoy her/him when family or friends discuss her/his use of alcohol or drugs?

Loss of Spiritual Potential

_____1. Has the use of chemicals diminished her/his enthusiasm for, and interest in, life?

_____2. Has the use of chemicals caused her/him to express shame about her/his sense of worth?

_____3. Does her/his use of alcohol or drugs result in a sense of isolation, loneliness, or shyness?

_____4. Are alcohol or drugs used as a regular source of fun, enjoyment, and entertainment?

_____5. Does she/he express remorse over excessive use of chemicals?

_____6. Has chemical use diminished her/his capacity to care for people, places, or things?

_____7. Does she/he need alcohol or drugs for solace, comfort, or inner strength?

_____8. Is chemical use disturbing her/his peace of mind?

_____ Total answered "Yes"

Scoring: In each category the questions represent characteristics used by the Hazelden Foundation to define the illness of chemical dependency. If one or two questions are checked "Yes" in each category, the person being described needs professional help. If, in each category, three or more are checked "Yes," or if the total score is eighteen, the person requires professional help or treatment.

Though this assessment is arranged in the order in which one's personal potentials are diminished, it is important to remember that losses occur simultaneously, not one at a time. Trying to establish which potential is most affected or how many of them are impaired, in hopes of assessing the degree of chemical dependency is not the point of the assessment. The sole purpose is to help the minister satisfy himself that there is a clear indication of alcohol or drug abuse. He is substantiating that:

1. There is a growing preoccupation with use.

2. There is a growing rigidity in lifestyle.

3. There is a growing tolerance to the drug.

4. There is a loss of control over use and the need to use, having harmful consequences to one's personal, social, and economic life.

The assessment is applicable to children as well as adults. Normal adolescence is a period of emotional storms and mood changes, making the diagnosis of chemical misuse and abuse difficult. This set of questions, however, will reveal clearly if a youngster's potential is being diminished by the use of alcohol or drugs. Once that picture is evident, professional help is imperative. The assessment reflects no judgment of right or wrong behavior, legal or illegal conduct (and neither should the minister be judgmental when using it). Its value is that, in a nonthreatening way, it quickly elicits evidence of chemical-dependency behavior. It is a problem-solving instrument, *not* a pastoral-counseling tool.

When the minister has satisfied himself that there is a chemical-dependency problem, the next step is to show the assessment to the concerned person and help him formulate desirable behavioral changes. Most often they will be articulated as, "I want him to stop!" That is not enough! The concerned person must state what changes he is committed to making to remedy his distress. It can't be stated often enough: *It is neither useful nor beneficial for the minister to act as the person's agent of change.* If changes are to be made and abstinence from alcohol or drugs is to be achieved, the successful outcome is directly proportional to the dependent's and codependent's investment and participation in the process.

Owing to denial, members of a distressed family very often will not be able to appreciate that they are just as much a part of the problem as the dependent person, that they are just as sick as he is. Their focus will be on "*his* drinking" or "*his* drug abuse." Consequently, once the minister, using the assessment, establishes there is a problem, he must help the social unit—be it a family or a lone spouse, mother, son, etc.—see that the whole unit has a problem, that it is suffering from codependency. If resolution of the problem depends on a change in the unit's behavior, it cannot hope to succeed unless its members can see the need to change.

EVALUATION OF CODEPENDENCY

There is nothing more difficult than trying to convince an "innocent victim" that he has, in fact, allowed himself to be victimized, as is the case with most adult codependents. It is useless for the minister to try to do so. If he does and his efforts are frustrated, his frustration signals his own codependency. Providing symptomatic evidence of the social unit's sickness, therefore, is the most expedient way of revealing a family member's illness. This goal is accomplished by asking each person to measure his own loss of personal potential. Again using Sharon Wegscheider's categories as a foundation, a field-tested "Evaluation of Codependency" is offered below as an objective diagnostic tool. The minister asks that the questionnaire be filled in without comment or interpretation. The point is to help a family member diagnose his illness without embarrassment or fear of judgment from others. The guilt and shame already are so acute that each is incapable of perceiving his own illness. For the evaluation to be beneficial, therefore, it must be answered in as nonthreatening an atmosphere as possible. That means within the security of one's own thoughts.

EVALUATION OF CODEPENDENCY

A tool to determine the effect of chemical dependency on members of the family. Make a check (√) for each question answered "Yes." Remember, you

are evaluating whether another person's chemical dependency is affecting you.
NOTE: "CD" = Chemical Dependency.

The Physical Potential

_____1. Have you either gained or lost weight as a result of the chemical-dependency problem?

_____2. Does the CD problem affect your sleeping?

_____3. Does the CD problem cause you to feel tired or weary?

_____4. Has your physical appearance been affected by the chemical dependency?

_____5. Are you using alcohol, tranquilizers, or any other drugs to counteract the effects on you of the person's chemical dependency?

_____6. Have you experienced digestive problems, ulcers, or colitis as a result of the chemical dependency?

_____7. Have you experienced tightness of chest, heart palpitations, headaches or backaches because of the CD problem?

_____8. Have you felt the need to see your doctor because of the chemical dependency?

The Emotional Potential

_____1. Does the CD problem make you feel angry?

_____2. Does it make you feel depressed? Suicidal?

_____3. Do you lose control of your temper with others as a result of the CD problem?

_____4. Has the person's chemical dependency diminished your sense of humor, your readiness to laugh?

_____5. Do you ever feel like you are "going crazy" because of the CD problem?

_____6. Has the chemical dependency affected your ability to care for those people, places, or things important to you?

_____7. Do you feel fearful or uncertain because of the person's chemical dependency?

_____8. Do you hide your feelings about the CD problem from other members of your family?

The Mental Potential

_____1. Are you having to manage more than your own responsibilities as a result of the chemical-dependency problem?

_____2. Do you have difficulty focusing on one thing at a time?

_____3. Do you have trouble finishing an idea, a project, or a task because of the person's chemical dependency?

_____4. Does the CD problem intrude on your thoughts?

_____5. Do you strive to keep an equilibrium in the household?

_____6. Is the CD problem affecting your professional, business, or school efficiency?

_____7. Do you feel that someone or something else is the cause of the person's chemical dependency?

_____8. Do you protect the chemically dependent person, cover up or hide the problem from others?

The Social Potential

_____1. Do you turn down invitations because of the CD problem?

_____2. Have you been embarrassed by a public display of the CD problem?

_____3. Do you find yourself trying to avoid the person suffering chemical dependency?

_____4. Does the CD problem affect your relationship with other members of your family?

_____5. Has the CD problem caused you to withdraw from your social circle?

_____6. Do you refrain from discussing your home life with others?

_____7. Are you hesitant to discuss the chemical dependency with members of the immediate family?

_____8. Do you feel like you are in a "cold war" with the chemically dependent person?

The Volitional Potential

_____1. Is the chemical dependency interfering with your opportunity to do the things you want to do?

_____2. Does the CD problem affect your decision-making ability?

_____3. Do you feel you are powerless over the CD problem?

_____4. Have you tried to find ways of dealing with the person's chemical dependency and failed?

_____5. To solve the problem, have you resorted to disposing of the chemically dependent person's supply?

_____6. Are you afraid of the chemically dependent person? His/her anger? His/her behavior?

_____7. Does the household revolve around the CD problem?

_____8. Do you feel responsible for solving the CD problem?

The Spiritual Potential

_____1. Do you feel guilty about the chemical dependency? That it is your fault?

_____2. Is the problem affecting your peace of mind?

_____3. Are you ashamed that you cannot seem to resolve the CD problem?

_____4. Do you feel your life is a matter of survival?

_____5. Does the problem cause you to lose your sense of joy?

_____6. Has your self-esteem been affected by the chemical dependency?

_____7. Is your ability to love the dependent person being jeopardized by the CD problem?

_____8. Has your relationship with a higher power or God been affected by the CD problem?

_____   Total answered "Yes"

Scoring: If there are a total of twelve answered "Yes," you and your behavior are being manipulated by the forces of another person's chemical dependency. You are, therefore, not in control of your own life. This is codependency. Outside help or treatment is required to change this behavior pattern.

When the members of the social unit have completed the evaluation, the minister has only to ask them their "scores" to help them appreciate their need for change; the answers make it self-evident. By reviewing the "Evaluation of Codependency" as well as the "Assessment of Chemical Dependency" with it, the minister can enable the social unit to see that its behavior has been controlled by the illness as much as the sick person's behavior has been controlled by the chemical. This objective evidence of loss of potential and the clear picture of powerlessness make the unit realize its need to change its behavior or else allow the family illness to progress. The minister, as problem-solver, can point out that no one can make another person stop drinking or stop doing drugs but that the unit can change by first admitting its own helplessness and then seeking outside help.

INTERVENTION

If an individual is suffering from chemical dependency, two obstacles usually prevent him from receiving the help he needs. First, because his behavior is so destructive to himself and so disrespectful or harmful to others, everyone close to him is put off by "his problem." Because they are put off, they usually do not see a need for a change in their own attitudes or behavior, and they do not want to help the sick person. The second reason a dependent person is so difficult to help is his deterioration. Because the dependent's rigid defenses of denial and his distorted memory get worse as he sickens, it becomes increasingly difficult to help him. What's more, the worse he gets, the less reason the family has for changing their opinion about helping him.

This downward spiral can only be broken by someone from the outside. The process is called "Intervention." It is the minister's function to refer, and one of his options is to suggest to the concerned person or family that an "Intervention" is required from outside the social unit and that only a more knowledgeable or trained person can provide it. To help the concerned person understand the Intervention, the minister can recommend Chapter 5, "The Dynamics of Intervention," in *I'll Quit Tomorrow*, written by the man who helped perfect the Intervention process, Vernon E. Johnson. The minister might also make available reprints of the *Reader's Digest* article "A Dynamic New Approach to the Alcoholic." It is a clear and concise explanation, which also applies to drug abuse.

> Intervention is a process by which the harmful, progressive and destructive effects of chemical dependency are interrupted and the person receives some kind of constructive help to terminate their active use of mood altering chemicals. Intervention implies that the person need not "hit bottom" before such help can be implemented.
>
> We are concerned here primarily with the family action and, where possible, action or support by the employer.
>
> Simply stated, Intervention is the method by which the realities of his illness can be presented in an acceptable way to a person who suffers. It is sitting down and discussing in a LOVING and CARING way the concerns of the family about the person's harmful use of alcohol and other mood-altering chemicals.[8]

It is the basic premise of an Intervention that the chemically dependent person *can* accept the reality of his illness if it is presented to him in a receivable form. The rules the Johnson Institute·follows for Intervention are:

1. Meaningful persons must present the facts or data. That is, they must be people who do exert real influence on the sick person. The persons may be members of the family. . . . They may be professionals such as physicians or clergymen, if they personally possess information which is useful.

2. The data presented should be specific and descriptive of events which

happened or conditions which exist. . . . Obviously evidence is strongest when it is firsthand. Opinions are avoided, along with generalizations.

3. The tone of the confrontation should not be judgmental. The data should show concern; in truth, the facts are simply items to demonstrate the legitimacy of the concerns being expressed.

4. The chief evidence should be tied into drinking (or drug use) wherever possible.

5. The evidence of behavior should be presented in some detail, and very explicitly, to give the sick person a panoramic view of himself during a given period of time. Since they are out of touch with reality, their greatest need is to be confronted by it.

6. The goal of Intervention, through the presentation of this material, is to have the dependent person see and accept enough reality so that, however grudgingly, the need for help can be accepted.

7. Now, the available choices (for help or treatment) are offered. The key person confronting the dependent may say, "Since abstinence is a basic requirement, these alternatives are before us: this treatment center, that hospital, or AA. Which will you use?"[9]

It is very important that the concerned person or family members include the steps they are taking for their own "treatment." This is a family illness and, therefore, a family recovery process. Including their intentions to get help and giving the dependent person the chance to be a part of that decision-making process make it clear that recovery is everyone's responsibility. The family, however, must anticipate the excuses and protests that may follow.

Prior to the Intervention, the family meets with the leader to establish what each person plans to say, to practice one's presentation, and to discuss ways of overcoming resistance or defusing anger. They must be prepared to remain firm in their intention to get help, and they must be willing to apply leverage to attain it. The leverage may be refusal to associate with the drug-dependent person unless he willingly seeks help, it may be to ask him to move out of the house, or it may be to report him to a superior or boss who will insist he gets treatment. Whatever it is, it must be the family's determination, and the family must be prepared to follow through on its ultimatum. This is no idle threat! If the Intervention gets this far and leverage is the last resort, it should be understood that it is the family's "bottom line."

Intervention is a loving but tough process the purpose of which is to save a life. Though once it was believed it was necessary to allow a chemically dependent person to sink lower and lower in his illness until he hit "bottom," that is no longer the case. With the model of Intervention used by the Johnson Institute, the downward spiral is stopped, the bottom is raised, as it were. Eight out of ten Interventions result in the dependent and codependents getting help. At the Johnson Institute, 97 percent of its interventions are successful. For ministers interested in a fuller description of interventions, both *I'll Quit Tomorrow* and Sharon Wegscheider's *Another Chance* include excellent educational chapters.

MINISTER AS INTERVENER

Though most ministers do not have the formal training to lead interventions, there will be times when one is suddenly thrust into the position of intervener. They are when a troubled person walks in the the minister's door or when the minister observes for himself there is an alcohol or drug problem (the behavior is so obvious it can no longer be denied, e.g., two arrests for driving under the influence). These occasions are ticklish because, as in the case of identifying the family's problem, unless the minister knows the symptoms represent a chemical-dependency problem, he is very hesitant to say anything about it. Usually he does not want to misjudge the situation, anger the person, and jeopardize the relationship. Even when the individual's behavior is observed to be alcohol or drug related, the minister is very hesitant to act; he fears he will violate the person's privacy and alienate him. Whenever one suspects that the problem is alcohol or drugs, however, it is very important to remember that the problem solver's effectiveness is *not* dependent on a continuing realtionship with the dependent person or the codependent family. The minister's role is to identify the problem, to articulate it in terms that can be understood and accepted, and then to refer the troubled person(s) to appropriate treatment. Consequently, in those circumstances where the minister is faced with the necessity of being an Intervener, it is important that he confront the individual not as an intervener but as a diagnostician acting for the impaired parishioner. He is an objective resource who has the knowledge to clarify if there is, in fact, a chemical-dependency problem.

The person who calls for help is seeking an authoritative evaluation. Usually he is willing to come in for a diagnostic interview. In the case of one whose behavior clearly reflects alcohol or drug problems but who does not call for help, the minister will need to invite him in for a visit. In both circumstances, counselors DiCicco, Unterberger, and Mack suggest the interaction include six elements:

1. An expresssion of warmth and concern for the person.

2. A description of the person's observable problem-drinking or drug-abusing behavior.

3. An explanation that the use of chemicals is the *source* of the person's problems (or at least of many of them) rather than its result.

4. An explanation that alcoholism or drug abuse is an illness and a discussion of some of the common signs.

5. An expression of hope about the illness and information about persons who have recovered.

6. Knowledge that outside help is needed, and a description of several options, including AA, Al-Anon, Ala-Teen, Narc-Anon contacts as well as counselors, clinics, or treatment centers.[10]

Just as the minister does not want to become involved in a discussion of feelings when identifying the family's problem, he also, when pointing out the individual's problem, does not want to get caught up in the sufferer's reasons or rationalizations for his alcohol or drug use. To aid the minister in his matter-of-fact determination, a composite of tested questions that diagnose loss of potential is provided below. This objective test serves two purposes: First, it gives the minister specific, clear-cut questions to ask, based on the known characteristics of chemical dependency, and second, it provides the person in need of help with a tangible profile of his deteriorating condition. It is his "Personal Inventory."

Personal Inventory of Chemical Dependency

A tool to help the individual ascertain if he has an alcohol or drug problem. To be used to determine if there is a need for professional help or treatment. Make a check (√) for each question answered "Yes."

The Emotional Potential

_____1. Do you use alcohol or drugs as an escape?

_____2. Is the use of chemicals making your family relationships unhappy?

_____3. Do you make certain you will not run out of your supply?

_____4. Do you ever feel remorse over things you've said or done while under the influence?

_____5. Does it take more for you to get the feeling you want than it once did?

_____6. Do you drink or use drugs alone?

_____7. Are you concerned or confused about memory lapses caused by chemical use?

_____8. Do you drink or use drugs to bolster your self-confidence?

The Physical Potential

_____1. Does your use of alcohol or drugs have an effect on your sleeping habits?

_____2. Do you ever drink or use drugs the next morning?

_____3. Do you want to have a drink or use your drug at a definite time each day?

_____4. Has your energy level been affected by your use of chemicals?

_____5. Have you ever gone to a doctor for problems related to your drinking or use of drugs?

_____6. Do you ever feel a need for a drink or a drug?

_____7. Have you ever had a case of the shakes as a result of chemical use?

_____8. Is drinking or using drugs having any effect on your physical health?

The Mental Potential

_____1. Have you ever had a blackout or period of amnesia (not to be confused with "passed out") as a result of drinking or drug use?

_____2. Have you felt the need to cut down on your drinking or use of chemicals?

_____3. Has your efficiency decreased as a result of using alcohol or drugs?

_____4. Has your drinking or use of drugs affected your job or school performance?

_____5. Have you had financial difficulties (money problems) as a result of drinking or use of drugs?

_____6. Have you ever lost time from work or school because of your chemical use?

_____7. Has your family or have your friends ever expressed concern about your drinking or use of drugs?

_____8. Have your family responsibilities or home obligations suffered as a result of your use of alcohol or drugs?

The Social Potential

_____1. Do you prefer to associate with those who drink or use drugs?

_____2. Is your use of alcohol or drugs affecting your reputation?

_____3. Have you gotten in a fight or lost a friend as a result of chemical use?

_____4. Do you use alcohol or drugs more than your friends?

_____5. Do you use chemicals to help you relax and relate to other people?

_____6. Have you ever been stopped for driving under the influence of alcohol or drugs?

_____7. Do you prefer to drink or use drugs alone as opposed to being a part of a social gathering?

_____8. Do you accept or refuse invitations depending on whether alcohol or drugs will be available?

The Volitional Potential

_____1. Are you unable to stop drinking or using drugs after one or two or when you want to?

_____2. Have you ever felt the need to cut down on your use of chemicals but failed to do so?

_____3. Does drinking or using drugs make you careless of your or your family's welfare?

_____4. Has your ambition decreased as a result of your use of alcohol or drugs?

_____5. Has your perseverance, your responsibility to follow through, or your ability to complete a task been affected by your use of chemicals?

_____6. Do you use alcohol or drugs for getting high?

_____7. Do you sometimes drink or use drugs more than you intended to?

_____8. Have any members of your family (grandparents, parents, aunts, uncles, brothers, sisters, children) ever had problems with alcohol or drug abuse?

The Spiritual Potential

_____1. Do you ever feel guilty about your alcohol or drug use?

_____2. Has your use of alcohol or drugs had any effect on your feelings of harmony and serenity?

_____3. Do you drink or use drugs to make you feel good? To have fun?

_____4. Has your use of chemicals affected your ability to care about people, places, or things?

_____5. Do you use alcohol or drugs for solace or comfort or to kill emotional pain?

_____6. Have you ever gone to anyone for help about your use of alcohol or drugs?

_____7. Has your drinking or use of drugs affected your enthusiasm for, or interest in, life?

_____8. Does your drinking or using drugs ever result in feelings of loneliness or isolation?

_____   Total answered "Yes"

Scoring: If there are one or two questions checked "Yes" in each category, you are suffering definite signs of chemical dependency. Professional help is needed. If, in each category, three or more are checked "Yes," or if the total score is eighteen, you are suffering the illness of chemical dependency. Treatment is required.

Having established there is a problem, the minister can then follow through with an explanation of chemical dependency as "an illness." He should be very clear and specific: "The inventory shows you are suffering from chemical dependency." To be diplomatic, indecisive, or fainthearted is to enable the illness to progress. What is needed is an unfaltering statement of the inventory's results. The minister is not offering merely his opinion here; acting on the authority and trust invested in him and using an objective, reliable instrument, he is presenting the reality of the problem in a way the sick person can see, can hear, can accept. With the inventory providing the data, he is in fact conducting an intervention.

The inventory is not an instrument to establish the *degree* of chemical dependency; its purpose is with tangible evidence to convince the dependent he *has* a problem. As the minister reviews the results with the person, a discussion of the signs and symptoms will reinforce that help is required and is available. The dependent is not faced with the choice to stop drinking—only to get help. It is not the minister's intention to force the person to seek the needed treatment. He can, however, induce the process by obtaining permission to alert the family, to set up a referral, or to call a parishioner who is a recovererd user. It is difficult to seek help alone; understanding this, the minister can invite the person to go with him to an AA or a Narc-Anon meeting. When the minister himself drives the person to an introductory meeting and stays with him, the referral process is usually successful. When he tells the person to go to a meeting or suggests they meet there, the sick person builds a rationale for missing the appointment, and usually he does not show. His reasons are valid, but the referral process fails. By offering to accompany the person to the referred resource, the minister is facilitating the process, not seeking to force or enforce it.

Though friendly persuasion is sucessful with adults, it is less so with teenagers. Once the inventory has revealed there is a problem, most youngsters fear their parents' reactions. Therefore, the minister must be forceful and use what Jay Haley calls a "directive": "I want your permission to talk with your folks about this. You need help, and I want to make sure you get it. The evidence is clear, and we can't afford to lose you. I want you to let me call them." If the young person refuses, as most do, the minister can use the leverage of his concern for the youngster; he can say, "I'm going to fight you for you. I plan to win because I don't want you to continue damaging yourself. You can tell your parents, or I'll go with you to explain the problem to them. The choice is yours, but that is the choice!" The focus is not on maintaining the relationship; it is on getting help for the child.

In the case of an alcohol problem, a youngster's recovery begins immediately—as soon as he stops drinking. But if it is a problem with marijuana, the teenager will not benefit from counseling until he has been "dried out," that is, until the THC has cleared out of his system. It usually takes twenty-one to twenty-nine days and requires professional treatment. In either case, he needs parental assistance and outside support to begin the process of recovery. The minister's task is to usher the dependent into a supportive environment. Though that task usually means helping the youngster despite his resistance, it does *not* mean being responsible for him once the parents have been called and the referral has been made. When the latter have been done, the minister's problem-solving responsibilities are complete.

Using problem-solving therapy as a technique for dealing with chemical dependency gives the minister a much-needed, expedient tool. Where once he had to rely on pastoral-counseling skills that avoided confrontation, he now has a means of addressing the issues in an objective, straightforward, goal-oriented way. The centripetal force of emotional involvement is not a danger because empathethic listening is not the goal. By employing the "Minister's Assessment," the "Evaluation of Codependency," and the "Personal Inventory," all compiled specifically to diagnose loss of personal potential because of chemical dependency, he can quickly determine there is a problem and deal with it effectively. The minister does not have to be a practitioner. He does not have to avow a moral stance. To be helpful he does not even need to be interested in dealing with alcohol- or drug-related problems. Problem-solving therapy is effective no matter what the personal or professional experience of the clergyperson, and he can use the diagnostic instruments provided here to deal successfully with the complexities of chemical dependency.

The starting point of all recovery is *recognition* of chemical dependency. The minister, more than any other care-giving professional, is in a position to make the initial diagnosis. Acting as a problem-solver, he has the means of focusing on behavior, identifying the illness, and effecting a change in the social unit, which result in referral to a suitable form of treatment. As he does so, he is an instrument of God's covenant that there is hope for those who suffer from this primary, progressive, chronic, and fatal family illness.

CHAPTER 8

Creating a Treatment Network

> Change begins with one person's recognition that there
> might be something better, that he or she might be some-
> one better, that the old ways are not working anymore and
> that the old self is not functioning well. Change begins with
> accepting what is and reaching out for something better.
> Change is almost always frightening, almost always pain-
> ful, but can lead to positive growth.[1]

Of all things we, the clergy, can do to help facilitate a change for the better, the
most powerful form of energy we can generate is that of prayer. Prayer! Praying
with, praying for, those in need of change. If we have anything at all to
contribute to the treatment process, it is in emphasizing that prayer and
meditation have greater predictive power relative to abstinence, recovery, and
family restoration than do any other factors (home life, marital status, job,
lifestyle, or friends). According to the Hazelden Foundation's model of treatment for chemical dependency, increased prayer and meditation—the "higher
power" variable—are critical means of remaining abstinent and improving
social and psychological functioning. We cannot, we must not, underestimate
the power of prayer. Too often we take God's "Good News," change it into good
advice, and suggest that drug discontinuance can be achieved by will power.
This advice is based on the erroneous belief that the illness is caused by a weak
or lacking will. Recovery from chemical dependency is accelerated when
everyone admits that they are powerless over the illness and that only a power
greater than themselves can change and restore them. As their spiritual
leaders, we can enhance this process of restoration by leading them to that
"higher power," to God, in prayer. By inspiring them to turn their will and lives
over to God's care, we can encourage them to continue reaching out for
something better despite the fear and pain. No matter where we are in the
process of facilitating change, each step for us and for those seeking recovery
must be guided by prayer.

NETWORKING

The starting point of recovery from chemical dependency is the moment when we respond to the cry for help by: (1) diagnosing the problem, (2) verbalizing the problem so everyone understands it, (3) eliciting a commitment to change, and (4) picking up the phone to make the referral. Though we are not responsible for the change to take place, as referral agents we *are* responsible for knowing where to steer our parishioners so change can begin. If we are successfully to link a person or family to the appropriate source of help, we cannot wait until the catastrophe presents itself to establish a network of resources; we need to be able to draw on those people, agencies, organizations, and treatment centers of which we have a personal knowledge and with which we have already established a working relationship. This means we are most useful when we have done our homework in advance and have made contact with a care-giver so that we know him and we know he knows us. The popular buzzword for this is "networking," and, fortunately or unfortunately, no one can do it for us; it requires a personal call and a visit. The place to begin is within our congregations.

If the chemical-education committee has not already seen the need, one can point out that every fellowship should have a current list of resources both within and without the community. The list is for the parish *and* the minister. It is a fulfilling project for one or two members of the parish to find out which professionals, organizations, or agencies are trained to deal with chemical dependency and which are not. But one word of caution is necessary: When charging the two parishioners with the responsibility of compiling this referral list, it must be made clear that unless the contacted care-giver has had specific training in, or extensive experience with, the treatment of chemical dependency, he or she should not be listed. As the preceding chapters have stressed, this subfield of health care requires specialized knowledge, training, and skills not ordinarily taught in medical schools or seminaries. What's more, the communication techniques commonly taught in such schools (e.g., empathetic listening) only complicate the family distress and prolong the illness of chemical dependency. Therefore, when compiling a resource list, great care must be taken to list only those agents known to be experienced in, or trained for, alcohol/drug work. Assuming that a doctor, psychologist, psychiatrist, minister, counselor, therapist, or social worker has the necessary qualifications is unacceptable; each professional's expertise in this unique field must be verified before he or she may be listed. Related professional organizations have directories that can be consulted. The Yellow Pages list counselors and consultants. A questionnaire that can be used to substantiate a practitioner's credentials is provided at the end of this chapter.

While the chemical-education committee is putting together a list for us, we can establish our own network by calling on members of the congregation whom we know to be members of Alcoholics Anonymous, Al-Anon, Narc-Anon, etc. Such people are invaluable as resources because their lives depend on maintaining sobriety and spiritual serenity. They are the congregation "in action," a source of support and strength. The primary goal of recovery is, of course, abstinence from alcohol or other mood-altering chemicals. Continual attendance at AA meetings and those of other support groups is, along with prayer and meditation, the most important factor in maintaining abstinence. The people who attend AA or Al-Anon are usually very knowledgeable about where to get help, i.e., which doctors are helpful, what agencies are most appropriate, which consultants are reliable, and what treatment programs are available. Recovering people are always happy to be of service, for their sobriety depends in part on helping others to recover. When we call on them, we need to ask for their permission to use them as a resource. Without their permission, we are not at liberty to divulge the fact that they are chemically dependent, nor are we free to violate their anonymity by saying they are members of Alcoholics Anonymous. (As a matter of interest, "Anonymous" means they themselves do not publicly reveal they are attending AA. They may say, "I am an alcoholic," but this is different from saying, "I am a member of AA.") Protection of the organization and the membership is at issue here. Just as doctors never tell who has what illness, neither can we reveal (without permission) who is an alcoholic. Furthermore, we do not have the right or the freedom to betray the confidentiality of privileged communications by revealing who goes to AA.

By contacting recovering members of our congregations, by securing their permission to use them for referral, we will have at our fingertips people we can call on at a moment's notice, people who are willing to respond just as quickly. These people are not afraid of chemical-dependency problems, nor are they suffering from the number one symptom of the illness-*denial*. They are among our most useful lay ministers because they, by virtue of their sickness, have the gift of discernment. They are not easily deceived by dependents' rationalizations. What's more, they do not concern themselves with trying to explain why an individual is chemically dependent or a family is distressed; they do not get bogged down in cause-and-effect analyses. Instead, they are willing to accept the problem as an unexplained illness; they are able to dismiss the rationalizations as symptoms of the illness, and they are able to focus everyone's energy where it is most needed—toward getting treatment for the illness. Their approach is the very essence of biblical theology. The emphasis is not on explanations of behavior, nor is it on judgments or blame. Just as the word "why" is not used in the commandments and is never asked in the confessional or in a corporate confession, recovering people do not use it to deal with chemical dependency. Rather, the emphasis is on helping those who are sick to take responsibility for their own behavior. This means they must admit their actions have been harmful to themselves and others. The sole purpose is to enable them to make choices that will change their behavior for the better. This means they must seek help for themselves. These helping people, therefore, the members of AA or Al-Anon or Alateen or Narc-Anon, are often the first ones we want to call. Because they have already suffered through the complex and trying process of changing their behavior, we can use them as guides to lead a distressed individual or family through the same process. It is astonishing that they expect no payment for their willingness to guide, to support, and to follow through with a distressed family. Their payment is sobriety.

UNDERSTANDING AND USING AA

Many people have misconceptions about who AA members are and what AA does. Consequently they hesitate to seek out recovering people for the special ministry the latter can offer. It is not uncommon, even today, for some of the clergy to picture the fellowship of Alcoholics Anonymous as a collection of derelicts who once drank booze out of a brown bag and slept their drunkenness off in gutters and doorways. AA members are still seen as uneducated bums who sit in their smoke-filled meeting halls, drinking gallons of coffee and exchanging "war stories." No picture could be further from the truth. With one out of eight people in the U.S. suffering Jellinek's disease, those who attend AA meetings are nothing more (but nothing less) than representatives of every classification of society: male and female; white, black, brown, yellow, and red; young, middle-aged, and old; married and unmarried; heterosexual and homosexual; Jewish, Roman Catholic, and Protestant; professional and nonprofessional; educated and uneducated; upper, middle, and lower class. To go to AA, Al-Anon, Alateen, or Narc-Anon is to meet a next-door neighbor or a member of the church or a doctor or an employer—or a minister. If we are going to use the recovering members in our parishes as primary resources, therefore, we need to attend their gatherings, meet them where they meet, understand their goals, and become familiar with their philosophy. We will then be able to understand how this nonsectarian, nondenominational fellowship can be a chief ally in helping us deal with chemical dependency in our parish. There are countless numbers of now sober people who owe their recovery to ministers who directed them to the fellowship of AA or put them in touch with parish members known to be in AA. These people's lives were saved by ministers who understood, appreciated, and knew how to take advantage of the AA program. For those who have yet to learn how, a brief introduction to AA, taken from an Alcoholics Anonymous pamphlet entitled "A Clergyman Asks About Alcoholics Anonymous," is offered here. For information on local AA meetings, see the Yellow Pages of the phone book.

QUESTIONS FREQUENTLY ASKED

1. *What is Alcoholics Anonymous?*

Perhaps the best brief description of AA is contained in the two-paragraph definition that is read at many group meetings: 'Alcoholics Anonymous is a fellowship of men and women who share their experience, strength and hope with each other that they may solve their common problem and help others to recover from alcoholism.'

'The only requirement for membership is a desire to stop drinking. There are no dues or fees for AA membership; we are self-supporting through our own contributions. AA is not allied with any sect, denomination, politics, organization or institution; does not wish to engage in any controversy; neither endorses nor opposes any causes. Our primary purpose is to stay sober and help other alcoholics to achieve sobriety.'

2. *How did AA get started?*

What was later to become known as the Fellowship of Alcoholics Anonymous came into being in Akron, Ohio, in 1935. It was founded by two men publicly identified only as Bill W., a former New York stockbroker, and Dr. Bob S., an Akron surgeon. . . . Both regarded as "helpless' alcoholics . . . the two men discovered that their own sobriety was strengthened when they offered to share it with others, stressing their own practical experience as recovered alcoholics. By the fall of 1935, a small group of sober alcoholics was meeting regularly in Akron.

3. *Why should members of the clergy be interested in AA?*

Because many alcoholics look to their spiritual advisors for guidance both before and after joining AA—and often by joining AA, the alcoholic may be able to help other alcoholics.

4. How can AA help?

AA can help in only one way: by making available to members of the clergy the practical experience of alcoholics who have learned to live without alcohol in any form. . . .

Many members of the clergy ask AA's to meet with alcoholics to describe the AA recovery program.

5. How do alcoholics attain sobriety in AA?

AA members follow to the best of their ability a suggested program of twelve steps. . . . The steps include elements found in spiritual teaching of many faiths. . . . They are not theoretical or dogmatic in tone, they simply state the actual experience of men and women who have been able to solve their own problems of alcoholism.

Members are also encouraged to attend meetings, at which they can share their experiences with one another and with newcomers. . . .

6. What are the Twelve Steps of AA?

These are the steps through which an estimated 1,000,000 men and women have achieved sobriety in the Fellowship of Alcoholics Anonymous:

1. We admitted we were powerless over alcohol—that our lives had become unmanageable.
2. Came to believe that a Power greater than ourselves could restore us to sanity.
3. Made a decision to turn our will and our lives over to the care of God, *as we understood Him.*
4. Made a searching and fearless moral inventory of ourselves.
5. Admitted to God, to ourselves, and to another human being the exact nature of our wrongs.
6. Were entirely ready to have God remove all these defects of character.
7. Humbly asked Him to remove our shortcomings.
8. Made a list of all persons we had harmed, and became willing to make amends to them all.
9. Made direct amends to such people wherever possible, except when to do so would injure them or others.
10. Continued to take personal inventory and when we were wrong promptly admitted it.

11. Sought through prayer and meditation to improve our conscious contact with God *as we understood Him,* praying only for knowledge of His will for us and the power to carry that out.

12. Having had a spiritual awakening as the result of these steps, we tried to carry this message to alcoholics and to practice these principles in all our affairs.

7. *Is AA a temperance society?*

No. The Fellowship takes no position on the so-called temperance question. Collectively, its members neither approve nor disapprove the use of alcohol by others. They have simply learned from experience that they cannot handle alcohol themselves. . . .

8. *Is AA a religious society?*

No AA is not a religious society or movement in the denominational sense, although the recovery program includes suggestions that reflect the insight of many spiritual leaders. . . .

9. *Is AA an evangelical movement?*

No, not in any sense of the term. . . .

10. *Does AA regard alcoholism as a sin?*

As a Fellowship, AA is committed to no theological concept of alcoholism. . . . Most members regard alcoholism as an illness that cannot be cured, but can be arrested by alcoholics who honestly attempt to practice the Twelve Steps in their affairs.

11. *What part do meetings play in the AA program?*

AA meetings evolved naturally out of the early members' desire to share their experience and problems with one another and with newcomers who sought sobriety. . . .

Most members believe that regular attendance at meetings is essential to the maintenance of sobriety. . . .

12. *Are members of the clergy welcome at AA meetings?*

They are most welcome at AA public meetings and (in some cases) at "open meetings." . . .

13. *Does AA have a formal creed?*

No. AA members are not asked to accept any formal creed or statement of belief beyond the admission that they have a drinking problem and want help. . . .

The unifying belief of the membership might be said to be the faith that a recovered alcoholic, by sharing his or her experience, can be uniquely effective in helping other problem drinkers. . . .

14. *Do AA members recognize the authority of a superior being?*

When alcoholics turn to AA for help, they are not asked about their personal religious beliefs.

Reliance upon a Higher Power is, however, central to the success of most men and women who have achieved sobriety in AA.

Early in the development of AA, it was recognized that many alcoholics are not prepared to accept the concept of a personal deity. . . .

Accordingly, the first members told newcomers, in effect: 'We have learned from experience that we need the help of a Power greater than ourselves if we are to stay sober. . . .'

15. *What do members mean by the "spiritual side" of the AA program?*

Most members use this phrase to describe the spiritual meaning of the Twelve Steps. . . .

16. *What is meant by 'the group conscience' in AA?*

Most AA's believe that they can find their most reliable guidance in a wisdom that rises above personal or factional desires and judgments.

17. *How is prayer used in the AA program?*

The Seventh Step reads: '(We) sought through prayer and meditation to improve our conscious contact with God, as we understood Him, praying only for knowledge of His will for us and the power to carry that out.' At most AA meetings, all in attendance are invited to close the gathering by reciting the Lord's prayer. . . .

Many members find spiritual strength in the following lines, which in recent years have come to be known as 'The AA Prayer':

> God grant me the serenity to accept the
> things I cannot change,
> The courage to change the things I can,
> And the wisdom to know the difference.

19. *May agnostics or atheists become members of AA?*

AA does not inquire into alcoholics' religious beliefs—or lack of them—when they turn to the Fellowship for help.

20. *Does AA support church programs in the field of alcoholism?*

AA traditionally has never been identified with or associated with private or tax-supported proposals, programs, propaganda or public fund raising in any area of alcohol prevention or control.

21. *Do any members of the clergy belong to AA?*

Yes. Alcoholism is no respecter of persons. Whatever their position, profession, or vocation in life may be. . . . There are a few groups composed entirely of such members.

22. *How may members of the clergy cooperate effectively with AA?*

There are several ways: by becoming familiar with AA's suggested recovery program through attendance at open meetings and through reading movement literature; by recognizing the spiritual (though nondenominational) aspects of their program; by calling on AA for help while appreciating the limitations of the work of AA members in the field of alcoholism; and by being patient with the human failings of individual members.

Some members of the clergy who have worked with many problem drinkers believe that it is essential to be acquainted personally with active AA members in the community; thus when AA help is desired, an alcoholic can quickly be placed in the care of a member who will take special interest in the recoverer and help the latter to get a good start toward recovery in AA.

23. *How may interested members of the clergy establish contact with AA?*

In many areas, an AA listing appears in the local telephone directory. . . . Doctors, law-enforcement officials, newspaper editors or reporters and welfare officials may also be able to provide information on AA locally.

Literature . . . and directions for getting in touch with a local group may also be obtained by writing to the General Service Office of AA, P.O. Box 459, Grand Central Station, New York, NY 10017.

24. *What can members of the clergy tell alcoholics who express interest in AA?*

Members of the clergy who have worked closely with AA would undoubtedly agree that the following points deserve emphasis:

First, try to impress upon alcoholics that AA probably can help them only if they are firm in their desire to stop drinking. . . .

Second, urge alcoholics to keep an open mind if the recovery program does not appear to make sense to them the first time they are exposed to it. . . .

Third, stress that AA has just one primary purpose—to help problem drinkers attain and maintain sobriety through sharing the personal experience of recovered alcoholics. . . .

Fourth, remind alcoholics that AA membership embraces a cross-section of society. . . .

Fifth, assure alcoholics that, in line with AA tradition, their personal anonymity will be respected and that their problem will not be disclosed ouside the Fellowship.

Finally, alcoholics should understand that, according to the best available medical evidence, they can never hope to drink normally again. They have two choices: progressive deterioration if they continue to drink, or a new and promising way of life if they will stop using alcohol in any form. In AA they will find thousands of men and women who will help them make the transition to this new life by sharing experiences with them."[2]

As the Reverend Samuel Shoemaker's tract suggests, we can learn a great deal from Alcoholics Anonymous. Not only is it itself a model of mental, emotional, and spiritual health but we can rely on its members as models. We can follow their example, and we can ask them to lead us. They are among our most beneficial resources. It is important to note that many members of the AA Fellowship today are recovering from alcoholism *and* other forms of drug addiction. They can be helpful no matter what the chemical dependency.

When Dr. George Vaillant completed his landmark study of Jellinek's disease (described in chapter 5), even he was surprised by some of his conclusions. First, he realized that his own profession, psychiatry, is inadequate to treat the illness. Second, traditional psychiatric approaches are nearly useless in dealing with the underlying causes of Jellinek's disease. Third, that expensive hospital treatment centers alone are not enough to bring about recovery. "Even though it's terribly unscientific," he says, "alcoholics do seem to need some kind of source of hope and self-esteem, or religious inspiration—whatever you want to call it—and that seems more important than hospital or psychiatric care."[3]

The key to treating Jellinek's disease, Vaillant believes, is in recognizing that it is neither a psychological symptom nor some vague, unnamed metabolic riddle waiting to be deciphered. It is not a sin but a progressive disease that may take years to manifest itself and from which it may take years to recover. Regarding recovery , Dr. Vaillant feels that the natural healing processes that relieve suffering and create hope are actuated best by Alcoholics Anonymous. He maintains that the initial step to recovery and sobriety starts with the acceptance of the first precept of AA: "I am powerless over alcohol." It is his professional judgment, based on extensive research, that "AA is the most effective means of treating alcoholism, and it worked for sophisticated, Harvard-educated loners as well as gregarious blue-collar workers."[4] Consequently, when we establish a network of resource people, the foundation of the network should be AA meetings and members of AA.

AL-ANON, ALATEEN, COA, AND NARC-ANON

Since chemical dependency is a family illness, we need to have personal contacts with family members who can be helpful to others distressed by the dependency. Here, our most useful resources are Al-Anon and Alateen. Though not as well known as AA, Al-Anon, which includes Alateen, is a well-established support program for the family no matter whether the dependent person seeks help or even recognizes the existence of a problem. It seeks to meet and alleviate the codependency problems that are an integral part of the illness. Although Al-Anon is an outgrowth of Alcoholics Anonymous and bases its programs on the same "Twelve Steps," it is a separate fellowship. Any person who feels his or her life has been affected by someone's chemical use is eligible for membership. The goals of both Al-Anon and Alateen are to:

1. Offer comfort, hope, and friendship to the families and friends of compulsive drinkers and drug users.

2. Provide the opportunity to learn to grow spiritually through living by the Twelve Steps.

3. Learn effective ways to cope with their problems through sharing experiences and discussing difficulties.[3]

As with AA members, we have within our parishes people who regularly attend Al-Anon. The resource list we compile should—with permission—include those whom we can call. They can help us help a distressed family. Again, Al-Anon and Alateeen are not exclusively for alcohol-related problems; in addition both organizations include family members affected by someone's drug use. The questions clergy frequently ask about Al-Anon are those they ask about AA, and the answers are the same. The only difference is that AA is for the recovery of the chemically dependent person, whereas Al-Anon is for the recovery of the chemically dependent person's family. Understanding Al-Anon and Alateen and how to use their programs as resources are best acccomplished by attending some of the local meetings.

In recent years still another self-help program has sprung out of Al-Anon; it is a group established to address the unique needs of a particular body of people—adult Children of Alcoholics (COA). Though chemical dependency runs in families, it does not necessarily mean *all* children of the chemically dependent person become dependent themselves. It does mean, however, that they have been hurt by the illness and that, as a result, they face a unique set of problems. Whether or not they drink or use chemicals, their adult lives are affected by the experience of growing up in a distressed home.

Considering that one out of eight adults is suffering from Jellinek's disease and that one chemically dependent person usually has a distressing effect on four or five other family members, there has developed a large population of adult children of alcoholics—22 million—who are suffering intellectual, emotional, or psychological problems without understanding the cause. Because they do not realize their problems stem from growing up in an alcoholic home, it never occurs to them that they can get help. To them distress feels normal, and yet it feels abnormal, too, because life seems like a perpetual war. Without insight into their problems, they remain victims of their past. But if we, their ministers, understand these difficulties, we can very usefully refer them to sources of help and support. According to the Johnson Institute's studies, there is a distinct psychological profile of the adult child of an alcoholic. It is offered here to help the reader recognize the symptoms.

PROFILE OF AN ADULT CHILD OF AN ALCOHOLIC

1. He/she guesses at what normal is, doesn't recognize what "normal" is when he/she sees it.

Traditional client-centered psychotherapy can be destructive because it assumes the answers lie within the person. The adult child doesn't have the answer, was never taught the answer because he/she never had the role models. He/she is used to stuffing and denying feelings—doesn't know they are OK.

2. He/she has difficulty in following a project from beginning to end.

Has the ideas, but no idea of the steps needed to carry the idea out. He/she has learned it was the "intentions" that count . . . not the behavior.

3. He/she lies when it would be just as easy to tell the truth.

Does this automatically without guilt. Truth doesn't have value.

4. He/she judges self without mercy.

Is never good enough.

5. He/she has difficulty having fun.

Never learned how to play.

6. He/she takes self too seriously.

Life is hard work.

7. He/she has difficulties with intimate relationships.

The fears of abandonment are too great to ease into a relationship. Doesn't know how to slowly develop a healthy relationship. Fears letting go of an unhealthy relationship.

8. *He/she constantly seeks approval and affirmation.*

Can never give it to self... looks to others for affection.

9. *He/she overreacts to changes over which he/she has no control.*

As a child he/she had no control over changes that often threatened his/her safety, security, survival.

10. *He/she is super-responsible or super-irresponsible.*

Can't say *no* because of need for approval—sets no limits, prime candidate for burnout. Super-responsible types have to get sick to break cycle.

11. *He/she has no sense of cooperation/working with others.*

Is used to doing things alone and for self, that's how he/she survived in [a] chaotic family. (Doesn't mean that they aren't cooperative people.)

12. *He/she is exceedingly loyal, even in the face of evidence the loyalty isn't deserved.*

Make great friends, employees, etc. Learned this from practice with drinking parent.

13. *He/she is often impulsive.*

Locks self into a course of action without thought of the consequences.

14. *He/she doesn't appear to have any more problems with sexuality or sexual behavior than anyone else.*

15. *He/she tends to look for immediate rather than delayed gratification.*

Learned as a child. ... if you wait, you don't get it.[4]

The common characteristics adult children of alcoholics list about *themselves* are useful for pastors to know.

ADULT CHILDREN OF ALCOHOLICS SPEAK FOR THEMSELVES

The Problem: Adult children of alcoholics seem to have several characteristics in common as a result of having been brought up in an alcoholic household.

1. We become isolated and afraid of people and authority figures.

2. We become approval seekers and lose our identity in the process.

3. We are frightened by angry people and any personal criticism.

4. We either become alcoholics, marry them, or both, or find another compulsive personality, such as a workaholic, to fulfill our sick abandonment needs.

5. We live life from the viewpoint of victims and are attracted by that weakness in our love, friendship, and career relationships.

6. We have an overdeveloped sense of responsibility, and it is easier for us to be concerned with others rather than ourselves. This enables us not to look too closely at our faults or our responsibility to ourselves.

7. We get guilt feelings when we stand up for ourselves instead of giving in to others.

8. We become addicted to excitement.

9. We confuse love and pity and tend to "love" people we "pity" and "rescue."

10. We have stuffed our feelings from our traumatic childhoods and have lost the ability to feel or express our good feelings, such as joy and happiness. Our being out of touch with our feelings is one of our basic denials.

11. We judge ourselves harshly and have a very low sense of self-esteem.

12. We are dependent personalities who are terrified of abandonment and will do anything to hold onto a relationship in order *not* to experience painful abandonment feelings which we received living with sick people who were never there emotionally for us.

13. Alcoholism is a family disease, and we became para-alcoholics and took on the characteristics of that disease even though we did not pick up the drink.

14. Para-alcoholics are reactors rather than actors.

If there is a single characteristic of adult children of alcoholics that undermines much of their sense of self-worth, it is a basic feeling of shame. Shame is inevitably at the basis of identity formation and has a drastic effect on the individual's search for value and meaning. The continual experience of shame, which occurs in an alcoholic household where the focus of the alcoholic's negativity is on the child himself and not on the child's behavior, results in a fundamental sense of being defective as a person.

The difference between shame and guilt is that guilt implies, "I did something wrong for which I feel bad," and shame says, "Basically, I am bad. That is why I did what is wrong." It is important for us to appreciate this difference if we hope to build a bridge of trust to the adult child of an alcoholic. As instruments of God's forgiving and redemptive love, we can help where other professional guides cannot. The adult child of an alcoholic feels defective and needs the affirmation of someone who accepts him as he is, not as he thinks he should be. By accepting him as God does, a bond of trust is established that enables us to refer him to those who understand his unique problems, appreciate him, and can help him. Because we accept him and he trusts us, even though he doubts himself, he is able to accept our suggestions for help.

By attending COA meetings, these people learn they can live their lives in a way that includes trust, openness, and vulnerability. They learn that having both positive and negative feelings is normal and healthy and that by changing former attitudes, patterns, and habits, they can rebuild their sense of worth, learn to accept themselves, find serenity and even happiness. (For further information about this special group, read *Adult Children of Alcoholics* by Janet G. Woititz.)

Narcotics Anonymous (NA) is yet another self-help group based on AA's principles and "Twelve Steps." As the name implies, its objective is to serve those who are recovering from drug dependency. Though its local chapters are not nearly as plentiful as AA's, Al-Anon's or Alateen's, the program Narc-Anon offers makes it important to include on our resource list. If no members of our parish attend NA meetings or if there are no local meetings, it is worthwhile to make contact with someone who goes, or to locate and attend the closest meeting. Narc-Anon is not just for the street junkies we see portrayed on television; it is for such people as the business person trying to stay off cocaine, the teenager abstaining from marijuana, the housewife letting go of sleeping pills, the athlete fighting off heroin, and the minister giving up tranquilizers. Though many people are frightened to address the problems of a drug addict, those who attend NA are not. Because of their experience, they can lead the way through fear and denial and make recommendations for appropriate treatment. [Note: a national hotline number for cocaine problems is 800–C–O–C–A–I–N–E. For a drug-treatment program, one of the finest in the U.S. is STRAIGHT, INC., P.O. Box 848, Marietta, GA 30061; (404) 434-8679.]

As the parish begins to compile its resource list and we build our own, it is worthwhile to consider asking one or two interested parishioners if they would be willing to become paraprofessionals in the drug-dependency field. The church or chemical-education committee will doubtless receive notices of both local and national training programs from which interested parishioners can acquire the knowledge necessary to become inhouse consultants. It is important that we not be perceived as the resident chemical-dependency experts. Training others to fill that role not only relieves us of the image but, more importantly, provides the congregation with its own expert, who will remain should we move to another post. The cost of this training can be paid by the parish, or the trainee may pay it as part of his offering to the church or synagogue. However it is done, it is important that the paraprofessional pass on his knowledge by giving presentations, preaching, and teaching in the parish. This reinforces the notion that his education is the congregation's education, that his expertise is available to parishioners.

A DIRECTORY OF REFERRAL RESOURCES

As was said at the outset, though we are not repsonsible for the change to take place as a result of a parishioner's treatment, we *are* responsible for knowing where to steer them so that change for the better can begin. Treatment sources are many and varied. To build a resource list that will help establish a network inside and outside the parish, we need to give those who are compiling it an idea of what kind of resources are needed. To that end a checklist of referral sources is provided here. Filling in the details rests with us and with those we have asked to compile the list. (*See* appendix A.)

REFERRAL RESOURCES

I. *Within the Congregation:*

Alcohol- and Drug-Related Problems:

Alcoholics Anonymous members
Al-Anon members
Alateen members
COA members
Narc-Anon members
Trained professionals
Chemical-education committee
Parish paraprofessionals

II. *Outside the Congregation:*

II. Alcohol- and Drug-Related Problems:

Alcoholics Anonymous meeting list. Available from AA.

Al-Anon group meeting list. Available from Al-Anon.

Alateen group list. Available from Al-Anon.

Adult Children of Alcoholics group. Available from Al-Anon.

Narc-Anon group

Tough Love group

Other self-help groups

Detoxification units

Treatment centers (alcoholism or drug abuse; for adults, adolescents)

Hotline numbers

Hospitalization facilities (private, state-run)

Emergency treatment

Outpatient treatment programs (for adults, adolescents)

Outpatient counseling centers

Evaluation consultants/centers

Halfway houses (male, female, mixed)

Salvation Army installations

Psychologists—with special knowledge

Psychiatrists—with special knowledge

Social workers—with special knowledge

Chemical-dependency counselors

Professional interveners

Intervention agencies/institutes

Ministers—with special knowledge

Other counselors

Family Service agencies

Training/teaching institutes

Training/teaching programs

Professional speakers/educators

Parents groups/organizations (state and national)

State agencies

Government agencies

Mental Health, Personal, Family Problems:

Community mental-health programs, resources

Private psychiatric hospitals

Private psychological hospitals

Nonprofit hospitals with psychiatric units
Psychiatrists
Psychologists
Pastoral counselors
Social workers
Family counselors/therapists
Family-service agencies
Grief groups
Dieters' groups
Exercise/dance groups
Other support/self-help groups
Emergency services
Vocational rehabilitation centers/programs
Marriage counselors
Child-welfare center/programs
Child-abuse prevention centers
Sexual-abuse counselors/centers
Rape counselors/centers
Services to the aging
Babysitting services
Child-care services
Educational/tutorial services

Medical Needs:

Hospitals
Clinics (profit and nonprofit)
Emergency services
Physicians
Visiting Nurse services
Homemakers services
Transportation to treatment services

Financial Needs:

Accountants
Attorneys
Public assistance agencies
Legal Aid
Consumer credit services
Veterans' services
Charities (local, state)

Foundations (local, state)
Scholarship funds
Private/community/state welfare funds

Legal Needs:

Private attorneys
Public defenders
Probation office/officers
Legal Aid
Police and fire officials

Deciding what form of treatment is needed or which treatment center to suggest is not as easy as it would seem. Each situation is unique. What is most appropriate for the dependent person may be inappropriate for family members. There are times when family members must get help because the dependent person will not be helped. In other situations, the dependent person must follow through with a recovery program even though the family members do not. Since the circumstances vary according to the people involved, suggestions for the most effective treatment will be just as varied. If we are to be useful, therefore, we need to be aware of the choices and of what effective treatment is.

One word of caution. A clergyperson might expect that because chemical dependency is a treatable disease and recovery a possibility, those involved would be glad to seek treatment. Nothing could be further from the truth. As has been pointed out, myths, misconceptions, and denial often prevent the dependent and his family from getting treatment. The most common hindrances are:

1. The difficulty of detecting the illness in relation to cultural values that encourage use, condone misuse, and accept abuse.

2. The misconception that chemical dependency is a self-inflicted problem and the dependent and the codependents are irresponsbile, weak-willed, and immoral. These attitudes cause the victims both to conceal and to deny the illness.

3. Inasmuch as the dependent is powerless over his chemical, he believes he cannot live a satisfying life without it. The thought of a life without alcohol or drugs is seen as the end of life altogether. This view accounts for the resistance and denial.

4. The shame, guilt, and remorse that accompany chemical dependency militate against exposing oneself to the possibility of help or the benefits of treatment.

In short, the victims of chemical dependency don't want treatment! The barriers described above render them incapable of wanting it. But ultimately their pain will become their greatest asset; it will drive them to seek help despite these obstructions. The minister suggests the choice of treatment, but it is up to those who need it to seek the changes that lead to recovery.

UNDERSTANDING TREATMENT

Three common misconceptions stand in the way of our recommending the most effective form of treatment: (1) that treatment means getting a chemically dependent person "fixed" so he becomes free of alcohol or mood-altering chemicals; (2) that the dependent person is "fixed" so he will no longer be a problem to family, friends, and associates; and (3) that once the dependent person is treated, abstinence from alcohol or drugs is assured. In each of these three, the belief is that chemical dependency is one person's problem. Though it assigns blame, it does not lead to recovery and health; instead, by suggesting that unless the dependent person gets "fixed" the entire situation is hopeless, it undermines the hope of treatment.

Though abstinence from alcohol or drugs is one of the primary goals of treatment, it is not as easily accomplished as sending the chemically dependent person to a hospital to have his addiciton cured. First of all, chemical dependency is *not* cured by *any* treatment; rather, the dependent person is afforded chemical-free time in which to regain the control of his life that alcohol or drugs have stolen from him. Whether he volunteers to go to twenty-eight AA meetings in as many days or to a twenty-eight-day hospital program, the goal of the procedure is the same: chemical-free time in which to regain control so the dependent can choose to begin recovering. During this period he also has the chance to learn how to improve his physical, emotional, and spiritual life and to begin reclaiming his personal potential so he can remain abstinent.

As was stated, the learned behavior patterns that contribute most to abstinence are prayer, meditation, and AA attendance. Also, chemical dependency is a family disease, and effectual treatment requires that all members of the social unit be helped to improve their personal and corporate lifestyles as well. For the family, the primary goal of treatment is the healing of their emotional wounds. This is best accomplished when each person understands the part he has played in perpetuating the illness, admits how the illness has caused him to act and react in negative, destructive, and delusional ways, and begins to build a new lifestyle that enhances personal growth and fosters healthy family interaction, honesty, openness, flexibility, acceptance, respect, and caring. Treatment, therefore, does not mean getting the dependent person "fixed" (i.e., sober or abstinent), although it is one of the primary goals; it means helping everyone in the family embark on a program to regain control of his life. And it teaches each where to go and how to establish a lifelong program of personal recovery and family restoration.

Concerning the second common misconception—that the dependent person is "fixed" so he will no longer be a problem to family, friends, and associates: This belief assumes that unless the dependent person is cured, everyone else's problems will continue. It is important to remember that the entire system is sick. If it had been healthy, the illness would not have affected everyone as it did. The point of recommending treatment for the dependent is not to alleviate the family's problems, but to provide him with the help he needs. Each member of the system must address his own sickness as well. If each family member's restoration depends on the dependent person getting sober and staying abstinent, then there can be no assurance of health for anyone. But when each person takes responsibility for his own recovery, regardless of what the others do, then the family system begins to change for the better. "Fixing" the dependent person so he is no longer a problem, asking him to change for the sake of the common good, does not bring lasting results. If he is to recover he must do it for himself. His abstinence cannot depend on another's wants, hopes, faith, or concern. By the same token, if there is to be lasting health, each member of the system—family, friends, and associates— must be responsible for getting well, too. The recovery of one's life cannot and must not depend on anyone else's health.

This leads us to the third common misconception—that once the dependent person is treated, abstinence from alcohol or drugs is assured. This belief is the one that causes most care-giving professionals, especially doctors and ministers, to give up on people suffering from chemical dependency. In dealing with alcohol or drug problems, it cannot be assumed that when a problem is solved or a sickness is cured all difficulty is ended. To make that assumption means that the resolution of the situation depends on the problem solver or the healer or else that it is the care-giver's responsibility to see to it that the sick person gets cured and stays healthy. Neither is realistic. Solving the problem does not assure that treatment will succeed. Treatment, no matter who suggests or provides it, is not recovery. Recovery from chemical dependency is not the doctor's responsibility, nor it is the minister's, nor anyone else's save that of the person in need of the treatment. Furthermore, one person cannot be responsible for another's restoration. Treatment is not a magical act that transforms an addicted person into an abstainer; it is the start of a lifelong recovery process in which each person in the system is responsible for his own progress, and there is no guarantee that the chosen path will sustain health. There are no contracts that can constrain a chemically dependent person to remain abstinent after treatment, just as no promises can prevent a family from falling back into the same old patterns of denial, delusion, compulsion, and control that were the symptoms of its illness.

The major difference between chemical dependency and all other pastoral problems is that with the former there is no such thing as recovered or healed or restored. An alcohol-dependent person does not *have* alcoholism, he *is* an alcoholic. An drug-dependent individual does not *have* an addiction, he *is* an addict. Family members do not *have* codependency, they *are* codependent. Chemical dependency is a chronic illness; it is never cured. Consequently, everyone involved is and always will be recovering.

Simply because the sufferer abstains does not mean the illness is stopped. Alcohol or drug dependency is a progressive illness, and the progression continues even though the chemical use is discontinued. There is always a potential for a relapse. Treatment, therefore, is no guarantee of recovery, and no one can be responsible for another's lifelong program of recovery. If we, the care-givers, accept this fact, if each person involved in the family illness accepts it, then no one will take it personally and give up should a slip occur. No one will blame the other for a relapse. No one will hold another responsible for a recurrence of his own sickness. This realistic understanding will remove the hurt, the anger that follow if expectations are frustrated and hopes dashed. It will also do away with blame.

We realize we cannot control another person's behavior, we are not responsible for the family system's health, and there are no guarantees health is permanent. The treatment program we recommend, therefore, is one aspect of a continuing journey. It points those in need toward recovery; it gives them the time to reclaim themselves; it suggests the steps that lead to continued health. But it does not guarantee restoration. Restoration happens as a new lifestyle and abstinence are practiced by each recovering person—one day at a time.

OBTAINING INFORMATION ON REFERRAL RESOURCES

Since those we recommend as referral resources will be an extension of our ministry, it is important to be certain of their expertise. To confirm their credentials or qualifications is not as difficult as it would seem. It is most efficiently accomplished when we can help the resources provide us with the information we seek. By asking our committee to send out a questionnaire (like the one provided below) and following it up with a phone call, much of the needed information can be culled. Other information can be collected from professional organizations and publications, mental-health associations, national denominational offices, national offices of AA, Al-Anon, and Narc-Anon, and nationally known treatment centers or training programs. Ironically, the fastest and easiest way to get information about potential referral resources is to ask the members of our own congregation for their suggestions and opinions. Whether we realize it or not, our people are already using many of the resources we will later recommend; they know who they are, what they do, and how well they do it. By sending our parishioners a questionnaire asking for their recommendations, we can get an immediate and accurate picture of what help is available. The following form is designed to accomplish this goal.

REFERRAL RESOURCE PROFILE

We would like to use you and your services as a referral. Please complete this form as completely as possible. If you want, you may attach any brochures or other information you use to describe your practice or services. If yours is a group practice, please have each practitioner who would like to be included as a referral resource complete a separate questionnaire.

I. *Identifying Data*

    1. Name of organization/service/practice/practitioner
    2. Office address
    3. Office telephone/Emergency telephone
    4. Staff on call

II. *Service Data*

    1. Type of service
    2. Full-time or part-time
    3. List days and hours of operation
    4. Duration of program/service/treatment
    5. Education/training programs offered
    6. Hospital-based: _____Inpatient _____Outpatient _____Clinic
    7. Services to: _____Adults _____Adolescents _____Children _____Families _____Schools _____Churches _____ Businesses _____Other (Please list):
    8. Modality: _____AA model _____Medical model _____Psychiatric/psychological model _____Group therapy _____Other (Please list):
    9. Detoxification: _____Yes _____No
    10. _____Profit _____Nonprofit
    11. _____Private _____Community _____State _____Federal
    12. Aftercare Services_____
        Describe:
    13. Please describe fee scale_____
    14. Eligibility for third-party payments _____Yes _____No
        Describe:

15. Are you able to provide services in cases where there is no ability to pay or where there is no insurance coverage? Please explain.

III. *Professional/Special Training*

1. Degree or degrees that qualify you for your service or practice:
2. Specific training that qualifies you for your service or practice:
3. Continuing-education programs, courses, workshops, or seminars that qualify you for your service or practice:

IV. *Professional Experience*

1. Years of experience in your field:
2. Please list last three forms of employment:
3. If your present professional work is different from that for which you were professionally trained, please explain how you became qualified for it.
4. If you do not have formal or professional certification but do have personal experience that qualifies you to work in your field, please explain.
5. List the organizations/services/practices/practitioners that you work for or that use your services:

Name
Address
Phone

V. *References*

1. Please list the names and addresses of three references from the professional community.
2. Please list the names and addresses of three references who have used or now use your services.
3. Please provide any further information you feel will help us in making referrals to you.

"LET GO AND LET GOD"

Building a resource list is of primary importance, and it is a necessary first step if we are to deal effectively with the problems of a chemical-using society. Because we are not experts and do not intend to be chemical-dependency practitioners, we need to have experts we can call on. The more we have, the more effective we can be. As was shown earlier, if we assume responsibility for a distressed family or a dependent person instead of shepherding them to the appropriate treatment, we prolong the illness and we become a part of the illness. The pastoral key to treatment, recovery and restoration is referral—referral to a chemical-dependency professional, treatment center, or organization that can help dependents and codependents to become responsible for their own health. We are neither responsible for the treatment nor the recovery. Referring dependents to treatment and then letting them continue with it constitutes the most beneficial pastoral care we can provide. We cannot make them get help; we cannot force them to follow through; we cannot control their behavior. What we *can* do as ministers is to accept them as God does, offering unconditional regard, praying with them and for them, and entrusting them to the parish or community resource most appropriate for them.

To be able to make the most appropriate recommendations, however, we need to build a network. Most of the research can be done by the members of the chemical-education committee, but we need to conduct our own research, too, both inside and outside the parish. To have tried and tested resources that we know are trustworthy and reliable is the equivalent of attending to the problem personally. It is caring enough to recommend the very best. Once we have recommended a resource and established contact for the chemically dependent person or suffering family member, our pastoral care is in the hands of the referral resource. We can, as is suggested in Alcoholics Anonymous, "Let go and let God."

> O blessed Lord, you ministered to all who came to you: Look with compassion upon all who through addiction have lost their health and freedom. Restore to them the assurance of your unfailing mercy; remove from them the fears that beset them; strengthen them in the work of their recovery; and to those who care for them, give patient understanding and persevering love. Amen.
>
> *The Book of Common Prayer*[6]

CHAPTER 9

Theological Perspectives, Spiritual Foundations

We Americans, who have been called by Dr. Herbert Ratner "the most over-medicated, over-operated, over-inoculated people in the world," have been brainwashed into believing that there is a pill, nostrum, or potion which will remedy any trouble, be it headache, insomnia, fatigue, depression, loneliness, anxiety, tension, flat feet, or body odor; and we have effectively taught this to our children.

David C. Hancock[1]

In the not too distant future, the motivational and emotional condition of normal daily life will probably be maintained in any desired state through the use of drugs.

B.F. Skinner
Harvard Psychologist[2]

THE CULT OF CHEMISTRY

The above quotations are not a very strong recommendation of the strength of the human spirit, nor are they a confident prospectus on our ability to cope with life. To all intents and purposes the cult of chemistry has become the primary religion of the day. That "better living through chemistry" is the culturally sanctioned means for dealing with trouble, sorrow, need, sickness, and adversity makes it appear that alcohol and drugs offer more expedient and immediate answers to life's problems than does the institutional Church. For too many people it is their religion. Each person is now capable of creating his own paradise, safe from intruding anxieties and worries, complete with comforting feelings of euphoria and security. Everyone can construct his own chemical cocoon, free from the pain of sickness, filled with well-being and tranquility.

Researchers Karen Dunnell and Ann Cortwright found that in any twenty-four- to thirty-six-hour period, from 50 to 80 percent of the adult American population takes at least one medical drug.[3] In a single day we can kill a morning headache with an aspirin, subdue hunger pains with a diet pill, find quick energy for work in a cup of coffee, enjoy a break with a cigarette, cement a business deal with a martini-soaked lunch, face a difficult meeting with a tranquilizer, sit more comfortably with a hemorrhoidal suppository, gain confidence at a cocktail party with a scotch-on-the-rocks, savor dinner with wine, kill the heartburn with an antacid, clear our sinuses with a decongestant, relieve constipation with a laxative, and sleep soundly with a pill. Drugs are *big business!* Lest there be any doubt that the bottom line is money, the FDA estimates that 1.5 billion prescriptions (seven for each American) will be written in a year for one or more of the twenty-six thousand licit drugs. This will amount to $11 billion spent on legal drugs per year. With regard to alcohol, the chief drug of use and abuse in our society, the six major producers spent $696.3 million in 1981 to convince the American public to drink. The amount spent on advertising by the entire alcoholic-beverage industry in that year was $1,014.9 billion.[4]

What is the primary message? It is not "Drink our brand," but "drink *more* of our brand." This is the goal, even though it is widely known that greater consumption is one of the key factors leading to alcoholism. To get Americans to drink and drink more, the power of persuasion is focused on the most vulnerable audiences—heavy drinkers, young people, and women. Americans respond avidly. The per capita consumption of alcoholic beverages in 1980 was 28.36 gallons, up 31.5 percent from 1970. That's 28.36 gallons drunk for every man, woman, and child in the United States.[5]

We have been proselytized by the cult of chemistry. We have been brainwashed into believing we do not have the spiritual, emotional, or intellectual resources to meet and overcome the vicissitudes of life. What's worse, the advertisers, focusing on our deficiencies, insecurities, vulnerabilities, and anxieties, have made us believe we are deficient as human beings. Ostensibly, unless we eat, drink, smoke, chew, sniff, or apply their product, we are incomplete or unacceptable. It makes no difference that we are all made in God's image and acceptable to him; we have been brainwashed with this pathological religion that says we are worthless as persons, our lives are without meaning or purpose, we cannot enjoy or find joy, there is no salvation . . . without chemicals.

Dr. Ratner's alarm is well founded. We are effectively teaching our children that health, welfare, and wealth come in the form of a magic potion. We allow our children to sit passively for countless hours in front of the TV. According to the A.C. Nielson Company, the rating service, daily TV watching per home averaged seven hours and two minutes in 1983—a new American record, surpassing 1982's record by fourteen minutes. What is so alarming about this amount of television viewing is that in 1982 the average ten-year-old spent only fourteen-and-a-half minutes in meaningful interaction with his parents, and twelve-and-a-half minutes of that time was spent by the parents correcting wayward behavior. TV is clearly the most influential force in young peoples' lives. Through it they first learn to expect the world to entertain them. This in itself is the basis for addiction! Because of TV's slow but relentless conditioning, children come to depend on the external world to give them pleasure, to make them feel good. Then they are saturated with every conceivable form of televised persuasion. From the shows that make light of drunkenness, to the sports heroes who push sugar-coated cereals, to the slick commercials that promise strength or health or escape from pain in a pill, the medium and the message are the same: "You need a chemical to be OK. Without it, you don't make it, you won't make it, you can't make it." By planting the seeds of dissatisfaction and discontent in our naive children, both the beverage and the pharmaceutical industries have "a customer for life."

Our parishioners are the media's congregation. They are the targeted market. For companies to make money, there must be consumers. To medicate Americans there must be the "Do Drugs" advertising messages. Every conceivable medium is employed: T-shirts, movies, music, sports events, magazines, newspapers, concerts, glassware, auto races, videos, college parties, etc. In monetary terms, this is where many of our pledging units are tithing their dollars. The pleasure and relief merchants have preached their gospel of salvation, and parishioners have joined their crusade-*en masse*.

Then there is the religious quest for a nirvana found only in illicit drugs. The numbers of people on this quest can be inferred from the fact that today illegally grown marijuana is the nation's fourth largest cash crop; it ranks just behind corn, soybeans, and wheat in market value. "Last year's marijuana harvest had an estimated street value of $8.5 billion. . . . California's harvest, worth an almost unbelievable but reasonably documented $1.5 billion at retail, led the list."[6] Those who were of the stoned, strung-out, or tripped-out generation of the sixties and the seventies are now grown up, and their habits have gone with them into the business world and the marketplace. An article in the August 22, 1983, issue of *Newsweek*, "Taking Drugs on the Job," estimates the cost of drug abuse to the American economy at $25.8 billion, $16.6 billion in lost productivity alone. Obviously, the tragedy of this religious quest is that the highs are short-lived. With diluted street cocaine selling at $2000 to $2500 an ounce, the price of quick contentment leads to an unquenchable hunger for more of this false freedom and results in spiritual, emotional, physical, and economic bankruptcy. Again, these are our people, this is happening to parishioners. The cult of chemistry is now a civil religion. As Pogo says, "We have met the enemy and they are us."

MANSLAUGHTER? SUICIDE?

Though the pharmaceutical producers, the brewers and distillers, the tobacco companies, and the illicit drug pushers would not have us believe it, it is nonetheless a basic principle of all religious traditions that human beings are made in the image of God. This likeness is found in the operation of intellect and creativity, in the exercise of memory and vision, in the growth of physical, emotional, and spiritual health, and in the use of free will. In short, we are replicas of God. Though we believe God is the creator of all and all his creation is good—including alcohol and drugs—to suggest that without chemicals we are something less than acceptable to ourselves and others is contrary to all theology.

We are created as whole human beings, wholly acceptable and holy as far as God is concerned. As unique individuals named and known by God, each of us has the potential to grow into the person he intends us to be. We have life in which to explore, develop, and fulfill that potential. We are called to share our uniqueness of body, mind, and spirit with each other. Anyone who undermines or negates this principle of growth and development by suggesting it is not attainable without chemicals is, in a manner of speaking, inviting us to die. That smacks of manslaughter. What's more, to misuse or abuse chemicals to the point of diminishing the right and responsible use of our Godlike functions or to the point of separating ourselves from our five senses and isolating ourselves from each other (and, ultimately, from our Creator) is going against the life principle itself. That is a form of suicide.

Not very pleasant words—manslaughter and suicide—but if we are to discuss the use, misuse, and abuse of chemicals in terms that will help us set standards and guidelines and give hope to our people, we need to explain the theological issues. It is immoral to destroy human life with alcohol or drugs; it is sinful. And it is just as sinful to lead, entice, or coax a person into manslaughter or suicide as it is to commit the act. The relief merchants promise gratification and the fullness of life in a can, a bottle, an elixir, or a pill, and in so doing they tempt us to die. We accept their religion, comply, and seek a haven or a heaven in chemicals. To the extent that we misuse drugs and interrupt or impede development of our God-given expression of selfhood, we are committing a form of suicide. (Note: It is not the agent, the chemical, that kills; it is the irresponsible use of it.)

"One should not preach of such things" (Micah, 2:6): Micah was told this when he pointed out the abuses in his society, and this is what we are told when we address the sin of our world. Nevertheless, unless we preach the theological principles that reveal the spiritual disease in each of us, we cannot proclaim the hope of restoration and redemption available to all of us. We can no longer disregard the cult of chemistry, for we are losing too many parishioners. We live in a drug-oriented culture that preaches one gospel—"instant gratification"— and this gospel is inconsistent with the assured promise of growth, fulfillment, and new life God offers us.

Dr. Kenneth L. Maudlin, minister of the First Presbyterian Church, Topeka, Kansas, expressed it well in his sermon of January 9, 1972, entitled "Discipleship and Discipline."

> Must we not admit that, as people, we are morally and religiously undisciplined? In the name of freedom and liberation we have fled every yoke and every restriction as though work, art, study, and religion are disciplines we can do without.
>
> The very concept of self-discipline has come under attack, and my personal conviction is that this is one reason that for many people life has lost its dimensions. The heights and depths are gone, and life has become flat and dull and cheap and frivolous. The pleasures sought are the pleasures of a smoking heart and a pulsating nerve—and when the thrill is gone, the refuge is drink and drugs.
>
> It may very well be that as adults we have been so captured by the cult of comfort ourselves that we are incapable of challenging a world that is bewildered, uprooted, beaten down, and more than half-starved. [7]

It is frightening to realize that a mere decade later, a life inside that "refuge" of drink and drugs has become the ultimate goal.

If we are going to help our parishioners find or rediscover the "heights and depths" of a meaningful existence, if we are going to challenge our young people to fill needs other than those for pleasure, we simply have to address the implications of the use, misuse, and abuse of chemicals and preach the creative alternatives God offers. We are preachers, yes, but we are also prophets like Micah. The value of a healthy, whole, and holy life can best be seen and appreciated when we expose the sin underlying the "dis-ease" and the disorder of a "dull and cheap and frivolous" life. We must do so not in a judgmental, condemning way but so that our perspective, which is God's, is the answer to urgent questions, which are our parishioners'.

THE SICKNESS OF OUR DAY

There is a spiritual sickness in America, one that is disabling much of our population. Though the symptoms are alcohol and drug misuse and abuse, the malaise is a pervading sense of hopelessness, a feeling that we are no longer in control of our lives, that our destinies are being decided by forces we are unable to influence, direct, or change. We are victims of the storms of our day, and, like a ship caught in a maelstrom, we are in distress. All the safe, stable social structures with which we were once able to identify are changed; the sense of belonging is gone. As the prominent social psychologists Stanton Peele and Archie Brodsky observe in their book *Love and Addiction*, our country, our government, our educational system, our economic programs, our social status, our families, our religious institutions, even God—all those certainties that once helped us structure our lives and define our meaning—are now beyond our control; worse, they are controlling us. Where once we had a say in the creation of our institutions, organizations, associations, and bureaucracies, we now are at their mercy. We are in a vacuum of uncertainty. The malaise we feel is isolation, loneliness, powerlessness, worthlessness, hopelessness.[8]

If the alcohol and drug problems of the day are not enough evidence of our desperate need for some external structure to belong to and depend on, the soaring adolescent suicide rate certainly exemplifies the young people's sense of instability and insecurity. According to an article in the *Boston Globe*, suicide is the second leading cause of death among college students. There has been a 300 percent increase in the suicide rate among young people ages fifteen to nineteen in the last twenty years.[8] Recently *Newsweek* reported that five thousand teenagers kill themselves every year, half a million more attempt to do so, and "the fifteen-to-twenty-five-year-old age group is the only segment of the population whose death rate has increased (by 13 percent) in recent years. Among fifteen-to-nineteen-year-olds, suicide is now the second leading cause of death, after traffic accidents—many of which are suspected suicides."[10]

These grim statistics indicate there is an urgent need for a sense of meaning and purpose. Life has gotten out of control. The social structures that once provided a sense of meaning, of purpose, have become too impersonal. The result is a feeling of being lost, isolated, disconnected. People simply are unable to function in such a spiritual wasteland, and because they cannot change the structures that have taken over their lives, some change the way they feel about them—with chemicals. Now that there no longer seem to be any constants with which to identify-not God, not country, not community, not even family—people are seeking solace and comfort in alcohol and drugs. The fact is, when all else fails, these drugs work. Or as one young man said:

> Drugs are the best friend I have. They are always there to help me; they never let me down. They always give me what I'm looking for, I can depend on them. They can be trusted to do the same thing for me over and over and most of all they are fun! Why not use them?

Chemicals offer people the control over their lives that the world has wrested from them. Even if they cannot control their destinies, they can control what they swallow, what they shoot, what they snort. They can control when they use alcohol or drugs. They can control the alteration of their minds. They can control whether to be passive or active; they can control whether to be absent or present for others; and they can control their feelings. What's more, they can control those around them, because family and friends stop relating in their usual way; they start reacting and slip into new patterns of overreaction. As a result, they, too, are controlled by the dependent's alcohol or drug use. Let it never be forgotten by those who are called on to minister to these family problems: *The alcohol or the drug is the controlling force. The chemical is in control of the person.* But it gives the user a feeling of control, since it is the means to his ends.

In trying to solve the problems of isolation and meaninglessness by using chemicals, parishioners are exacerbating their spiritual problems; in fact, they *are* the problem. The misuse of alcohol or drugs causes isolation. It isolates man from himself, from others, from his family and community, from organizations, institutions, and associations. Worse, it separates man from the primary source of his meaning and purpose—from God. That is true hopelessness!

THE WAY TO TRANSCENDENCE

Most people want a meaningful, satisfactory, happy existence free of all trouble, sorrow, need, sickness, and adversity. For many, though, the only hope is in instant gratification—chemicals. Of the utmost importance but often forgotten is that this lamentable solution is sought for pleasure and avoidance or reduction of emotional pain. Pleasure and pain! With the exception of hunger for food or sex, these are the most powerful drives motivating human beings.

We know people seek relief because they are isolated or in pain, but what we ignore or forget is that they choose to use alcohol or drugs when they are happy, pleased, or when they want to be happy—to celebrate, to relax and have fun. "Let's have a party" is synonymous with "Let's have fun." For many today, fun means getting wasted, stoned, drunk. Though the penalty is the inevitable morning-after hangover, the instant gratification is deemed worth it because it offers an interval of happiness. And how the ads take advantage of this: Fun equals friends getting together, not for fellowship but to drink. The ads sell the idea and people use every occasion imaginable to celebrate accordingly. It is pleasurable! It is fun! Still, it is fleeting, and it does nothing for self-fulfillment or a fulfilling life.

Inner strength does not come in a pill! Confidence does not come in a bottle! Personal satisfaction does not come in a joint! Self-worth does not come in a powder! Instant relief or instant pleasure does, but the period of chemically induced well-being and spiritual contentment is fleeting. Pleasure, however, reinforces itself. It has a power all its own; power in that momentary, pleasant relief is always available. It can be obtained at any time. Therefore, it controls behavior. It exerts a powerful influence over choices and decisions. When the option for pleasure is ever-present, seldom (if ever) do people choose self-disciplined behavior, which is not necessarily pleasureable but leads to a more gratifying life. Instead they opt for instant gratification, which is merely a short-term solution to their need. Thus, the quest for a heaven must start over again . . . and again and again. That is not spiritual health; it is chemical dependency.

Before we can preach the theological truths that offer our people hope and God's promise of a meaningful life, it is very important to analyze how religion and drug use are, for many people, interchangeable. Both can serve the same purpose, and for those who are chemically dependent, this is often the case. To be pastors as well as preachers and prophets, it is useful to realize that alcohol and drugs, no matter what their ultimate effect, offer answers to the same problems as religion does. Clearly, this is why their use has become the religion of such a vast population.

Howard J. Clinebell, Jr., in *Understanding and Counseling the Alcoholic*, describes the areas in which alcohol and religion offer mutual answers. Because his book is about Jellinek's disease, his comparisons are with alcohol; the same principles, however, apply to other drugs.

> In the first place both give answers to the problems of weariness, boredom, drudgery, rejection, and loneliness in our dog-eat-dog society. . . . [Alcohol] offers the illusion of unity with one's fellows, temporary deadening of anxiety, and the quieting of inner conflict. Its relief is temporary and illusory, but available to many who have found no other. A fluid which for a time can banish disappointment, frustration, and feelings of inadequacy, which can give feelings of self-confidence and the illusion of strength has tremendous appeal, an appeal which those who seek a better way must take into account.[11]

Note how many of these feelings the merchants of relief exploit in their media promotions: weariness, boredom, drudgery, rejection, loneliness, unity with one's fellow, deadening of anxiety, quieting of inner conflict, disappointment, frustration, and feelings of inadequacy. In their powerfully persuasive presentations, all these spiritual sicknesses are remedied by alcohol or drugs.

Then there is the use of chemicals to anesthetize us against the social, political, and economic miseries of the day—"Sweet Blindness," as the song by the Fifth Dimension expresses it. The tragedy, says Dr. Clinebell, is that "the cure is recognized as a cause of further chaos!" Yet all of us in the ministry know that religion can furnish principles that provide an abiding sense of comfort, strength, and security. Like alcohol and drugs, religion promises a haven, and a heaven, too, but one that is free of charge, constantly available, permanent and everlasting.

Addressing the "ultimate anxiety" of all people, specifically one's isolation, finitude, and impotence in the face of the forces of life and death, Clinebell says:

Man is the animal who knows that he will die; he is the animal who wants to transcend his animality—to become something larger, more powerful, to feel infinite. Alcohol can give an illusion of transcendence.[12]

Again, the media presentations play on this theme constantly. Realizing that death and its symbols—darkness, riderless horses, colorless people, ghostlike figures, blank, lifeless faces—all provoke anxiety and that anxiety creates its own need for peace, they offer their products as the only paths to infinite quietness, mystical salvation, and ecstasy.

The predisposition that makes the alcohol or drug experience religious is primarily the innate desire for transcendence—transcendence of anything and everything, anyone and everyone. Human beings ever since Adam have wanted to be in control, have sought the power to play God, have wanted the knowledge of God so they could be God or, at the very least, be one with Him. The problem since antiquity has been how to transcend the boundaries of our finitude and gain this control. Would an answer be found within, or could one be created from without through the use of a sacred substance?

The ancient Greeks sought magic in an opiate derived from the poppy and used it in their religious ceremonies. They used wine and beer, too, in their Bacchic rites, to represent larger life. In the Roman and Jewish traditions wine was used as the gateway to the abundant life. In the Christian religion Jesus blessed the wine to recall His sacrifice and God's promise of new and eternal life. As the sacrament of the Lord's Supper, it is the sacred symbol of the mystical union between God and His people—union with the Holy—Holy Communion. In India the divine potent of the *Rig-Veda* was a beverage— *soma*—pressed from a plant whose source is still unknown. Religious sects in the Middle East used a drug called *hashish*, derived from *Cannibis sativa*. The Celts of the Germanic tribes drank a sacred alcoholic brew made from the fermentation of plants. Peyote provided the transcendent high of Mexican Indians and the Kiowa Indians of North America. For the Indians of both North and South America tobacco was the symbol of divine presence.[13] In the 1960s, LSD was the gateway to higher consciousness.

Today, for the Rastafarians of Jamaica and millions of young people in the United States, Great Britain, and Europe, marijuana is the sacred medium. And there is alcohol, which, as Clinebell says, "has symbolized the ecstatic element in religion. . . . Alcohol has the ability to give temporary feelings of mutual acceptance and unity among men, and between man and the rest of creation."[14] When a person feels lost and alone, estranged from himself, from others, and from his God, alcohol has the strange effect of reuniting him; with it he can "get it all together." It satisfies a very basic and powerful human need.

The enjoyment of chemicals is now a civil religion in America. The use of licit or illicit drugs to pursue pleasure or avoid pain is the Gospel. With the media as persuasive preachers, many consumers are just as avid to buy as the merchants are to sell. People want to transcend the cares of this world, and if they can swallow, smoke, sniff, or shoot something that will immediately do it, that is power, that is control, that is omnipotence.

The problem is, this substitute religion does not remedy the spiritual unrest. The falsity of the doctrine lies in that: 1. it is in fact an ephemeral solution, therefore always elusive, always attractive; 2. it is totally self-serving and often self-destructive; 3. reliance on its transcendent power retards the growth of personal strength and personality; 4. its mind-altering effect separates us from ourselves, from others, and from God; and 5. it can and does lead to chemical dependency.

FRUITLESS DISCUSSIONS, INEFFECTIVE ANSWERS

Though it is clear, as Howard Clinebell suggests, that both chemicals and religion offer answers to the same problems and therefore serve the same purpose, it is also clear that the misuse of alcohol and drugs does not provide a lasting solution. In fact, reliance on these chemicals can be the cause of greater chaos. What is not taken into account by the Church or its ministers but needs to be recognized, is the alarming fact that religious answers, too (those proclaimed in the past *and* those preached today), have not been effective in curing the spiritual sickness of the day!

For far, far too long the Church has tried to solve the social problems of a chemical-abusing culture as well as the personal complexities of chemical dependency by moralizing, i.e., by applying rigid, Scripture-based rules to enforce appropriate, acceptable, moral behavior. It has sought to use these religious beliefs like a vestment, draping it over this vast problem. The goal has been to make the sacred fabric cover *all* the issues, suit *all* the circumstances, or at least give the appearance that substance use, misuse, and abuse are encompassed by moral theology. The Church has not and still cannot agree, however, on which religious view is correct or applicable. Left, right, and center have argued over questions such as drinking versus abstinence, excess versus moderation, the practical versus the theological definition of drunkenness, the virtue of responsible social drinking versus the godliness of temperance, chemical dependency as a sin or a sickness, the freedom to choose versus the compulsion to use, responsibility versus liability, liability versus culpability, and the moral versus the immoral use of chemicals. While these theological polemics have been endlessly debated, the problems of chemical use and abuse have become a national crisis. As the Gallup and United Presbyterian polls point out, the insitutional Church has not acted to prevent or reduce the destruction wrought by alcohol and drugs. The religious sectors' influence, regrettably, has been inconsequential.

There is no queston there has been an ecumenical expression of the Church's concern. After much internal debate, the Church has prescribed for its *acedia* an entire tablet full of "oughts" and "shoulds." They have included:

1. Develop a national consensus on the right and proper use of alcohol and drugs.

2. Educate pastors and youth directors to be proficient in recognizing and preventing alcohol and drug abuse.

3. Act as a political group to urge legislators to regulate the advertising and sale of licit and illicit drugs.

4. Become a support system for those whose lives are damaged by chemical dependency.

These prescriptions have been promoted in denominational plans and churchwide policy statements as being *the* remedy—theologically sound answers and pastorally effective approaches. Nevertheless, *these dictums have had no appreciable effect on alleviating or resolving any aspect of the problem.* Children's lives continue to be wasted! Adults' lives continue to be ruined! Families continue to be destroyed! While the institutional Church argues over the appropriate answers, the devastation continues right before the eyes of the local priests, ministers, and rabbis.

Local churches have not been any more effective in ministering to alcohol- and drug-related problems than the religious denominations have been in addressing them. Orthodoxy has been inadequate to cure the epidemic spiritual sickness or stem the increase of personal and family illness. The primary reason for this inadequacy is that religion is of divine origin and religious answers depend on our maintaining a faithful and trusting relationship with the ground of being, a diety—with God. That is the prerequisite to eternal salvation. People who have lost their sense of meaning and purpose and are seeking salvation in a pleasurable fix, however, have already turned away from the source of ultimate meaning; their faith is in a chemical. Furthermore, they are eroding the possibility of sustaining an ongoing relationship with a higher power by continually building a reliance on substances.

As for those whose spiritual sickness has led them to misuse, the alcohol or drug has become their only hope for a safe haven or heaven. Faith in God does not put an end to emotional pain, nor does it produce the instant pleasure that transforms loneliness into fun. If a drug-dependent person has ever belonged to a church or synagogue, it is usually at this point that, because of his shame, lack of faith, feelings of isolation, and sensitivity to congregational disapproval, he breaks his ties with the fellowship and withdraws. If the person has any belief in God left, it is usually superseded by faith in a quicker and more dependable solution to his need—the next chemical high.

Finally, there is the person who is chemically dependent, who is already physically sick. The only relationship of value in his life is with his chosen chemical. In fact, this chemical is the ultimate value to him, because he must have it to survive. But his feelings of isolation and guilt are such that he does not feel worthy to be in relation to anyone or anything other than the sustaining substance. God is perceived as unloving and vengeful. Any religious answers offered by God's ministers are mistrusted. Seeing the clergy as self-righteous, sanctimonious, or judgmental, the dependent expects the pastor to disapprove of him as much as he disapproves of himself. There are no religious precepts to counter these feelings, any more than there are any to cure his illness. When the minister does not succeed in helping him, which is most often the case, in self-defense the sick person rejects the minister, the Church, and God. In so doing he feels he is the one rejected by all three. That is why there are so many self-proclaimed agnostics or atheists in AA. It is also why Alcoholics Anonymous and the other self-help groups are so successful. AA accepts the sick person without asking him to be someone or to believe in someone. A relationship with a "higher power" is not required for membership.

For as long as the denominations have been wrangling over moral guidelines and appropriate forms of engagement, for as long as the local churches have been wrestling with their problems of disengagement and congregational apathy, the parish priests, ministers, and rabbis have been asked to take a stand and exorcise the cult of chemistry. Or they have been directed to defend against the spiritual sickness of the world by imposing their religious value systems, i.e., prohibition, abstinence, moderation, or responsible use. In ministering to and treating chemical dependency, they have been expected to be counselors. Here again, the studies documenting the soaring increase of alcohol and drug abuse in America in the last twenty-five years make it painfully apparent just how little impact religious values have had on the prevention of substance abuse. As to chemical dependency, a survey from the Yale Summer School of Alcohol Studies provides embarrassing evidence that even trained ministers cannot agree on how to define the disease, much less suggest religious answers to cure it. Finally, what the surveys and polls do not show is how mistaken the institutional Church is in assuming that ecclesiastical professionals would be interested in being practitioners of alcohol and drug-abuse education, prevention, and treatment. It has expected shepherds to be veterinarians. The overall resistance by the majority of local ministers trumpets loud and clear that the clergy are not called by God to fulfill that ministry. It is for specialists.

A REALISTIC, ATTAINABLE GOAL

If the Church has any business at all in the substance-abuse field, if it has any calling to minister to alcohol- and drug-related problems, its most important religious role, its most useful pastoral role, is to do one and only one thing: *create a local Church environment in which there is the hope of redemption.* This means it must establish an atmosphere in which a person being lost to the destructive effects of chemicals can still associate with, and be accepted by, parishioners who know enough and care enough to understand the problem as a sickness and will show him the options by which he can regain control of his life. The Church's primary function in this matter is to address today's spiritual malaise by proclaiming the *hope* that life can be better. It can accomplish this goal by making its congregations aware that the problems of alcohol and drug abuse are not the result of individual immorality but of a spiritual sickness that pervades the world. Drugs are symptoms of a "dis-ease" of the spirit, a disease that infects every member of the parish and can only be healed when lifestyles are changed in fellowship, *when people stop judging each other and start caring for one another.*

The local Church has no other business in the arena of alcohol and drug dependency than to establish a "life-changing fellowship," as Samuel Shoemaker calls it, from which no one is cast out because he seeks answers to his problems in chemicals, and no one is cut adrift because his chemical dependency prevents him from meeting his responsibilities. It would be a compassionate community in which weaknesses are acknowledged without blame and there is no shame in being spiritually or physiologically ill. It would be an inspirational community that promotes spiritual values instead of dogmas and teaches healthy, life-enhancing choices that include responsibility, contribution, and fulfillment, as opposed to moralistic rules that demand banishment for weakness, sickness, or failure. It would be a "do-it-yourself" Greek family in which people are so intimately interrelated that as one person suffers, there are others who, having been affected by similar problems, will witness that there can be something better, that the victim can be someone better, and that they are there as resources to bring about the change.

The "oughts" and "shoulds" the ecumenical Church has prescribed for itself are not realistic. It is futile to try and establish a national consensus on the right and proper use of alcohol and drugs. Unless the Church has an advertising budget of $1,014.9 billion, access to the mass media, and universal agreement on all the issues, there is no way to create a common opinion, much less promote a united position. As to educating the pastors and youth directors, the Church's programs will continue to be disregarded until the local religious leaders are taught a methodology that enhances their primary calling and does not ask them to become a specialist in an alien field. If the Church wants to exert its influence as a political action group whose goal is to lobby for legislation, it must know it is duplicating the efforts of more knowledgeable pressure groups, e.g., the Consumer Federation of America, the National Parent Teachers Association, the National Congress of Parent and Teachers, Action for Children's Television, and the National Council on Alcoholism. It also must be aware of the countervailing forces, the lobbys for the alcoholic-beverage industry, which are so powerful that for the last three decades (though alcohol revenues have increased markedly) they have been able to freeze the government's alcohol excise tax at the 1951 level. Finally, the Church need not try to be a support group for the victims of chemical dependency, for other groups (previously described in this book) are already highly successful at it and are always willing to help. Chemical dependency is a sickness requiring special forms of treatment and after-care. If the Church wants to help, it can offer its local premises as meeting places for these self-help groups. Beyond that, recovering people will go to the support groups of their choice.

The Church's business is to create a local church environment in which there is the hope of redemption. That is a realistic, attainable goal. By helping its members understand that substance abuse is a spiritual sickness and chemical dependency a medical one, by transforming the prejudices that stigmatize those afflicted with the sickness, the Church can do more to promote the possibilities of something better (and, therefore, the potential of a redeemed life) than by any other form of engagement. If the Church were to deflect people from the judgments that hold "alcoholism" and "drug addiction" to be sins and moral weaknesses and make them aware that these are treatable illnesses, it would make manifest God's promise of salvation to those who are the victims. Whereas it is the avowed function of the organized Church to promise salvation, it is the divine service of the local church to promise redemption—in short, life after birth as well as life after death.

The development of methods and materials useful in creating a resurrected and tolerant congregation can be the educational task of each national denomination, but the person who must ignite the torch that will enlighten the local church is the parish clergyperson. His or her inspiration is necessary to raise up hope.

Dispelling fears and prejudices while creating a local environment in which there is hope of redemption is the parishioners' responsibility. This is the reason for choosing a "spark plug" from the congregation and establishing a core group to serve as the chemical-education committee. The committee's task will ultimately be its main reason for being; its members will be the primary agents of change for the better. It rests with the clergy, however, to open the way for parishioners to know that redemption is available. It is up to us to provide the theological foundation of a new and more hopeful outlook.

The most fundamental characteristic of religion is God's self-initiated movement into human existence, establishing a relationship with each one of us through revelation and grace. Just as fundamental a characteristic, however, is our response to Him, our faith in Him, in terms of acceptance and commitment. To be effective in creating a life-changing fellowship in which hope is available, it is paramount to understand that substance misuse and abuse is a spiritual sickness, not a religious problem. Though the core of faith says, "God cares," it is the sickness of the spirit that says, "No matter. It is not enough. I need something more definite to define my purpose and give me pleasure."

The problem with *any* religious answer is not the question of whether or not God moves into our lives, it is our inability to believe there is any worthwhile reason to respond. The main task of religion is to describe the ways God calls us and to inspire people to answer. Among the throngs who pursue the cult of chemistry, however, if there is not a total loss of inspiration involving a lack of joy, enthusiasm and dedication, there is enough uncertainty about the meaning and purpose of work, money, status, prestige, and the future to make it seem futile to try to relate to God. To what end? It is not a matter of a lack of faith in God's activity, it is a loss of trust that the effort makes a difference. The spiritual sickness is a lack of faith in life itself and one's value in life.

To dispirited people looking for immediate answers to life's struggles,

God's interest in a relationship does not provide the needed instant gratification. Consequently they turn to the only hope they know that gives immediate and definite satisfaction and at the same time alleviates the pain of hopelessness—alcohol and drugs. Religion, specifically the Jewish and Christian faiths, calls believers to relate to God through trust and love and service to others, but those who are spiritually sick or chemically dependent are incapable of any trusting, loving relationship other than that with a mind-altering chemical. Their needs are so great they can only serve themselves. If we hope to build a life-changing fellowhship, we must understand that those who are dispirited and affected by the illness of chemical dependency are not capable of caring for anyone or anything other than for whom or what will meet their immediate needs. To establish a redemptive community, therefore, we must make it known that God cares for them, that we care for them, that the congregation cares for them, even though they do not feel deserving of it and are incapable of returning the love we extend. Before there can be atonement with God, there must be reconciliation between persons.

THEOLOGICAL PERSPECTIVES AND SPIRITUAL FOUNDATIONS

Building a redemptive community is an ongoing process that takes more than an annual chemical-education program. It is a ministry of "raising the consciousness" of the congregation. It is a matter not only of teaching people how to care but of providing them with the basis for caring. As long as there are people who feel that Jellinek's disease or drug addiction is a depravity, as long as there are parishioners who insist that the drunkard or the druggie is a sinful degenerate responsible for his own troubles and should be cast adrift, the very essence of reconciling love is negated. Our most successful means of revealing that God cares and that we care is to be an example of openness and compassion grounded not in personal opinion but in biblical theology. Because people are looking for a foundation on which to build their lives, because they are searching for guidelines, we have the opportunity to provide a theological foundation for caring that can change people's attitudes and beliefs. Just as there are positive attitudes that help a practitioner address chemical dependency, so are there Biblical principles that help the minister convey the nonjudgmental attitudes so necessary to the establishment of a redemptive community.

It is known that Bible-based dogmatic rules on the use of alcohol and drugs are fruitless, for the Bible does not address such questions specifically. What *is* helpful, however, is to offer biblical insights that inspire new awareness based on God's concerns. The principles are not a religious vestment, they are spiritual foundations. In his booklet *A Biblical Perspective on the Use and Abuse of Alcohol and Other Drugs* (an invaluable preaching tool), T. Furman Hewitt provides an excellent analysis of the most helpful Biblical principles. A brief summary of his theological principles provides a plan for establishing the spiritual foundation of a redemptive fellowship.

1. The first principle which must be affirmed is the goodness of the created order . . . "And God saw that it was good." (Gen. 1:12, cf. 2:9, Psalm 104)

God created all, and it was good. It ill-serves us to attribute evil or sinfulness or destructiveness to the substances of God's creation. If we do so, there is no possible hope that people who use alcohol or drugs will feel worthy of redemption. One who chooses evil feels himself to *be* evil. If we say alcohol or drugs are evil because they cause so much destruction, we are implying that those who use it intend to destroy themselves. That fixes blame. The value of a substance—whether it is in the form of an automobile, a gun, or a chemical—is that it has its own behavior and purpose. When it is used in a way that does not respect its behavior or disregards its purpose, the responsibility or irresponsibilty lies with the person using it, not with the substance. When we insist on blaming people for using a potentially harmful substance or for using a "good" substance in a "bad" way, then we are missing the opportunity to communicate the goodness of creation as God intended it and we are closing the door on those who use God's good creation in a way He did not intend. Ours is to enlighten, not to condemn.

2. Another principle upon which all could agree is the ultimate value of persons, all of whom are made in the "image of God" (Gen. 1:26-27; 9:6). The Judeo-Christian tradition is united in its belief that persons have inherent worth before God and, therefore, for other persons. . . . Jesus was remembered for saying, "I come that they may have life, and have it abundantly" (Jn. 10:10). The goal of "abundant life" surely points to a potential for developing personhood, the blocking of which would be immoral.

Clearly, whenever a chemical is used in any way that diminishes a person's six "personal potentials," it can be said that the substance is eroding the person's inherent value. And if the abuse or chemical dependency is having a detrimental effect of the "personal potential" of members of the family, that, too, is counter to the Jewish and Christian view of personal value. To harm or impede one's growth and development or that of others, to isolate oneself from or numb oneself to experience, to cut oneself off or to be cut off from relationship with self, with others, and with the source of life itself is inconsistent with God's intention for His creation.

The joy in life is found not so much in what we do as in how we do. God offers us life. He calls us to share that life, to live in meaningful relationships with others and, especially, with Him. Abundant life is not found in instant gratification. It comes when we seek a meaningful relation with God, which in turn is self-fulfilling and fosters more wholesome relationships with others. Before we can suggest that the spiritually sick and chemically dependent seek reunion with God and therefore regain abundant life, however, we must first reestablish a meaningful, caring, accepting association with them. If we don't see them as created in the image of God and valuable as persons, surely they will not believe God offers anything better. Redemption begins when the sick person is considered worthy of being better, even if he does not feel he is of value to anyone, including God.

3. A third priniciple is that of personal freedom of the believer from the law as a source of justification or solution. It is not the keeping of rules which renders us acceptable to God, but rather His gracious love which accepts us in spite of our failure and pretension of goodness. . . . Clearly, it is possible to be free, yet use that "freedom" in a destructive way. . . . The thoughtful believer knows that he or she is not made more righteous or good by not drinking, nor is he or she barred from the Kingdom of God because of incidental use. . . . In that sense we are free. But freedom implies boundaries which keep us from doing damage to self and to another. When does an act of indulgence done out of personal freedom run counter to one's obligation to the neighbor?

The question is often raised, "Does a son or a daughter, a husband or a wife have the right to use chemicals to the degree that it destroys personal potential?" Another question, asked almost as frequently is, "Does a person have a right to use chemicals to the degree that it destroys the lives of others?" The theological answer to both these questions is continually disputed in the Church; there is no clear answer. The issue is not dissimilar to the hotly debated questions of abortion and euthanasia. It recalls the "manslaughter" and "suicide" perspectives already discussed. In the commandment "You shall love your neighbor as yourself" (Lev. 19:18 and Mk. 12:31), however, God's intentions are clear: Rights and freedoms are not given so we may hurt ourselves or our neighbors. God never intended for individual freedoms to be exercised to the detriment of personal or social health. Consequently, whether the theological question is decided or not, to allow youngsters to exercise their rights before they are capable of responsibility for their actions, to let them choose to drink and use drugs without their knowing the ramifications, is not in their best interests. Certainly, to allow a child or an adult to abuse himself with alcohol or drugs and to jeopardize his potential is totally against God's interests. And when anyone's destructive abuse of chemicals begins to destroy the life of another, that, too, is contrary to God's concerns—for all involved. Caring in such circumstances is not a matter of taking charge of the abuser; it is a matter of saying, "*No!*" when such free acts run counter to wholeness. We cannot be responsible *for* the life and health of another, but we can be responsible *to* another by caring enough to challenge and oppose his abuse of freedom—for his sake and ours.

4. The command to "love your neighbors as yourself" leads us to a fourth principle which should be taken into consideration, the reality of social repsonsibility. The commandment . . . which Jesus chose as a part of his summary of the Law, was a predictable part of a religious tradition which insisted that we are our "brother's keeper."

In our culture we have gotten away from the notion that one person's actions have an impact on another's life. Owing to the "now" generation's pursuit of instant gratification in the 1960s and the self-help, self-awareness movements' emphasis on self-gratification in the 1970s, there is now barely any thought at all for the effects of personal conduct on other people—family, community, or society. Such heedless individualism is compounded by the isolation and loneliness endemic in a depersonalizing society. The result is a hardheartedness that scoffs at a "brother's keeper" attitude and instead pro-claims, "Everyone for himself!" This attitude is not only contrary to the commandment, it is the cause of the spiritual sickness that infects America. To "do your own thing," an individual must separate himself from others to the point that he does not care what others think. But separatism not only keeps others out, it closes the individual in.

To establish a redemptive community requires that the parishioners be encouraged to feel they are part of a family. There is room for self-determina-tion, but there is room for mutual respect, concern, and interdependence, too. It is obvious that selfish individualism has not worked and that people hunger for that which isolationism cannot provide—acceptance and love. God created us as social animals who need one another. He made us mutually responsible and interdependent. To that end we have a social responsibility to one another; we are our "brother's keeper." When a person knows he is part of a community that will not give up on him, he has a sense of belonging that nurtures health and motivates him to see himself in relation to others. It rests with us to create the caring environment in which people feel they belong. In terms of being our "brother's keeper," it may be that a chemically dependent person is no longer capable of the insight needed for him to seek remedial care. It may be he is insensitive to the effects of his actions on others. It may be that an adult child of an alcoholic does not realize he, too, is highly susceptible to chemical dependency. It may be that an older person does not know his medication should not be mixed with alcohol. Or it may be that a pregnant woman is not aware of the damage alcohol can do to an unborn infant. In all these circumstances, and under any circumstance where ignorance or stupidity results in the hazardous use of chemicals, we have a responsibility to care as God cares for us. He allows us the freedom to choose, but He intervenes in our lives whether we like it or not, and His initiative is always to promote health and wholeness.

5. A fifth principle is found in Isaiah's distinction between the thoughts of God and man (Is. 55:8), in Paul's realistic understanding of his own limitations ("For now I see in a mirror dimly. . . . Now I know in part. . . . " I Cor. 13:12) as well as in the Christian affirmation of the need for the Holy Spirit as a source of continuing diving guidance (Jn. 14:26). That principle, in short, is the incompleteness or relativity of many of our moral judgments. . . . Our moral judgments emerge from a unique set of circumstances which include our own intellectual and spiritual maturity, our cultural heritage, our individual personality, and the circumstances with which we are faced.

Dogmatic claims to infallibility must give way to candid sharing of the truth as we see it and a genuine listening to those who disagree with us.

Does God ever give up on us because of our behavior or beliefs? Because people in the Church hold differing opinions of what is right or wrong, moral or immoral, unselfish or selfish, strong or weak, healthy or sick, righteous or sinful, there is constantly an undercurrent of judgment and condemnation that keeps people from revealing their frailty. As Samuel Shoemaker says, "Today the last place where one can be candid about one's faults is in church." And he deliberately stings us by pointing out that such Pharisaism is "just as definite and just as hideous as anybody's drunkenness can ever be, and a great deal more . . . dangerous."

If any immorality is rampant in the realm of alcohol and drug dependency, it is the willful disregard of those who need care by those who might care for them. To eliminate by ignoring, to exterminate by casting out, to purge by blaming is the epitome of ungodliness. Debating the moral issues of the use and abuse of chemicals without seeking to address the sins of prejudice, malice, contempt, and hypocrisy is moral delinquency. God calls us to care, not to kill one another with our self-righteous judgments—judgments in themselves imperfect. Caring, in God's terms, means understanding, appreciating, accepting, and, most of all, forgiving. We do not have to like the troubled person, but we are expected to love him as we are loved. And we are expected to forgive him as God forgives us. That means being responsive to him in spite of our judgments and enabling him to see the hope of redemption whether we want to or not.

The irony of judging those who suffer from the misuse of alcohol or drugs is that they need no condemnation to feel worthless; already they are laden with guilt, shame, and remorse. These diseases of the spirit are inevitable byproducts of the self-destruction wrought by the chemicals. To care for the dependents as God does requires that we offer them compassion, not recrimination. The forgiveness they so desperately need is a matter of extending our concern when we don't feel like it and they least deserve it.

For the most part the victims of substance abuse, although sickened by feelings of shame and worthlessness, have within them a flicker of spiritual hope. Call it the "life force" or the "creative energy of God," it is a restorative power that endures despite the destruction wrought by chemicals. It is a spark of spiritual health that can be the basis of redemption. If there is any chance at all of it becoming a life-sustaining force, it occurs when a member of a life-changing fellowship offers a measure of concern and communicates regard, forgiveness, and acceptance to the sufferer. Being the recipient of another's understanding and compassion is an affirming, healing, highly inspiring experience. When one individual, who believes in a spiritual power, cares enough to relate to another without judgment, it can be sufficient to mobilize a victim's spiritual energy and bring him into a relationship with a "higher power" who will restore him completely.

It is not our intention to duplicate Alcoholics Anonymous, but since our goal is to inspire faithful relationships, we can be a community of enlightened people who are tolerant and forgiving enough to be faith-filled and faithful guides to the treatment programs and support groups that provide remedial care.

6. A final principle is the fact that biblical writers viewed moral demands as emerging from the character and redemptive activity of God. In the Old Testament the right to demand certain forms of behavior was based on God's prior activity in bringing Israel out of the land of Egypt. . . . (cf. Ex. 20:2-17). In the New Testament the standard of behavior, "to love one another as I have loved you" (Jn. 15:12), was the right response to God's redemptive activity in Jesus of Nazareth. Relating this to the use of alcohol and other drugs, the issues are not resolved by citing this or that text, but by the more difficult struggle of asking, as Luther put it, what it means to be "Christ to my neighbor," what it means to be a loving servant in the twentieth century.[15]

The cult of chemistry has become the primary religion of the day. It has grown out of the spiritual sicknesses that pervade human existence—isolation, loneliness, meaninglessness, hopelessness. If we are to have any impact at all on this malaise, if we are to be Christlike to our neighbors, loving servants in the twentieth century, we need to get out of the chemical-dependency business and into the life-changing fellowship business. We have something to offer that no secular organization proclaims—*hope*. We know by the knowledge and belief in our faith that life can be better, that a person can be better, and that there is a realistic possiblity of betterment in the future. That is hope. A person is more than he has been, and the same is true for society. Do we believe God has given up on His creatures? Do we believe He has given up on His creation? If not, the message of hope we proclaim as loving servants in this age is that we, a redemptive community, can provide that which the world cannot—the assurance that there is something better. And just as God does not give up on helping us toward that "something better," neither will we give up on those who need it.

Our primary objective in ministering to alcohol- and drug-dependent people is to create a parish environment in which the possibility of redemption is open. The creation of hope. By establishing a nonjudgmental and forgiving climate, we can help parishioners discover that spiritually oriented lifestyles can lead to more fulfilling lives, that loving, caring relationships are the answer to isolation and loneliness, that chemical dependency is treatable family illness, and that each person can be an effective guide to God's possibilities.

RANSOMED, HEALED, RESTORED, FORGIVEN

No body of professionals is better equipped to offer the building blocks of a fulfilling life than the clergy. We are the group people trust most. As the Gallup pollsters' 1983 annual survey revealed for the eighth year, the U.S. public ranks the clergy highest in terms of honesty and ethical standards. Our parishioners are looking to us for some sense of direction, they are crying out for something firm they can hold onto, rely on. Standards. Guidelines. Foundations. Faith. A believing hope.

People are looking to us for leadership. God has called us to care for His people. The operative word here is "care." In the face of the fact that alcohol and drugs are the top family concerns of our day, we are in the unique position of being the only professionals who have regular access to the whole family (half the people in America). We are looked on and trusted as channels of God's grace. At a time when our parishioners wonder if they are important, if there is any place where they are valuable as human beings, we are the ones who have a meaningful answer. In God's eyes each person is unique, each life has meaning, and each serves His purpose. The good news is that no matter how drastic the problem, we offer the possibility for anyone and everyone to become a new person—"ransomed, healed, restored, forgiven," as the hymn *Praise, My Lord* proclaims. We have only to care—not as alcohol or drug experts but as knowledgeable, informed *ministers*.

Doubt. Guilt. Fear. Death. These are the dark forces that cause spiritual disease. These are the sicknesses people are trying to remedy with pills, bottles, cigarettes, solutions, powders. Caring requires that we understand and respond to these spiritual maladies with the grace only we are in a position to provide.

To feel wanted

To belong

To be needed

To feel accepted

To be understood

To be creative

To feel capable of achievement

To be appreciated for our achievements

To feel worthwhile

To feel worthy

To know boundaries

To have limits

To share

To have friendships

To give and receive pleasure

To have freedom

To forgive

To be forgiven

To be recognized for who we are

To have faith

To be loved

To love

Here are the basic hungers that must be satisfied. The misuse and abuse of chemicals furnishes only momentary relief and, ultimately, estrangment, whereas the grace of God provides lasting nourishment.

As Paul Tillich says in his sermon, "You Are Accepted," Grace is the reunion of life with life.

Grace is the reconciliation of a life with a life. Grace is the overcoming of separation and isolation. It is the restoration of sickness to health. Grace intervenes, in spite of our wants, in response to our needs. Grace accepts that which is rejected; it forgives where no forgiveness is warranted. Grace transforms the futility of our lives into meaningfulness. And even to the victims and the vanquished, grace offers victory.

God calls us to care. We have been chosen to shine His light into the darkness. We are a beacon of hope to those whose own spiritual brightness is dim or extinguished. We need not be alcohol and drug experts to share the hope God offers; we need only be what He has chosen us to be—instruments of His grace. To ransom, to heal, to restore, to forgive, we need only say, "You are accepted. You are accepted as is. You are accepted for what you were and what you shall be. You are accepted by me and by others. You are accepted by God." Therein lies our ministry to alcohol- and drug-dependent people. Therein lies redemption

> For thus says the Lord God: Behold I, I myself, will search for my sheep and will seek them out. As a shepherd seeks out his flock when some of his sheep have been scattered abroad, so will I seek out my sheep; and I will rescue them from all places where they have been scattered on a day of clouds and thick darkness. . . . I will seek the lost, and I will bring back the strayed, and I will bind up the crippled, and I will strengthen the weak, and the fat and the strong I will watch over; I will feed them in justice. (Ezekiel 34:11-12, 15-16)

APPENDIX A

A PROGRAM FOR CHEMICAL HEALTH

GOALS OF PRIMARY PREVENTION

When the "spark plug" and the core group (see p. 32) sit down to develop a parish program of chemical health, there is often a temptation to opt for ordering authoritative books that provide scientific information on the problems or hazards of alcohol and drug use. The thrust of this preventive measure is to address the issues of chemical abuse by using a book as a pill-like remedy. That was the temperance movement's approach, and it failed.

Another temptation is to send for tracts, pamphlets, or service-bulletin inserts that impart factual information about chemical dependency and what one can do about it. This is a form of secondary prevention, the effort to intervene in a preexistent problem. Though it is useful to the one-in-four families in which chemical dependency is a problem, it is pertinent only to those who have a vested interest; it is not a program for the parish at large.

Still another approach (usually a panicky reaction to the immediate need for a solution to teenage alcohol and drug abuse) is to bring in an expert to lecture the parish youngsters. This is the chemical-education program many secondary schools are following today—a two-, three-, or four-period presentation by a specialist and a recovered person, whose design is to fill the youngsters' heads with slanted "facts" instead of ideas to think about. More often than not, it serves only to reinforce the teenagers' natural feelings of indomitability, for each believes he cannot be harmed by alcohol or drugs. He hears the "drunkalogue" but sees the speaker as a wholesome, engaging entertainer, and he imagines himself as someone who also can do drugs and survive. He, too, can build a hero's identity that will win him prestige, glory, and the same spotlight the speaker now occupies.

An outside speaker can be very effective as long as his presentation equips the audience to think, does not try to tell it how to think, nor purports to be an exemplar of new or restored thinking. As long as the expert's presentation is but one of many strategies to promote healthy behavior, the parish's program will not succeed or fail on the basis of it alone.

A specialist is most effective when he presents objective information or offers concepts with which young people can examine their feelings and attitudes toward chemical use and abuse. The most appropriate time to begin alcohol and drug education is during preadolescence. It is when young people are first confronted with the pressures to drink and do drugs. (The average age children begin to drink is thirteen.) It is also when youngsters must learn how to cope with a parent's or a close relative's dependency. Finally, children at the elementary-school level are more open to learning about healthy attitudes toward chemical use. By the time they enter junior high school, the pervasive influences of our chemical-using society have led them to accept prejudices and opinions they are much less willing to change.

No single strategy can be adopted to remedy the chemical problems of a parish. And this is not the overriding aim of chemical education. A parish program needs to encompass many interrelated events, all of which are designed to promote spiritual, emotional, and physical health rather than to prohibit chemical abuse. The extent of the chemical-education program will depend on the time, money, and energy the members of the congregation are willing to expend. Some core groups will have only enough time and money to develop a program that consists of supplying educational tracts, pamphlets, and books to parishioners in need. (The reader will find a list of the most useful publications at the end of this chapter.) Others will be motivated to develop a comprehensive program that: (a) begins with classes on strengthening the family, (b) investigates family lifestyles, (c) includes sermons on the spiritual and moral aspects of chemical use and misuse, (d) provides accurate information on alcohol and other drugs, (e) suggests guidelines for reaching responsible decisions about the use of alcohol and drugs, (f) offers insight into the influence of the media on mass consumption, and (g) suggests ways of getting help for alcoholics and drug addicts. No matter how limited or extended the program, four primary goals are to be achieved:

1. To raise parishioners' consciousness about the role of chemicals in society (that is, use, nonuse, misuse, and abuse).

2. To present up-to-date, accurate information on which people can base responsible decisions.

3. To offer the tools with which to prevent or deal with alcoholism or drug abuse in the family, the religious institution, and the community.

4. To provide biblical and theological principles by which families can set spiritual and moral standards on chemical use.

Those who do not know how much or how little to include in a parish program may benefit from David Hancock's list of topics, below. It is based on the course Hancock teaches at Rutgers School of Alcohol Studies—a "wholistic [sic] approach to the primary prevention of alcohol and drug abuse."

1. Causality: What causes harmful chemical dependence? The chemical? The person? Genetics?

2. Drug taking for self-defined use: Why? Which drug? What are the hazards?

3. The role of alcohol and other drugs and the appropriateness of drug use for creative comfort in time of stress.

4. The role and function of work, stress, fear, anxiety, guilt, tension, pain, and wistfulness in one's life.

5. The role and appropriateness of alcohol and other drugs in the pursuit of pleasure.

6. The "medicalization" of human problems, which then require drugs for relief or solution.

7. The social impact of self-defined drug use on family, friends, employers, employees, the public, automobile drivers.

8. Social pressure to use alcohol and drugs.

9. Examining attitudes, folklore, superstitions, prejudices, mythology, and magic about drinking customs and practices in the U.S.

10. The role of the peer group, its power, pressure, meaning, significance, influence, authority, caring.

11. Ethical and moral issues involved in risk-taking behavior of all kinds.

12. The concept of responsible use.

13. The place and role of education. What to teach our children about alcohol and other drugs.

14. Developing inner (i.e., nonchemical) resources for handling life's problems.

15. Other issues to be identified and explored, e.g., parent-effectiveness training, values clarification, the stewardship of life, health, the earth, etc.

The complete outline of this course is available on request from David Hancock, Prevention of Alcohol Problems, Inc., 4616 Longfellow Avenue, South Minneapolis, MN 55407. It is also found in the manual *The Church and Chemical Health*, listed below under required texts. It is an excellent guide for any educational program.

As catalysts, we must provide our appointed "spark plug" and the chemical-education committee with information that will help them build their own program. It is not necessary to comb through an entire library of material, nor is it necessary to "reinvent the wheel" by creating new programs. Many excellent resources are available that the chemical-education committee can use as guidebooks. They are the committee's tools of the trade. They are listed below as *Required Texts*, *Recommended Reading*, and *Resources*.

REQUIRED TEXTS *(Buy all)*

A. *Manuals/Workbooks*

The Church and Chemical Health. A resource manual about alcohol- and drug-related problems, to help pastors, church councils, and other governing bodies develop programs for individuals and families of the chemically dependent. Order from: The Synod of Lakes and Prairies, 8012 Cedar Avenue South, Bloomington, MN 55420; (612) 854-0144. Cost (postpaid) $5.00.

The Religious Community and Chemical Health (1983). An interfaith guide to alcohol and drug issues, to help the interfaith community develop appropriate and effective responses to chemical-use problems. The guide not only contains ideas for specific programs but discusses alcohol and drug problems and spiritual life. Order from: Minnesota Prevention Resource Center, 2829 Verndale Avenue, Anoka, MN 55303; (612) 427-5310. Cost (postpaid) $5.00.

N.F.P. Educational and Public Speaking Manual for Drug Education Presentations (1982). Prepared by Pat Barton. To help parents give educational talks and institute a variety of programs on adolescent drug abuse. Order from: National Federation of Parents for Drug-Free Youth (N.F.P.), 9805 Dameron Drive, Silver Spring, MD 20902; (301) 593-9256. Cost (postpaid) $5.00.

Delaine, John K., *Who's Raising the Family?* (1981). A workbook for parents and children. Information and exercises to help parents help children develop positive self-concepts, express feelings, make decisions, solve problems, and accept responsibility for their actions. Order from: Wisconsin Clearinghouse, 1954 East Washington Avenue, Madison, WI 53704. Cost (postpaid) $5.00.

Rusche, Sue, *How to Form a Families-in-Action Group in Your Community* (1979). This manual details a step-by-step procedure for starting a parents' group. It includes checklists and procedures, defines committee responsibilities, and outlines a speech. Order from: Families in Action, Inc., 2845 North Druid Hills Road, Suite 300, Decatur, GA 30033. Cost (postpaid) $10.00.

B. *Study Program/Kits*

Schneider, Karl A., *Alcoholism and Addiction: A Study Program for Adults and Youth* (1976). A four-session program to raise consciousness on the subject, to help realize the congregation's potential to educate its members, and to present methods of intervention. Order from: Fortress Press, 2900 Queen Lane, Philadelphia, PA 19129; (800) 523-3824. Cost (plus postage) $2.50.

The U.S. Jaycees, *All in the Family*, plus "Chairman's Guide." A program to help adults, parents, and youths understand the factors that influence a child's attitudes, awareness, and behavior toward alcohol, whether by imitation, identification, conversation, or observation. Order from: The U.S. Jaycees, P.O. Box 7, Tulsa, OK 74121; (918) 584-2481. (Catalogue no. 747-1; "Chairman's Guide"—catalogue no. 753-1.) Cost (plus postage) $3.20.

PRIDE Drug Information Kit. A resource kit to help parents combat drug abuse. PRIDE (National Parents Resource Institute for Drug Education) is a nonprofit organization established to stem the epidemic of drug use, especially among adolescents and young adults. It offers accurate health information, acts as a reference source for parents and children, and helps form parent and youth networks. Order from: PRIDE, 100 Edgewood Avenue, Suite 1216, Atlanta, GA 30303; (800) 282-4241. Cost (postpaid) $12.00.

Eakin, J. Thomas, *Alcohol Education Within the Church: Applying an Interactive Method.* Outline of a six-session, process-oriented course successfully used by St. Paul's United Methodist Church in State College, Pennsylvania. The course addresses: (a) the Church and alcohol problems; (b) the historical and biblical perspective; (c) alcohol—the substance; (d) alcohol and the family; (e) alcohol's impact on personal and social circumstances; and (f) the gospel of prevention. The guiding presuppostion is the strong belief that the Church needs to be a caring and healing community. J. Thomas Eakin is director of Religious Affairs at the Eisenhower Chapel of Pennsylvania State University. Order from: The North Conway Institute, 14 Beacon Street, Boston, MA 02108; (617) 742-0424. Free.

RECOMMENDED READING

A. *Books*

Alcohol/Alcoholism

Cross, Wilbur, *Kids and Booze—What You Must Know to Help Them* (New York: E. P. Dutton, 1979). Very useful in helping parents and teenagers address the issues of drinking.

DuPont, Robert L., *Getting Tough on Gateway Drugs—A Guide for the Family* (Washington, D.C.: American Psychiatric Press, 1984). Focuses on the three drugs which open the gates to drug dependence for American youth: alcohol, marijuana, and cocaine. Excellent. Cost $16.95.

Johnson, Vernon E., *I'll Quit Tomorrow* (New York: Harper & Row, 1973). Defines the stages of alcoholism and explains the process of intervention families follow to help alcoholics. Very useful to families and friends of the chemically dependent person. Cost $10.95.

Milam, James R., and Ketchum, Katherine, *Under the Influence* (Seattle: Madrona Publishers, 1981). Sound evidence detailing the physiological causes of chemical dependency. Very helpful to correct those who believe alcoholism is the result of a character weakness or a lack of will power. Cost (paperback) $3.50.

Wegscheider, Sharon, *Another Chance* (Palo Alto, CA: Science and Behavior Books, 1981). Depicts the effect of alcoholism on the family and defines the role each member plays in relation to the dependent person and the other members of the household. This book is most helpful for clergy interested in understanding the family problems caused by chemical dependency and the hope available to those involved. Superb, both in style and content. Cost $12.95.

Drugs

Mann, Peggy, *Pot Safari* (New York: Woodmore Press, 1982). Evidence for the layperson who doubts marijuana is harmful. Peggy Mann is the writer whose articles in Reader's Digest and *Post Magazine* alerted the nation to the hazards of marijuana. Many of her data are included. Cost $6.95.

Cretcher, Dorothy, *Steering Clear, Helping Your Child Through the High-Risk Drug Years* (Winston Press, 430 Oak Grove, Minneapolis, MN 55403, 1982). A comprehensive work that not only defines the hazards of licit and illiict drugs but discusses the problems of a rapidly changing society, their effect on young people, and what can be done to prevent drug abuse. Cost $4.95.

Monatt, Marsha, *Parents, Peers and Pot* (National Institute on Drug Abuse [NIDA], Division of Research Development, Room 10A56, 5600 Fishers Lane, Rockville, MD 20857, 1980). A useful description of a parents' organization formed to combat drug use among adolescents. Its value is in its description of the results of parent/peer-group power. [Note: When writing to NIDA for this book, ask for a free copy of "A Family Response to the Drug Problem," Research Issues 4: Drugs and Family/Peer Influence.] Cost $2.00.

Family/Parenting

Glenn, Stephen H., *Strengthening the Family* (Potomac Press, 7101 Wisconsin Avenue, Suite 1006, Bethesda, MD 20014). Dr. Glenn, quoted earlier in this book, discusses the problems impairing young people and offers specific ideas parents can follow to reduce those problems' effect on children. Cost $2.50.

Kuzma, Kay, *Prime-Time Parenting* (Wade Publishers, Inc., 1980). Tells how a working mother spends high-quality time with her children. Its many practical suggestions, examples, and anecdotes make it an excellent resource for anyone raising children.

Wegscheider, Don, *Families in Stress* and *Chemical Dependency: A Family Illness* (Nurturing Networks, 4728 Maryland Avenue North, Crystal, MN 55428). The author is a family therapist with an expert's understanding of chemical dependency. All his works are excellent.

Counseling/Guidance

Myrick, Robert D., and Emery, Tom, *Caring and Sharing: Becoming a Peer Facilitator* and *Youth Helping Youth: A Handbook for Training Peer Facilitators* (Educational Media Corporation, P.O. Box 21311, Minneapolis, MN 55421). Complete classroom materials and guidance for the leader of a peer-helping program. Although not specifically for drug prevention, the principles of peer counseling are applicable. Cost $6.95 each.

Block, Claudia, *It Will Never Happen to Me* (Thomas W. Perrin, Inc., P.O. Box 423, Rutherford, NJ 07070). Insights into the children of alcoholics as youngsters, adolescents, adults. Cost $7.95.

York, David and Phyllis, *Tough Love* (Community Service Foundation, Inc., P.O. Box 70, Sellersville, PA 18960; (215) 257-0421). What to do when a drug-dependent child has gained control of the family. Describes how to set up parents' support groups.

B. Booklets

A Parent's Guide to Preventing Alcohol and Other Drug Problems (Regional Council on Alcoholism, 3101 Euclid Avenue, Suite 707, Cleveland, OH 44115, 1979). $3.00.

Fornaciari, Suzanne, *How to Talk to Kids About Drugs, Prevention* (Potomac Press, Suite 1006, 7101 Wisconsin Avenue, Bethesda, MD 20014, 1979). $2.50.

National Institute on Alcohol Abuse and Alcoholism (P.O. Box 2345, Rockville, MD 20852), *How to Talk to Your Teenager about Drinking and Driving*. Free.

National Institute on Drug Abuse-NIDA (National Clearinghouse for Drug Abuse Information, 5600 Fishers Lane, Rockville, MD 20852), *Drug Abuse Prevention for Your Family; For Parents Only: What You Need to Know*

About Marijuana; For Kids Only: What You Need to Know About Marijuana; This Side Up: Making Decisions About Drugs. All free.

C. *Tracts*

Alcoholics Anonymous, P.O. Box 459, Grand Central Station, New York, NY 10017. Consult the telephone directory for local offices. The following are free from any local AA:

> *A Brief Guide to AA*
> *44 Questions and Answers*
> *Do You Think You're Different?*
> *Letter to a Woman Alcoholic*
> *Young People and AA*

Al-Anon Family Group Headquarters, P.O. Box 182, Madison Square Station, New York, NY 10010. Consult the telephone directory for local offfices. The following are free from any local Al-Anon:

> *Alcoholism, the Family Disease*
> *How Can I Help My Children?*
> *So You Love an Alcoholic*
> *To the Father and Mother of an Alcoholic*
> *What Do You Do About the Alcoholic's Drinking?*

Channing L. Bete Co., Inc., 200 State Road, South Deerfield, MA 01373; (413) 655-7611. Send for its catalog of scriptographic booklets on alcohol and drug education. Especially useful are:

> *About Alcohol* (no. C1145)
> *ABC's of Drinking and Driving* (no. C1041)
> *Teenager/Alcohol* (no. C1216)
> *Women and Alcohol* (no. C1214)
> *About Alcohol* (no. C1107)
> *Drug Abuse* (no. C1122)
> *Parents/Drug Abuse* (no. C1135)
> *About Preventing Drug Abuse* (no. 1268A)
> *Drug Abuse Information Center* (no. C9070)

[Note: Any of the Channing L. Bete booklets make excellent resources for talks, lectures, sermons, or classes because they present accurate information in a step-by-step format.]

Hazelden, Box 176, Center City, MN 5502; (800) 328-9000. Send for catalog. Its materials cover every aspect of chemcial-dependency education, prevention, and intervention. Especially useful are:

> *Alcoholism—A Merry-Go-Round Named Denial* by J.L. Kellerman
> *I Can't Be an Alcoholic Because . . .* by D. Hancock

I Had to Stop Because I Couldn't Quit by V.E. Johnson
Drugs—Use, Misuse, Abuse by M. Hill
For Troubled Teens with Problem Parents by Anonymous
Reconciliation with God and Family by J.L. Kellerman
Points for Parents Perplexed About Drugs by D. Hancock
Teen Drug Use: What Can Parents Do?
What Shall We Teach the Young About Drinking? by R.D. Russell
Setting Limits: Parents, Kids and Drugs by W.L. Fountain
The Woman Alcoholic by B.J. Kimball
The Liberated Woman by P. McGrine

The Johnson Institute, 10700 Olsen Memorial Highway, Minneapolis, MN 55441; (612) 544-4165. Send for order form and sample packet. Especially useful are:

Chemical Dependency and Recovery Are a Family Affair (booklet)
Women, Alcoholism and Dependency (booklet)
Sober Days, Golden Years (booklet)
Alcoholism: A Treatable Disease
Some Perspectives on Alcoholism
The Family Enablers
Recovery of Chemically Dependent Families
Dynamics of Addiction
Intervention: A Professional's Guide

National Council on Alcoholism, 733 Third Avenue, New York, NY 10017; (212) 986-4433. Send for catalog.

Alcoholism—Know These Early Warning Signs
The Alcoholic Is a Sick Person Who Can Be Helped
Facts on Alcoholism
How to Help the Alcoholic
The Alcoholic Spouse
The Effects of Alcohol on Children
A Guide for the Family of an Alcoholic
To the Mother and Father of an Alcoholic
How Teens Set the Stage for Alcoholism
You and Your Alcoholic Parent
What Is Alcohol Education?
When Your Teenager Starts Drinking
Danger Signals for Women Drinkers
The Woman Alcoholic

The Reader's Digest, Pleasantville, NY 10570; (914) 769-7000. Reprints available. Send for price list. At approximately $5.00 to $9.00 per 100 reprints and $15.00 per 500 reprints, they provide some of the best information avail-

able at the cheapest price. At the very least every member of the congregation
should be given:

"A Dynamic New Approach to the Alcoholic" by J.G. Hubbell
"The Rising Tide of Alcoholism" by W.B. Terhune, M.D.
"Marijuana Alert: Brain and Sex Damage" by P. Mann
"Marijuana Alert II: More of the Grim Story" by P. Mann
"Marijuana Alert III: The Devastation of Personality," by P. Mann.
"Marijuana and Driving" by P. Mann
"Cocaine and the Middle-Class High"

RESOURCES/INFORMATION

Alcoholics Anonymous World Services, Inc.
P.O. Box 459, Grand Central Station
New York, NY 10017
(check local telephone directory)

Addicts Anonymous
Education Building
St. Marks United Presbyterian Church
10701 Old Georgetown Road
Bethesda, MD 20014

Alcohol and Drug Resource Center, Inc.
1819 Peachtree Road, N.E., Suite 601
Atlanta, GA 30309
(404) 351-5463

Al-Anon Family Group Headquarters
P.O. Box 182, Madison Square Station
New York, NY 10010
(check local telephone directory)

Alcohol and Drug Problems Association of North America (ADPA)
1101 Fifteenth Street, NW
Washington, DC 20005
(202) 452-0990
[Publishes a directory of treatment facilities, $7.50 + .50]

National Association of Gay Alcoholism Professionals
P.O. Box 376
Oakland, NJ 07436
(201) 337-1087

National Black Alcoholism Council
100 Maryland Avenue, NE
Washington, DC 20005

National Center for Alcohol Education
1901 North Kent Street
Arlington, VA 22209

National Clearinghouse for Alcoholic Information
P.O. Box 2345
Rockville, MD 20852

National Clearinghouse for Drug Abuse Information (NCDAI)
P.O. Box 416
Kensington, MD 20795

National Clearinghouse for Smoking and Health
Center for Disease Control
Building B., Room 222
Atlanta, GA 30333

National Episcopal Coalition on Alcohol
P.O. Box 50989
Washington, DC 20004

National Federation of Parents for Drug-Free Youth
P.O. Box 722
Silver springs, MD 20901
(301) 593-9256

Prevention of Alcohol Problems, Inc.
4626 Longfellow Avenue South
Minneapolis, MN 55407
(800) 729-3047

PRIDE (National Parents Resource Institute for Drug Education, Inc.)
100 Edgewood Avenue, Suite 1216
Atlanta, GA 30303
(800) 282-4241

The North Conway Institute
14 Beacon Street
Boston, MA 02108
(617) 742-0424

THE OPPORTUNITIES TO CHANGE AND TO GROW

With so many resources to choose from, a "core group" may feel over-whelmed by the task of selecting those that will be useful for a program of chemical health. It is helpful to remind the group that it is not responsible for designing a program for the entire congregation; such a task would overwhelm anyone who is not a professional in chemical dependency or education. The best advice the core group can follow is: *Start small.* It should begin by choosing the one thing it feels is most important and then devote its time and energy to it. To settle on a program that is small enough to manage *and* a good start toward other, more complicated efforts, the following decisions need to be made:

1. What is the object of the educational program?
2. At whom is the program directed?
3. What are the needs of the people who will come to the program?
4. What should the educational method be?
5. How should the learning process progress?
6. Who will facilitate the learning process?
7. What materials or resources will be necessary?
8. How and where will the educational program take place?
9. How will the program be evaluated?
10. What sort of fellowship is expected to follow?

No matter how large or small the initial program in a parish, the four primary goals for the promotion of chemical health must be the basis of the educational process. If growth and change are to result, those who participate will need to have:

1. *The opportunity to begin with one's own needs and concerns.* Learning occurs when we are able to start with our own needs and concerns and to reflect on, analyze, and understand them. This philosophizing symbolizes our personal experiences, provides the basis for new insights, and creates a receptivity to change. When a chemical-education program begins where the group or individual is and builds from there, the insights and learning that result are more "life-effective" than those gained from the imposition of another person's views.

2. *The opportunity to focus on attitudes and feelings without threat of judgment or criticism.* We cannot objectively investigate attitudes different from our own unless we are assured ours will not be criticized. Fear of judgment leads to distrust and intolerance; freedom from fear leads to openness and receptivity. Most of our attitudes and feelings toward chemical use are not based on rational considerations but on historical and personal prejudices. To have them challenged or judged, therefore, is threatening. When an educational program offers an open and accepting atmosphere in which the participants feel free to express their opinions, they are better able to understand their prejudices in relation to other attitudes and they can appreciate the benefits of changing their unhealthy biases.

3. *The opportunity to learn about chemical use, nonuse, misuse, and abuse in an objective setting.* If the object of a program of chemical education is to control the learning process, then the participant has no investment in the structure or material of the class, no motivation to learn, no opportunity to value the experience, and no commitment to try new behavior. The lesson to be learned from the temperance movement is that moralizing about chemical use, overstressing the dangers of misuse, and focusing on the evils and hazards of abuse are counterproductive. A chemical-education program is most beneficial when it emphasizes healthy behavior, when the positive aspects of responsible alcohol and drug use are investigated alongside the ramifications of abuse, when responsible abstinence as well as responsible use are discussed, and most importantly, when the emphasis is on the making of responsible decisions rather than on promoting specific attitudes or behaviors.

4. *The opportunity to gain insights into biblical concepts and theological principles that can be used for personal strengthening and guidance.* When structuring a program of chemical education, we need to reflect on the needs of the people who will come to it, i.e., to ask ourselves, "Why are they coming to their religious institution for a class on chemical health?" If change and growth are to occur, it must be as the result of faith that there is (and will continue to be) something better. We cannot know who we will become or what will happen, but we can trust in the biblical assurance that there is a power greater than ourselves that creates all things, restores all aspects of our world, and gives meaning, direction, and purpose to life. When our chemical-education program is grounded in a theology that emphasizes the presence of a God or a "higher power" in our lives and proclaims that he has intentions and a purpose for us, then we can dare to change, confident that growth and health will be nourished and sustained by that power which causes and maintains all life.

A Life-Changing Fellowship

The role of the clergy in the initiation of a chemical-education program is to create the environment in which these opportunities can become a reality. Our purpose is not to be the educators but to contribute to the learning process by publicizing the programs, preaching about them, and promoting an atmosphere of openness, honesty, and caring that minimizes judgment, fear, denial, and prejudice. If we want to build a do-it-yourself "Greek Family," one that draws on AA's model, one in which success is measured not by the number of people in attendance but by the number of lives redeemed, then we will want to communicate that all persons deserve acceptance, respect, concern, and love.

Preventing problems through education before they begin is most effective when *everyone* knows that *everyone* matters. Consequently, it is essential to the creation of a caring, nonjudgmental community that we share how we feel about alcohol and drug use. Finally, how we respond to parishioners with alcohol or drug problems and to those affected by another's chemical dependency will demonstrate whether or not the Church is a redemptive community. For it is in our charitableness toward the extreme forms of chemical use and abuse that people will see our unconditional positive regard for *all* persons.

Unless we are in the business of redeeming lives, we are out of business. Though it is one of the Church's primary tasks to develop the faith of those who come to worship, none will grow unless it is commonly believed that the Church is a community in which people may not only learn to trust in God but dare to trust one another. As was stated previously, the success of the Church is gauged not by the number in attendance, but by the lives redeemed. When we can accept people in weakness and return them to the world in strength, we are proclaiming our faith in God's redeeming power and establishing a basis for faith in each other. This is the lesson, as Samuel Shoemaker points out, the Church needs to learn from AA—that men are redeemed in a life-changing fellowship."

On the one hand, the goal of a program of chemical health in a parish is to equip the members to deal with the complex problems of chemical use and at the same time strive to prevent problems before they begin. On the other hand, it is to establish an environment in which there is the unlimited possibility for redemption. That means, in essence, demonstrating the Church's response to the weak, the sick, the impaired, the unacceptable. Rest assured, as the program of chemical health becomes established, alcoholics, drug abusers, family members, friends, neighbors, fellow employees, bosses will all rush forward to be accepted, heard, and helped. Whether we accept them as sick people or as sinners will reveal the depth of our faith. Whether we receive them or reject them will proclaim how deeply we, as leaders of a redemptive community, are committed to serving God's purpose of redemption. It begins when we come to terms with our own attitudes toward chemical dependency.

APPENDIX B

A DIRECTORY OF RESOURCES

CENTRAL OFFICES OF CHURCHES/DENOMINATIONS/RELIGIONS

American Baptist Churches in the
  U.S.A.
Valley Forge, PA 19482
(215) 768-2305

American Lutheran Church
1568 Eustis Street
St. Paul, MN 55108
(616)645-9173

Christian Council (Disciples of Christ)
P.O. Box 1986
Indianapolis, IN 46216
(317) 353-1491

Church of the Brethren
1451 Dundee Avenue
Elgin, IL 60120
(312) 742-5100

The Episcopal Church
815 Second Avenue
New York, NY 10017
(212) 867-8400

Greek Orthodox Archdiocese of North
  and South America
8-10 East 79th Street
New York, NY 10021
(212) 570-3500

Lutheran Church in America
231 Madison Avenue
New York, NY 10016
(212) 481-9895

Presbyterian Church Center
341 Ponce de Leon Avenue NE
Atlanta, GA 30308
(404) 873-1531

Reformed Church in America
Room 1818
475 Riverside Drive
New York, NY 10115
(212) 870-2851

Seventh-Day Adventist Church
6840 Eastern Avenue NW
Washington, DC 20012
(202) 723-0800

Union of American Hebrew Congregations
838 Fifth Avenue
New York, NY 10021
(212) 249-0100

Unitarian-Universalist Association
24 Beacon Street
Boston, MA 02108
(617) 742-2100

United Church of Canada
315 Queen Street, East
Toronto, Ontario M5A 1S7, Canada
(416) 366-9221

United Church of Christ
105 Madison Avenue
New York, NY 10016
(212) 683-5656

United Methodist Church
Room 1370
475 Riverside Drive
New York, NY 10115
(212) 663-8900

United Presbyterian Church U.S.A.
Room 1948
475 Riverside Drive
New York, NY 10115
(212) 870-2037

United Synagogues of America
155 Fifth Avenue
New York, NY 10010
(212) 533-7800

U.S. Catholic Conference
1011 First Avenue, 13th Floor
New York, NY 10022
(212) 644-1880

NATIONAL ORGANIZATIONS

(For local meetings refer to yellow pages of the local phone book.)

Alcoholics Anonymous
General Service Office
468 Park Avenue South
New York, NY 10016
(212) 686-1100

Al-Anon Family Group
P.O. Box 182, Madison Square Garden
New York, NY 10159
(212) 481-6565

Narcotics Anonymous
World Service Office
P.O. Box 622
Sun Valley, CA 91325
(213) 768-6203

Narc-Anon Family Group
P.O. Box 2562
Palos Verdes, CA 90274
(213) 547-5800

Alcohol and Drug Problems Association
of North America (ADPA)
1101 15th Street, NW
Washington, DC 20005
(202) 452-0990

National Association of Alcoholism
Counselors
951 S. George Mason Drive
Arlington, VA 22204
(703) 920-8338

National Association of Gay Alcoholism
Professionals
P.O. Box 376
Oakland, NJ 07436
(201) 337-1087

National Association of Alcoholism
Treatment Programs
2082 Mickelson Dr., Suite 200
Irvine, CA 92715
(714) 975-0104

National Alcoholism Treatment Direc-
tory $5.00
Alcoholism/The National Magazine
Box C 19051
Seattle, WA 98109
(800) 528-6600, ext. 100

National Black Alcoholism Council
100 Maryland Avenue, NE
Washington, DC 20005

National Episcopal Coalition on Alcohol
P.O. Box 50489
Washington, DC 20004

National Clearinghouse for Alcohol
Information
Box 2345
Rockville, MD 20852
(301) 468-2600

National Clearinghouse for Drug Abuse
Information
P.O. Box 722
Kensington, MD 20901

National Coalition of Hispanic Mental
Health and Human Services Organizations
1010 15th Street, NW, Suite 402
Washington, DC 20005

National Council on Alcoholism, Inc.
(NCA)
733 Third Avenue
New York, NY 10017
(212) 986-4433

National Indian Board on Alcohol and
Drug Abuse
P.O. Box 8
Turtle Lake, WI 54889

National Institute on Drug Abuse
(NIDA)
5600 Fishers Lane
Rockville, MD 20857

National Federation of Parents for
Drug-Free Youth
P.O. Box 722
Silver Spring, MD 20901
(301) 593-9256

National PTA
Alcohol/Drug Education Project
700 North Rush Street
Chicago, IL 60611
(312) 787-0977

North Conway Institute
14 Beacon Street
Boston, MA 02108
(617) 742-0424

Prevention of Alcohol Problems, Inc.
4616 Longfellow Avenue, S
Minneapolis, MN 55407
(612) 729-3047

PRIDE
100 Edgewood Avenue, Suite 1216
Atlanta, GA 30303
(800) 282-4241

STATE AND TERRITORIAL AUTHORITIES*

Alabama

Alcoholism Program
Department of Mental Health
145 Moulton Street
Montgomery, AL 36104
(203) 265-2301

Alaska

Office of Alcoholism
Division of Mental Health
Pouch H-05F
Juneau, AK 99801
(907) 456-3020

American Samoa

Samoa Comprehensive Health Planning
Pago Pago, Samoa 96799

Arizona

Alcoholism Program
Division of Behavioral Health Services
2500 E. Van Buren Street
Phoenix, AZ 85008
(602) 271-4525

Arkansas

Office of Alcohol Abuse and Alcoholism
Dept. of Social and Rehabilitation Services
1515 W. 7th Street, Suite 202
Little Rock, AR 72202
(501) 371-2003

California

Office of Alcohol Program Management
825-15th Street

* Source: The National Alcoholism Treatment Center Directory, 1983–84. Produced by "Alco-
holism/the national magazine" in cooperation with the National Association of Treatment Programs.

Sacramento, CA 93814
(916) 445-1940

Colorado

Alcohol and Drug Abuse Division
4210 East 11th Avenue
Denver, CO 80220
(303) 388-6111

Connecticut

State Alcohol Council
90 Washington Street
Hartford, CT 06115
(203) 566-3464

Delaware

Alcoholism Services
Delaware State Hospital, Briggs
   Building
New Castle, DE 19720
(302) 421-6421 or -6422

District of Columbia

Mental Health Administration
1875 Connecticut Avenue, NW
Room 822
Washington, DC 20009
(202) 629-3595 or -3594

Florida

Bureau of Alcoholism Rehabilitation
Division of Mental Health
1323 Winewood Boulevard, Room 324
Tallahassee, FL 32301
(904) 488-8922, -8924, or -8925

Georgia

Alcohol and Drug Abuse Section
Division of Mental Health
618 Ponce de Leon Avenue
Atlanta, GA 30308
(404) 894-4785

Guam

Guam Memorial Hospital
Agana, Guam 96910

Hawaii

Substance Abuse Agency
1270 Queen Emma Street, Room 404
Honolulu, HI 96813
(808) 548-7655

Idaho

Bureau of Substance Abuse
Health and Welfare Department X
Statehouse
Boise, ID 83720

Illinois

Alcoholism Division
Department of Mental Health and
   Development Disabilities
188 West Randolph Street, Room 1900
Chicago, IL 60601
(312) 793-2907

Indiana

Division of Addictive Services
3000 West Washington Street
Indianapolis, IN 46222
(317) 633-4477

Iowa

Division of Alcoholism
508-10th Street, 5th Floor
Des Moines, IA 50319
(515) 281-5831

Kansas

Commission on Alcoholism
535 Kansas Avenue, Room 1106
Topeka, KS 66603
(913) 296—3991

Kentucky

Alcohol Section
Department of Human Resources
Bureau for Health Sevices
275 East Main Street
Frankfort, KY 40601
(502) 564-7450

Louisiana

Bureau of Substance Abuse
Division of Hospitals
Health and Human Services
   Administration
200 Lafayette Street
Baton Rouge, LA 70801
(504) 389-6453

Maine

Office of Alcoholism and Drug Abuse
   Prevention
32 Winthrop Street
Augusta, ME 04330

Marianas Islands

Marianas Island Division of Mental
   Health
Saipan, Marianas Islands 96950

Maryland

Division of Alcoholism Control
201 West Preston Street, 4th Floor
Baltimore, MD 21202
(301) 383-2781, -2782, or -2783

Massachusetts

Division of Alcoholism
755 Boylston Street
Boston, MA 02116
(617) 536-6983

Michigan

Office of Substance Abuse Services
Department of Mental Health
3500 N. Logan-Baker-Olin, West
Lansing, MI 48914
(517) 373-8600

Minnesota

Chemical Dependency Program
   Division
402 Metro Square Building, Room 402
St. Paul, MN 55101
(612) 296-4610

Mississippi

Division of Alcohol Abuse and
   Alcoholism
619 Robert E. Lee Office Building
Jackson, MS 39201
(601) 354-7031

Missouri

Division of Alcohol and Drug Abuse
Department of Mental Health
2002 Missouri Boulevard
Jefferson City, MO 65101
(314) 751-4942

Montana

Department of Institutions
Alcohol Services Division
Capitol Station
Helena, MT 59601
(404) 525-3178

Nebraska

Division of Alcoholism
Box 94728
Lincoln, NE 68509
(420) 471-2851

Nevada

Bureau of Alcohol and Drug Abuse
Capitol Complex
1803 North Carson Street
Carson City, NV 89701
(702) 885-4790

New Hampshire

Program on Alcohol and Drug Abuse
61 South Spring Street
Concord, NH 03301
(603) 271-3531

New Jersey

Alcoholism Control Program
P.O. Box 1540, John Fitch Plaza
Trenton, NJ 08607
(609) 292-8947

New Mexico

Commission on Alcoholism
P.O. Box 1731
Albuquerque, NM 87103
(505) 877-1000

New York

Division of Alcoholism
44 Holland Avenue
Albany, NY 12208
(518) 474-5417

North Carolina

Alcohol and Drug Abuse Services
Division of Human Resources
325 N. Salisbury Street
Raleigh, NC 27611
(919) 829-4670

North Dakota

Division of Alcoholism and Drug Abuse
909 Basin Avenue, Expressway Office
   Building
Bismark, ND 58505
(710) 224-2767

Ohio

Alcoholism Unit
450 East Town Street
P.O. Box 118
Columbus, OH 43216
(614) 466-3445

Oklahoma

Division of Alcoholism
P.O. Box 53277, Capitol Station
Oklahoma City, OK 73105
(405) 521-2811

Oregon

Programs for Alcohol and Drug
   Problems
Mental Health Division
2570 Center Street, NE
Salem, OR 97310
(503) 378-2163

Pennsylvania

Governor's Council on Drug and
   Alcohol Abuse
No. 1 Riverside Office Center, Suite N
2101 North Front Street
Harrisburg, PA 17120
(717) 787-9857

Puerto Rico

Department of Addiction Services
Box B-Y, Rio Piedras Station
Rio Piedras, Puerto Rico 00928
(809) 764-5014 or -7575

Rhode Island

Services for Alcoholism
Department of Mental Health, Retar-
   dation and Hospitals
P.O. Box 8281
Cranston, RI 02920
(401) 464-2656

South Carolina

Commission on Alcohol and Drug
   Abuse
P.O. Box 4616
Columbia, SC 29240
(803) 758-2521

South Dakota

Division of Alcoholism
Pierre, SD 57502
(605) 224-3459

Tennessee

Alcohol and Drug Abuse Section
300 Cordell Hull Building
Nashville, TN 37219
(615) 741-1921

Texas

Commission on Alcoholism
809 Sam Houston State Office Building
Austin, TX 78701
(512) 475-2577

Utah

Division of Alcoholism and Drugs
554 South 300 East
Salt Lake City, UT 84111
(801) 533-6532

Vermont

Alcohol and Drug Programs
Agency of Human Services
79 River Street
Montpelier, VT 05602
(802) 828-2741

Virgin Islands/U.S.

Mental Health Services
P.O. Box 1442
St. Thomas, Virgin Islands 00801
(809) 774-0117

Virginia

Bureau of Alcohol Studies and
    Rehabilitation
James Madison Building
109 Governor Street
Richmond, VA 23219
(804) 770-3082

Washington

Office of Alcoholism
Department of Social and Mental
    Services
P.O. Box 1788, M.S. 45-1
Olympia, WA 98504
(206) 753-5866

West Virginia

Division of Alcoholism and Drug Abuse
State Capitol
Charleston, WV 25305
(304) 348-3616

Wisconsin

Bureau of Alcoholism and Other Drugs
1 West Wilson Street
Madison, WI 53702
(608) 266-3442

Wyoming

Alcoholism and Alcohol Abuse
Mental Health and Mental Retardation
    Services
State Office Building
Cheyenne, WY 82002
(307) 777-7351

STATE AND TERRITORIAL AGENCIES

Alabama

Division of Alcoholism and Drug Abuse
Department of Mental Health
502 Washington Street
Montgomery, AL 36104
(205) 834-4350

Alaska

Dept. of Health and Social Services
Office of Alcoholism and Drug Abuse
Pouch H-05F
213 South Franklin
Juneau, AK 99811
(907) 586-6201

American Samoa

Mental Health Clinic
Government of American Samoa
Pago Pago, AS 96799

Arizona

Drug Abuse Section
Dept. of Health Services
Bureau of Community Services
2500 E. Van Buren Street
Phoenix, AZ 85008
(602) 255-1238

Arkansas

Arkansas Office on Alcohol and Drug
    Abuse Prevention
1515 W. 7th Street, Suite 300
Little Rock, AR 72202
(501) 371-2604

California

Department of Alcohol and Drug
    Problems
111 Capitol Hill Mall
Suite 450
Sacramento, CA 95814
(916) 445-1940

Colorado

Alcohol and Drug Abuse Division
Department of Health
4210 East 11th Avenue
Denver, CO 80220
(303) 320-66137

Connecticut

Connecticut Alcohol and Drug Abuse
    Council
90 Washington Street, Room 312
Hartford, CT 06115
(203) 566-4145

Delaware

Bureau of Alcoholism and Drug Abuse
Division of Mental Health
1901 North Dupont Highway
Newcastle, DE 19720
(302) 421-6101

District of Columbia

D.C. Dept. of Human Resources
Mental Health, Alcohol and Addiction
    Services Branch
421 8th Street, NW
2nd Floor
Washington, DC 20004
(202) 724-5637

Florida

Drug Abuse Program
Mental Health Program Office
1316 Winewood Boulevard
Tallahassee, FL 32301
(904) 487-1842

Georgia

Alcohol and Drug Abuse Section
Division of Mental Health and Mental
    Retardation
Georgia Dept. of Human Resources
618 Ponce de Leon Avenue, NE
Atlanta, GA 30308
(404) 894-4785

Guam

Mental Health and Substance Abuse
    Agency
P.O. Box 20999
Guam, GU 96921
(404)477-9704

Hawaii

Department of Health
Substance Abuse Agency
Alcohol and Drug Abuse Branch
1270 Queen Emma Street, Room 505
Honolulu, HI 96813
(808) 548-7655

Idaho

Bureau of Substance Abuse
Department of Health and Welfare
450 West State Street, 4th Floor
Boise, ID 83720
(208) 344-4368

Illinois

Illinois Dangerous Drugs Commission
300 North State Street
Suite 1500
Chicago, IL 60606
(312) 822-9860

Indiana

Division of Addictive Services
Department of Mental Health

5 Indiana Square
Indianapolis, IN 46204
(317) 232-7818

Iowa

Department of Substance Abuse
Insurance Exchange Bldg., Suite 202
505 5th Avenue
Des Moines, IA 50319
(515) 281-3641

Kansas

Alcoholism and Drug Abuse Section
Dept. of Social Rehabilitation Service
2700 West Sixth Street
Topeka, KS 66606
(913) 296-3925

Kentucky

Mental Health/Mental Retardation
    Section
Department of Human Resources
275 East Main Street
Frankfort, KY 40621
(502) 564-2880

Louisiana

Office of Mental Health and Substance
    Abuse
Dept. of Health and Human Resources
655 North 5th Street
Baton Rouge, LA 70829
(504) 342-2590

Maine

Office of Alcoholism and Drug Abuse
    Prevention
Department of Human Services
32 Winthrop Street
Augusta, ME 04330
(207) 289-2781

Maryland

Maryland Drug Abuse Administration
201 West Preston Street
Baltimore, MD 21201
(301) 383-3959

Massachusetts

Massachusetts Dept. of Mental Health
Division of Drug Rehabilitation
160 North Washington Street
Boston, MA 02114
(617) 727-8614

Michigan

Office of Substance Abuse Services
Department of Public Health
3500 North Logan Street
Lansing, MI 48909
(517) 373-8600

Minnesota

Chemical Dependency Program
    Division
Dept. of Public Welfare
4th Floor Centennial Building
658 Cedar Street
St. Paul, MN 55155
(612) 296-4610

Mississippi

Division of Alcohol and Drug Abuse
Department of Mental Health
619 Robert E. Lee Office Building
Jackson, MS 39201
(601) 354-7031

Missouri

Division of Alcoholism and Drug Abuse
Department of Mental Health
2002 Missouri Boulevard
Jefferson City, MO 65102
(314) 751-4942

Montana

Alcohol and Drug Abuse Division
Department of Institutions
1539 11th Avenue
Helena, MT 59601
(404) 449-2827

Nebraska

Nebraska Dept. of Public Institutions
Nebraska Division on Alcoholism and
    Drug Abuse

801 West Van Dorn
Box 94728
Lincoln, NE 68509
(420) 471-2851

Nevada

Bureau of Alcohol and Drug Abuse
Department of Human Resources
505 East King Street
Carson City, NV 89710
(702) 885-4790

New Hampshire

Office of Alcohol and Drug Abuse
   Prevention
Health and Welfare Buliding
Hazen Drive
Concord, NH 03301
(603) 271-4626 or -4630

New Jersey

New Jersey Division of Narcotic and
   Drug Abuse Control
129 East Hanover Street
Trenton, NJ 08605
(609) 292-8930

New Mexico

Substance Abuse Bureau
Behavioral Health Service Division
Health and Environment Department
P.O. Box 968
Santa Fe, NM 87503
(505) 827-5271, ext. 226

New York

New York Office of Alcoholism and Sub-
   stance Abuse
Division of Substance Abuse Services
Executive Park South, Box 8200
Albany, NY 12203
(518) 488-4270

North Carolina

Alcohol and Drug Abuse Services
Div. of Mental Health/Mental Retardation and Substance Abuse
325 N. Salisbury Street

Albemarle Bldg., Room 1100
Raleigh, NC 27611
(919) 733-4670

North Dakota

Division of Alcoholism and Drug Abuse
State Department of Health
909 Basin Avenue
Bismarck, ND 58505
(710) 224-2768

Ohio

Bureau of Drug Abuse
Dept. of Mental Health and Mental
   Retardation
65 South Front Street, Suite 211
Columbus, OH 43215
(614) 466-9023

Oklahoma

Division of Alcoholism and Drug Abuse
   Programs
Department of Mental Health
4545 North Lincoln Blvd., Suite 100
P.O. Box 53277
Oklahoma City, OK 73152
(405) 521-2811

Oregon

Programs for Drug Problems
Oregon Mental Health Division
2575 Bittern Street, NE
Salem, OR 97310
(503) 378-2163

Pennsylvania

Governor's Council on Drug and Alcohol Abuse
2102 North Front Street
Harrisburg, PA 17120
(717) 787-9857

Puerto Rico

Department of Addiction Control
   Services
P.O. Box B-Y
Rio Piedras Station, PR 00928
(809) 764-5014

Rhode Island

Division of Substance Abuse
General Hospital, Building 303
Rhode Island Medical Center
Cranston, RI 02920
(401) 464-2091

South Carolina

South Carolina Commission on Alcohol
    and Drug Abuse
3700 Forest Drive
Landmark East, Suite 300
Columbia, SC 29204
(803) 758-2183

South Dakota

Division of Drugs and Substance
    Council
Department of Health
Joe Foss Building, Room 119
Pierre, SD 57501
(605) 773-3123

Tennessee

Division of Alcohol and Drug Abuse
Tennessee Department of Mental Health
501 Union Building
Nashville, TN 37219
(615) 741-1921

Texas

Drug Abuse Prevention Division
Texas Department of Community
    Affairs
Drug Abuse Prevention Division
210 Barton Springs Road
Austin, TX 78704
(512) 475-6351

Trust Territories

Department of Health Services
Office of the High Commissioner
Saipan, TT 96950
(615) 741-1921

U.S. Virgin Islands

Division of Mental Health, Alcoholism
    and Drug Dependency

P.O. Box 520
Christiansted
St. Croix, VI 00820
(809) 773-1192, 774-4888

Utah

Division of Alcoholism and Drugs
150 West North Temple, Suite 350
P.O. Box 2500
Salt Lake City, UT 84110
(801) 533-6532

Vermont

Alcohol and Drug Abuse Division
Department of Social and Rehabilita-
    tion Services
103 South Main Street
State Office Building
Waterbury, VT 05675
(802) 241-2170

Virginia

Division of Substance Abuse
Virginia Department of Mental Health
    and Mental Retardation
P.O. Box 1797
109 Governor Street
Richmond, VA 23214
(804) 786-5313

Washington

Bureau of Alcoholism and Substance
    Abuse
Washington Department of Social and
    Health Services
Mailstop OB-44W
Olympia, WA 98504
(206) 753-3073

West Virginia

Department of Health
Alcoholism and Drug Abuse Program
State Capitol
1800 Kanawha Boulevard E
Charleston, WV 25305
(304) 348-3616

Wisconsin

Bureau of Alcoholism and Other Drug
    Abuse
One West Wilson Street, Room 523
Madison, WI 53702
(608) 266-3442

Wyoming

Substance Abuse Program
Hathaway Building, 4th Floor
Cheyenne, WY 82002
(307) 777-7115

TRAINING PROGRAMS

Rutgers University
Summer School of Alcohol Studies
New Brunswick, NJ 08903
(201) 923-2190
Three-week school, June/July

Seattle University
Alcohol Studies Program
Seattle, WA 98122
Wide variety of courses

University of Utah
School of Alcoholism and Drug
    Dependency
P.O. Box 2604
Salt Lake City, UT 84110
One-week school, June

International School of Alcohol Studies
Division of Alcoholism and Drug Abuse
909 Basin Avenue
Bismarck, ND 58505
One-week school, July

Hazelden Foundation
Center City, MN 55012

(612) 257-4010; (800) 328-9000
Variety of short- and long-term courses
    throughout year

Johnson Institute
10700 Olson Memorial Highway
Minneapolis, MN 55441
(612) 544-4165
Variety of seminars and training courses
    throughout year

North Conway Institute
14 Beacon Street
Boston, MA 02108
(617) 742-0424
One-week assembly, June

The Reverend Doctor Stephen P. Apthorp
Foundation for Personal Freedom
Box 442, 12 Trapelo Road
Lincoln, MA 01773
(617) 259-8895, 259-9128
Clergy and Church workshops
School programs

DIRECTORIES OF TREATMENT CENTERS

National Directory of Drug Abuse
    Treatment Programs, 1980
National Directory of Drug Abuse and
    Alcoholism Treatment and Prevention
    Programs, 1982
Superintendent of Documents
U.S. Government Printing Office
Washington, DC 20404
(202) 783-3238 (price on request)

APPENDIX C

FIVE SERMON OUTLINES*

ALCOHOLISM—AN ILLNESS

Introduction: Dispelling myths and misconceptions

I. Alcoholism
  A. Definition
    1. Biochemical—Milam, Ketchum
    2. Genetic—Vaillant
    3. Hereditary—Mann
  B. Extent of the illness
    1. National Council on Alcoholism figures
      a. Affects 1 in 4 families in America
      b. 1 out of 8 adults
      c. 3.3 million teenagers
      d. 10 million adults
      e. 4 million women
    2. Traffic fatalities
      a. 27,400/year, 75 citizens/day
      b. College of American Pathologists—90% of fatal auto accidents involve alcohol
  C. Public's attitude
    1. General Mills Survey—personal, emotional, weakness
    2. Mental, emotional problem
    3. Moral degeneracy, lack of will—Milam, Ketchum
  D. Professional's attitude
    1. AMA's approach—psychiatric treatment
    2. Churches' beliefs—sin or sickness?

*May also be used or adopted for talks.

       3. *Human Behavior* magazine survey
         a. Alcoholic, the cause of his own problem
         b. Least acceptable disorder
    E. Jellinek's disease
       1. Dr. E.M. Jellinek
       2. First definition of alcoholism as a medical illness
       3. Established at Yale University

II. Description of chemical dependency—Johnson Institute
    A. Primary
       1. Identifiable symptoms
       2. Not the symptom of a more serious problem
    B. Progressive
       1. No observable plateau effect
       2. Illness gets worse
         a. Physical
         b. Emotional
         c. Spiritual
       3. Symptoms can be arrested
       4. Victim must abstain
    C. Chronic
       1. No cure, lifelong illness
       2. Always susceptible—"Once a pickle, never again a cucumber."
       3. Symptoms can only be arrested
       4. Recovery requires abstinence
    D. Fatal
       1. Ultimately terminal
       2. Misrepresentations
         a. Physical deterioration
         b. Accidents
         c. Suicides
       3. Disease can only be arrested

III. Identification characteristics—Hazelden
    A. Preoccupation with use
    B. Protects the supply
    C. Use of alcohol as medicine
    D. Solitary use
    E. Rapid intake for effect
    F. Increased tolerance
    G. Blackouts, memory loss
    H. Episodes of unplanned, excessive drinking

IV. Effects of disease
    A. Individual—Wegscheider
        1. Physical potential
        2. Emotional potential
        3. Social potential
        4. Mental potential
        5. Spiritual potential
        6. Volitional potential
    B. Family
        1. Enablers
        2. Unspoken rules
        3. *Denial*—No. 1 symptom
        4. Codependent

V. God wants us to be well
    A. A sickness—not a sin
    B. Resources are available
    C. "Call me. I can get you the help that will save your life."

LICIT DRUG ABUSE

Introduction: Drug abuse means the use of any drug to the point that it damages the user's health, work, education, personal relationships, judgment, or ability to cope with daily life.

I. Drug Abuse
    A. Alcohol abuse equals drug abuse
        1. Alcohol a drug
        2. Central nervous-system depressant
    B. Legal drugs that are abused
        1. Alcohol
        2. Tranquilizers
        3. Stimulants—amphetamines
        4. Depressants—barbiturates
        5. Narcotics
    C. Drug gourmands
        1. Polydrug abuse rampant among adults
        2. The Betty Ford example
        3. Approximately 2,500 deaths per year

II. Reasons for polydrug abuse
   A. Combining alcohol and prescriptions
      1. Antagonistic reaction
      2. Synergistic effect
      3. Dangerous mixes
   B. Medication of women
      1. Sixty-nine percent of tranquilizer and sedative prescriptions are for women
      2. Double standards: men's vs. women's drinking
      3. Psychological and emotional problems have chemical solutions, e.g., financial difficulties, unhappiness, etc.
   C. Alcohol abuse among women
      1. Four million alcoholics
      2. Prescriptions plus alcohol

III. Drug abuse among older generation
   A. Extent of their problem
      1. Two to ten percent will have chemical-dependency problems
      2. Use of minor tranquilizers, 10 percent women, 5 percent men
      3. Abuse of alcohol: men 5 to 1
   B. Cause of drug abuse
      1. Loss of activity, loneliness, retirement
      2. Medical prescriptions
      3. Allowances by family members
      4. Oversight of the doctor

IV. Theological perspective
   A. Proper use of drug
      1. To correct health problems
      2. To protect against disease
      3. To strengthen or stabilize
   B. Rule of thumb
      1. Does it enhance the individual's life?
      2. Does it detract from the individual's life?
   C. God's intentions
      1. Life is a gift and a trust
      2. Each person has opportunity to fulfill his or her potential
      3. Damaging one's body, mind, and spirit is contrary to God's purpose

Conclusion: Help is available. Drug abuse is a treatable illness and recovery is possible.

ADOLESCENTS AND ALCOHOL

Introduction: The number one drug of choice among adolescents is alcohol (beer).

I. Teenage drinking
  A. Misuse and abuse
    1. Thirty-one percent of high-school students considered misusers
    2. Fifteen percent of high-school students are heavy users (five drinks at least once a week)
    3. Average age kids begin to drink—13
    4. Approximately 3.3 million teenagers showing signs of potential alcohol problems
  B. Alcohol, the chemical
    1. Ethyl alcohol—toxic
    2. Central-nervous-system depressant
    3. Colorless liquid plus congeners and processing equals beer, wine, liquor
  C. Alcohol content
    1. One-half the proof equals alcohol content
    2. One beer, one five-ounce glass of wine, one highball have the same alcohol content
    3. One drink equals a Blood Alcohol Content (BAC) of 2 percent
    4. Five drinks in one hour by a 150-pound person = BAC of 10 percent; legally drunk
    5. BAC drops 2 percent per hour
  D. Drinking and driving
    1. Underestimating the effects of beer vs. liquor
    2. Overestimating driving ability
    3. At BAC of 5 percent, chances of accident double; at 10 percent, they increase seven times
    4. After two beers, marked loss of depth perception and peripheral vision
    5. BAC varies according to many factors, e.g., body weight, gulping, etc.
    6. Over half the drivers killed in auto accidents had BAC of 9 percent

II. Misuse and abuse
  A. Proper use
    1. Beverage with meals
    2. Social gatherings

      3. Celebrations

      4. Religious ceremonies

      5. Medicinal purposes

  B. Goal of teerage drinking

      1. Message of drug culture

      2. "Get high," "get wasted"

      3. "Having a party" means getting drunk

      4. Many teenagers know no other reason to drink

  C. Hazards of abuse

      1. Separates the youngster from his own psycho-social growth

      2. Less able to gain a sense of self

      3. Relies on it to feel good

      4. The more consumed in quantity, the greater the chances of becoming addicted

      5. Five ways alcohol affects adolescents differently than adults

      6. The earlier the drinking age, the greater the chances of problems

III. Responsible decisions

  A. Parents' role

      1. The decision is the parents'

      2. How do the parents use alcohol themselves?

      3. Do they provide alcohol for their kids?

  B. Responsible abstinence

      1. Saying, "No, thank you"

      2. Peer influence

      3. Parental influence

      4. Teaching the steps to a responsible decision

  C. Question of drinking and driving

      1. "No! Absolutely not!"

      2. Safe transportation home

Conclusion: Use of liquor, beer, wine to get drunk is drug abuse. Ultimately it results in loss of self. In the final analysis, who is reponsible?

ADOLESCENTS AND MARIJUANA

Introduction: There is no such thing as repsonsible use of marijuana among teenagers. Any use at all is considered drug abuse because it has such a harmful effect on the adolescent's growth and development.

I. Marijuana use
   A. Extent of use
      1. Over half of all high-school students have used marijuana
      2. One out of three uses it monthly
      3. One out of fourteen high-school seniors are daily users
   B. Reasons for use
      1. Escape
      2. Control of one's life
      3. Fun
      4. *Pleasure*
   C. Professional opinions about use
      1. Dr. Carlton Turner
      2. Dr. Robert Dupont

II. The chemical and its effects
   A. Delta 9–Tetrahydrocannabinol (THC)
      1. THC is the psychoactive chemical producing the high
      2. THC is fat-soluble; it is absorbed by the fatty tissues in the brain, lungs, and reproductive system
      3. THC is metabolized in half-lives; it takes 21 to 29 days to clear out of the system
      4. THC content 10 percent to 20 percent
      5. Higher the THC content, the greater the damage
   B. Effect of marijuana on growth and development
      1. Loss of motivation
      2. Distorts perception of self and world
      3. Loss of short-term memory
      4. Emotional regression
      5. Stunting of psychological growth
      6. Irreversible immaturity
   C. Physical effects of marijuana use
      1. Brain cell congestion; decrease of cellular activity
      2. Interferes with male hormone (testosterone)
      3. Damages sperm
      4. Damages ova. Interferes with ovulation
      5. Respiratory system (lung) damage
      6. One joint equals 16–20 cigarettes

III. Theological perspective
   A. Loss of personal potential

    1. Adolescence a period of rapid emotional, intellectual, psychological growth
    2. Marijuana retards this process; permanent immaturity
    3. No social interaction and feedback
    4. Separates user from self, family, friends
    5. Cannot relive the lost years
    6. User does not grow into the person God intended

B. What to do
    1. Explain hazards to young children and parents
    2. Say *No* to use of marijuana
    3. Learn signs and symptoms
    4. Be prepared to fight youngster for himself
    5. Take him to treatment, no matter what
    6. We are our children's keepers

Conclusion: Marijuana use is drug abuse. It results in chemical dependency, which leads to the loss of personal potential—forever. We are our brother's keepers.

ILLICIT DRUG ABUSE

Introduction: The use of illicit drugs has become an accepted way of life that costs the American economy nearly $26 billion annually.

I. Illicit drug abuse
  A. Extent of problem
    1. Entertainment industry
    2. Business world
    3. Doctors, lawyers
    4. Secretaries
    5. United States military
    6. Professional sports
  B. Reasons for abuse
    1. Drug habit of the 60s and 70s
    2. Pain is bad, pleasure is good
    3. Escape
    4. Manipulate feelings
    5. Overcome boredom, loneliness
  C. Bridge to drug abuse
    1. From no drug to beer and wine (38 percent)

      2. Beer and wine to hard liquor and cigarettes (40 percent)

      3. Hard liquor and cigarettes to marijuana (27 percent)

      4. Marijuana to opiates, cocaine, LSD, heroin (26 percent)

II. The drugs
- A. Marijuana
    1. Smoked
    2. Euphoria
    3. Stunts emotional, intellectual, psychological growth
    4. Damages brain cells, reproductive organs
    5. Results in permanent immaturity
- B. Cocaine
    1. Sniffed, injected
    2. Rapid, short-lived, overpowering high
    3. Cost $100–$125/gram
    4. Addictive, leads to dealing and association with criminals
    5. Withdrawal results in depression, paranoia
- C. Hallucinogens—LSD, STP, DMT
    1. Taken by mouth
    2. Distort senses
    3. Expand consciousness
    4. Affect judgment
    5. Cause unpredictable behavior
- D. Narcotics
    1. Legal—codeine, Demerol, Methadone, Percodan
    2. Illegal—heroin
    3. Injected, swallowed, smoked
    4. Produces euphoric high, i.e., orgasm
    5. Addictive, withdrawal very unpleasant
- E. PCP—Angel Dust
    1. Animal tranquilizer
    2. Stimulant, anesthetic, hallucinogen
    3. Inhaled, smoked, swallowed
    4. Extreme perceptual distortion
    5. Produces aggressive, violent behavior

III. Theological perspectives
- A. Hazards of drug abuse
    1. Chemical dependency
    2. Life loses its value
    3. Disrupts families, friends, communities

    4. Destroys personal potential

B. What to proclaim
    1. The value of life, the ultimate value of persons
    2. Joy is found *not* so much in *what* we do with our time and talents as in *how* we do it
    3. Using oneself in relation to others as an instrument of God's love

C. What to do
    1. Take a theological stand
    2. Explain the disruption to personal potential
    3. Describe the help available
    4. Offer pastoral assistance
    5. Express *hope*

Conclusion: Unless the use of chemicals enhances the individual's life, as God intended, it leads to illness in the person and sickness in society.

NOTES

CHAPTER ONE: A MINISTER'S DILEMMA

1. Karl Menninger, *Whatever Became of Sin?* (New York: Hawthorn Books, 1973), 146.

2. David C. Hancock, "The Role of the Church in Alcohol Problems—Involved or Uninvolved?" (Paper presented to the International Conference of Religious Leaders, Indiana, 27 November 1979, 1. Sample from the author, 4616 Longfellow Avenue, South Minneapolis, MN 55407).

3. Ibid., 2.

4. Ibid., 3.

5. Ibid., 4.

6. Ibid.

7. Harold A. Mulford, "Drinking and Deviant Drinking, U.S.A." *Quarterly Journal Studies, Alcohol* 15 (1964): 634–50.

8. C. Peter Brock, "The Johnson Institute's Program for Adolescents with Alcohol Problems," in *Adolescent Substance Abuse* (Columbus, OH: Ross Laboratories, 1983), 70.

9. White House Conference on Families,, *Listening to America's Families: Action for the 80's.* The Report to the President, Congress and Families of the Nation, Jim Guy Tucker, Chairperson (Washington, DC, 1980) 18.

10. J.R. Deluca, ed., *Fourth Special Report to the U.S. Congress on Alcohol and Health* (Washington, D.C.: U.S. Dept. of Health and Human Services, publication no. ADM 81-1080, 1981).

11. L.D. Johnson, J.G. Bachman, and P.M. O'Malley, *Student Drug Abuse in America: 1975–1981* (Washington, DC: U.S. Dept. of Health and Human Services, publication no. ADM 82-1205, 1981), 231.

12. Karl A. Schneider, *Stumbling Blocks or Stepping Stones: Overcoming Clergy Inhibiting Attitudes to Involvement in Early Intervention and Training in Alcohol and Drug Problems* (New York: National Council on Alcoholism , 1982), 3–8.

13. Samuel W. Blizzard, "The Minister's Dilemma," *The Christian Century*, 15 April 1956, 508–9.

14. James D. Anderson and Ezra Earl Jones, *The Management of Ministry* (New York: Harper and Row, 1978), 8–9.

15. Ibid., 24–25.

16. Ibid., 195–97.

17. Keith Shuchard, "The Floodtide of Drugs and the Very Young: *Rebuilding the Protective Dikes at Home and Abroad*," in *Drug Abuse in the Modern World*, edited by Gabriel G. Nahas and Henry Clay Frick (New York: Pergamon Press, 1981), 320.

CHAPTER TWO: THE CLERGY AS CATALYST

1. Jim Castrelli, "Study Finds Religion Major Factor in U.S.," *Boston Globe*, 2 March 1981, 27.

2. Samuel M. Shoemaker, *What the Church Has to Learn from Alcoholics Anonymous* (Baltimore: Diocese of Maryland). Reprinted with permission of Helen Shoemaker.

3. Stephen Glenn, *Strengthening the Family* (Bethesda: Potomac Press, 1981), 5.

4. Ibid.

5. Ibid.

6. Ibid.

7. Jean Seligmann, review of *Growing Up Old: Children Without Parents*, by Marie Winn, *Newsweek*, 8 August 1983, 72.

8. Glenn, *Strengthening the Family*, 15.

9. Ibid., 9–16.

10. Virginia Satir, *People Making* (Palo Alto: Science and Behavior Books, 1972), 303.

CHAPTER THREE: PROHIBITION OR PREVENTION?

1. David C. Hancock, *Alcohol and the Church* (Minneapolis: Prevention of Alcohol Problems, 1980), 357, 361.

2. Paul C. Conley and Andrew A. Sorenson, *The Staggering Steeple* (Philadelphia: Pilgrim Press, 1971), 30.

3. Ibid., 59.

4. Ibid., 81.

5. Hingson et al., *Adolescent Substance Abuse*, 46–54.

6. Robert Maddox, "The War Against Demon Rum," in *American History Illustrated* (Gettysburg, PA: The National Historical Society, June 1979).

7. *Problem Drinking: Report of the Task Force on Alcohol Problems* (New York: National Council of Churches of Christ, 1973), 15.

8. Ibid., 11.

9. Howard J. Clinebell, Jr., *Understanding and Counseling the Alcoholic* (Nashville: Abingdon, 1978), 323.

10. George Bach and Peter Wyden, *The Intimate Enemy* (New York: William Morrow and Company, 1969), 207.

11. Robert L. DuPont, "Learning from the Passt to Cope with the Future," in *Drug Abuse in the Modern World* (New York: Pergamon Press, 1981), 271.

CHAPTER FOUR: ALCOHOLISM—SIN OR SICKNESS?

1. Michael Satchell, "Doctors in Trouble," *Parade Magazine*, 17 October 1982, 26.

2. LeClair Bissell, *Some Perspectives on Alcoholism* (Minneapolis: Johnson Institute, 1982), 12.

3. Vernon E. Johnson, "The Johnson Institute Philosophy Regarding Alcoholism and Drug Abuse" (Johnson Institute, Minneapolis, Mimeographed).

4. *Facts on Alcoholism*, (New York: National Council on Alcoholism , 1979).

5. James R. Milam and Katherine Ketchum, *Under the Influence* (Seattle, WA: Madrona Publishers, 1981), 32, 41–42.

6. Jane O 'Reilly, Mary Carpenter, and Ruth Mehrtens, "New Insights into Alcoholism," *Time*, 25 April 1983, 88–89.

7. George A. Mann, *The Dynamics of Addiction* (Minneapolis: Johnson Institute, 1983), 12.

8. Milam and Ketchum, 9.

9. Kathleen Whalen Fitzgerald, "Living with Jellinek's Disease," *Newsweek*, 17 October 1983, 22.

10. *ABC's of Drinking and Driving* (Greenfield, MA: Channing L. Bete Co., 1971), 3.

11. Milan and Ketchum, 9.

12. Clinebell, *Understanding and Counseling the Alcoholic*, 168–69.

13. Ibid., 167.

14. Milam and Ketchum, 9.

15. Johnson Institute, "The Nature of Chemical Dependency" (Minneapolis, Mimeographed).

16. Clark J. Laudengran, *Easy Does It* (Minneapolis: Hazelden Foundation, 1982), 13–14.

17. Sharon Wegscheider, *Another Chance* (Palo Alto: Science and Behavior Books, 1981), 32–33.

18. Ibid., 34–43, 70–75.

19. Ibid., 81–82.

20. Ibid., 221.

21. Ibid., 239.

CHAPTER FIVE: THE MISUSE AND ABUSE OF LICIT DRUGS

1. Dorothy Cretcher, *Steering Clear* (Minneapolis: Winston Press, 1982), 5.

2. William Stockton, "Dual Addiction," *New York Times Magazine*, 6 August 1978, 4.

3. Ibid.

4. Ibid.

5. Ibid.

6. Edith Lisansky Gomberg, *Sober Days, Golden Years* (Minneapolis: Johnson Institute, 1982), 12–13, 16.

7. Ibid., 9.

8. Ibid., 21.

9. *Facts on Teenage Drinking* (New York: National Council on Alcoholism , 1982).

10. Mann, *Dynamics of Addiction*, 4, 6.

11. National Council on Alcoholism, *Teenage Drinking*.

12. "Drinking Not Responsible," *PRIDE Newsletter* 5, no. 3 (September 1983): 9.

CHAPTER SIX: ILLEGAL DRUG USE

1. "Stages of Drug Use," *PRIDE Newlsetter*, 3.

2. Denise Carter, "Why Do Kids Use Drugs and Alcohol and How to Help Them Stop," *PTA Today*, October 1983, 27.

3. Cretcher, *Steering Clear*, 5.

4. Peggy Mann, *Pot Safari* (New York: Woodmere Press, 1982), 21, 121.

5. Ibid., 120–21.

6. Pat Barton, *NFP Educational Kit and Public Speaking Manual for Drug Education Presentations* (Silver Springs, MD: National Federation of Parents for Drug Free Youth, 1982), 44–45.

7. Ibid., 10–13.

8. John Buecher et al., "Taking Drugs on the Job," *Newsweek*, 22 August 1983.

CHAPTER SEVEN: THE CRY FOR HELP

1. Jay Haley, *Problem Solving Therapy* (New York: Harper and Row, 1976), 2.

2. Ibid., 2–3.

3. Ibid., 5.

4. Lena DiCicco, Hilma Unterberger, and John Mack, "Confronting Denial: An Alcoholism Intervention Strategy," *Psychiatric Annuals* 8 (11 November 1978: 603)

5. Haley, *Problem Solving Therapy*, 9.

6. Ibid., 27–28.

7. Wegscheider, *Another Chance*, 33–34.

8. *What Is Intervention?* (Minneapolis: Johnson Institute, 1980), 2.

9. Vernon E. Johnson, *I'll Quit Tomorrow* (New York: Harper and Row, 1980), 55–57.

10. DiCicco, Unterberger, and Mack, "Confronting Denial," 603.

CHAPTER EIGHT: CREATING A TREATMENT NETWORK

1. Sharon Nale, *A Cry for Help* (Philadelphia: Fortress Press, 1982), 47.

2. *A Clergyman Asks About Alcoholics Anonymous* (New York: Alcoholics Anonymous World Service, 1978), 3–17.

3. O'Reilly, Carpenter, and Mehrtens, "New Insights Into Alcoholism," *Time*, 89.

4. Ibid.

5. *Purpose and Suggestions* (New York: Al-Anon Family Group Headquarters, 1974), 2.

6. *Adult Children of Alcoholics* (Minneapolis: Johnson Institute, 1983).

7. Ibid.

8. *The Book of Common Prayer, According to the Use of the Episcopal Church* (New York: The Church Hymnal Corporation, 1979), 831.

CHAPTER NINE: THEOLOGICAL PERSPECTIVES, SPIRITUAL FOUNDATIONS

1. David C. Hancock, *Points for Parents Perplexed About Drugs* (Center City: Hazelden Educational Service, 1975), 6.

2. Howard J. Clinebell, Jr., *The Pastor and Drug Dependency* (New York: Council Press, 1968), 15.

3. Stanton Peele and Archie Brodasky, *Love and Addiction* (New York: New American Library, 1975), 172.

4. Michael Jacobson, George Hacker, and Robert Atkins, *The Booze Merchants* (Washington, DC: Center for Science in Public Interest, 1983), 153.

5. Ibid., 3.

6. Jonathan Beaty and Lee Griggs, "Grass Was Never Greener," *Newsweek*, 9 August 1982, 15.

7. Menninger, *Whatever Became of Sin?*, 197.

8. Stanton Peele and Archie Brodasky, *Love and Addiction* (New York: New American Library, 1975), 151–55.

9. Jean Dietz, "An Alarming Trend in Teenage Suicide," *Boston Globe*, 5 December 1982, section A, 1.

10. B.K. Gangelhott and David Gelman, "Teenage Suicide in the Sun Belt," *Newsweek*, 15 August 1983, 70–72.

11. Howard J. Clinebell, Jr., *Understanding and Counseling the Alcoholic* (Nashville: Abingdon, 1978), 154–55.

12. Ibid., 156.

13. 13. Herbert L. Stein-Schneider, "Drug Abuse, Religion and Mysticism," in *Drug Abuse in the Modern World* (New York: Pergamon Press, 1981), 189.

14. Clinebell, *Counseling the Alcoholic*, 157.

15. T. Furman Hewitt, *A Biblical Perspective on the Use and Abuse of Alcohol and Other Drugs* (Raleigh Department of Human Resources, 1980), 20–30.

BIBLIOGRAPHY

ABC's of Drinking and Driving. Greenfield, MA: Channing L. Bete Co., 1971.

A Clergyman Asks About Alcoholics Anonymous. New York: Alcoholics Anonymous World Service, 1979.

Adult Children of Alcoholics. Minneapolis: Johnson Institute, 1983.

All in the Family: Chairman's Guide. Tulsa: The U.S. Jaycees. (Catalogue no. 753-1).

All in the Family: Understanding How We Teach and Influence Children About Alcohol. Tulsa: The U.S. Jaycees. (Catalogue no. 747-1).

Anderson, James D., and Jones, Ezra Earl. *The Management of Ministry*. New York: Harper and Row, 1978.

Bach, George, and Wyden, Porter. *The Intimate Enemy*. New York: William Morrow and Company, 1969.

Barbour, John. *Marijuana and Your Child: A Primer for Concerned Parents*. New York: Associated Press, 1981.

Barton, Pat. *NFP Educational Kit and Public Speaking Manual for Drug Education Presentations*. Silver Springs: National Federation of Parents for Drug Free Youth, 1982.

Beaty, Jonathan, and Griggs, Lee. "Grass Was Never Greener." *Newsweek*, 9 August 1982, 15.

Bissel, LeClaire. *Some Perspectives on Alcoholism* . Minneapolis: Johnson Institute, 1982.

Blizzard, Samuel W. "The Minister's Dilemma." *The Christian Century*, 15 April 1956, 508–9.

Brecher, John, et al. "Taking Drugs on the Job." *Newsweek*, 22 August 1983, 52–60.

Brock, Peter C. *The Johnson Institute's Program for Adolescents with Alcohol Problems. Adolescent Substance Abuse*. Ohio: Ross Laboratories, 1983, 68–72.

Carter, Denise. "Why Do Kids Use Drugs and How to Help Them Stop." *PTA Today* , October 1983.

Castelli, Jim. "Study Finds Religion Major Factor in U.S." *Boston Globe*, 2 March 1981, 27.

Clinebell, Howard J., Jr. *The Pastor and Drug Dependency*. New York: Council Press, 1968.

———. *Understanding and Counseling the Alcoholic*. Nashville: Abingdon, 1978.

Conley, Paul C., and Sorenson, Andrew A. *The Staggering Steeple*. Philadelphia: Pilgrim Press, 1971.

Cretcher, Dorothy. *Steering Clear*. Minneapolis: Winston Press, 1982.

Cross, Wilbur. *Kids & Booze—What You Must Know to Help Them*. New York: E.P. Dutton, 1979.

Delaine, John K. *Who's Raising the Family?* Madison: Wisconsin Clearinghouse, 1981.

Deluca, J.R., ed. *Fourth Special Report to the U.S. Congress on Alcohol and Health*. Washington, DC: U.S. Dept. of Health and Human Services, publication no. ADM 81-1080, 1981.

DiCicco, Lena; Unterberger, Hilma; and Mack, John. "Confronting Denial: An Alcoholism Intervention Strattegy." *Psychiatric Annuals* 8, 11 November 1978.

Dietz, Jean. "An Alarming Trend in Teenage Suicide." *Boston Globe* 5 December 1982, 4.

"Drinking Not Responsible." *PRIDE Newsletter* 5, no. 3 (September 1983): 9.

DuPont, Robert L. *Getting Tough on Gateway Drugs—A Guide for the Family*. Washington, D.C.: American Psychiatric Press, Inc., 1984.

———. "Learning from the Past to Cope with the Future." In *Drug Abuse in the Modern World*, edited by Gabriel G. Nahas and Henry Clay Frick. New York: Pergamon Press, 1981.

Facts on Alcoholism. New York: National Council on Alcoholism, 1979.

Facts on Teenage Drinking. New York: National Council on Alcoholism, 1980.

Fitzgerald, Kathleen Whalon. "Living with Jellinek's Disease." *Newsweek*, 17 October 1983, 22.

For Parents Only: What You Need to Know About Marijuana. Rockville: National Institute on Drug Abuse, 1980.

Gangelhoff, B.K., and Gelman, David. "Teenage Suicide in the Sun Belt." *Newsweek*, 15 August 1983, 70–74.

Glenn, Stephen. *Strengthening the Family*. Bethesda: Potomac Press, 1981.

Gomberg, Edith Linsky. *Sober Days Golden Years*. Minneapolis: Johnson Institute, 1982.

Haley, Jay. *Problem Solving Therapy*. New York: Harper and Row, 1976.

Hancock, David C. *Alcohol and the Church*. Minneapolis: Prevention of Alcohol Problems, 1980.

———. *Pointers for Parents Perplexed About Drugs*. Center City: Hazelden Education Service, 1975.

———. "The Role of the Church in Alcohol Problems—Involved or Uninvolved?" Paper presented to the International Conference of Religious Leaders, Indiana, 17 November 1979. Sample from the author, 4616 Longfellow Avenue, South, Minneapolis, MN 55407.

Hewitt, T. Furman. *A Biblical Perspective on the Use and Abuse of Alcohol and Other Drugs*. Raleigh: Department of Human Resources, 1980.

It Starts with People. Rockville: National Institute on Drug Abuse, 1979.

Jacobson, Michael; Hacker, George; and Atkins, Robert. *The Booze Merchants*. Washington, DC: Center for Science in Public Interest, 1983.

Janeczek, Curtis L. *Marijuana—Time for a Closer Look*. Columbus: Healthstar Publications, 1980.

Jellinek, E. M. *The Disease Concept of Alcoholism*. New Brunswick: Hillhouse Press, 1960.

Johnson Institute. "The Nature of Chemical Dependency." Minneapolis: Johnson Institute. Mimeograph.

Johnson, L. D.; Bachman, J. G.; and O'Malley, P. M. *Student Drug Use in America: 1975–1981*. Washington, DC: U.S. Dept. of Health and Human Services (publication no. ADM 82-1208), 1982.

Johnson, Vernon E. *I'll Quit Tomorrow*. New York: Harper and Row, 1980.

———. "The Johnson Institute Philosophy Regarding Alcoholism and Drug Abuse." Minneapolis: Johnson Institute. Mimeograph.

James Hardin, and James, Helen. *Sensual Drugs*. Cambridge: Cambridge University Press, 1977.

Kellerman, Joseph L. *Alcoholism: A Guide for the Clergy*. New York: National Council on Alcoholism , 1958.

Laudergan, Clark J. *Easy Does It*. Minneapolis: Hazelden Foundation, 1982.

Maddox, Robert. "The War Against Demon Rum." In *American History Illustrated*. Gettysburg: The National Historical Society, 1979.

Mann, George A. *The Dynamics of Addiction*. Minneapolis: Johnson Institute, 1983.

Mann, Peggy. *Pot Safari*. New York: Woodmere Press, 1982.

McDarby, Dario. *Drug Abuse: A Realistic Primer for Parents*. Phoenix: Do It Now Foundation, 1980.

Menninger, Karl. *Whatever Became of Sin?* New York: Hawthorne Books, 1973.

Milam, James R., and Ketchum, Katherine. *Under the Influence*. Seattle: Madronna Publishrs, 1981.

Mulford, Harold A. "Drinking and Deviant Drinking, U.S.A." *Quarterly Journal Studies. Alcohol* 25 (1964): 634–50.

Nale, Sharon. *A Cry for Help*. Philadelphia: Fortress Press, 1982.

O'Reilly, Jane; Carpenter, Mary; and Mehrtens, Ruth. "New Insights Into Alcoholism." *Time*, 25 April 1983, 88–89.

Parents Peers and Pot. Rockville: National Institute on Drug Abuse, 1979.

Peele, Stanton, and Brodasky, Archie. *Love and Addiction*. New York: New American Library, 1975.

Problem Drinking: Report of the Task Force on Alcohol Problems. New York: National Council of Churches of Christ, 1973.

Purpose and Suggestions. New York: Al-Anon Family Group Headquarters, 1974.

Russell, George K. *Marijuana Today*. New York: The Myrin Institute for Adult Education, 1980.

Satchell, Michael. "Doctors in Trouble." *Parade Magazine*, 17 October 1982, 26.

Satir, Virginia. *People Making*. Palo Alto: Science and Behavior Books, 1972.

Schneider, Karl A. *Stumbling Blocks or Stepping Stones: Overcoming Clergy Inhibiting Attitudes to Involvement in Early Intervention and Training in Alcohol and Drug Problems*. New York: National Council on Alcoholism, 1982.

Schuchard, Keith. "The Floodtide of Drugs and the Very Young: *Rebuilding the Protective Dikes at Home and Abroad*." In *Drug Abuse in the Modern World*, edited by Gabriel G. Nahas and Henry Clay Frick. New York: Pergamon Press, 1981.

Seligmann, Jean. Review of *Growing Up Old: Children Without Parents*, by Marie Winn. *Newsweek*, 8 August 1983, 72.

Shoemaker, Samuel M. *What the Church Has to Learn from Alcoholics Anonymous*. Baltimore: Diocese of Maryland, Diocesan Committee on Alcoholism.

"Stages of Drug Use." *PRIDE Newsletter* 5, no. 3 (September 1983): 3.

Stein-Schneider, Herbert L. "Drug Abuse, Religion and Mysticism." In *Drug Abuse in the Modern World*, edited by Gabriel G. Nahas and Henry Clay Frick. New York: Pergamon Press, 1981.

Stocton, William. "Dual Addiction." *New York Times Magazine*, 5 August 1978.

The Book of Common Prayer, According to the Use of the Episcopal Church. New York: The Church Hymnal Corporation, 1979.

Wegscheider, Sharon. *Another Chance*. Palo Alto: Science and Behavior Books, 1981.

What Is Intervention? Minneapolis: Johnson Institute, 1980.

White House Conference on Families. *Listening to America's Families: Action for the 80's*. The Report to the President, Congress and Families of the Nation, Jim Guy Tucker, Chairperson, Washington, DC, 1980.

Woodward, Nancy Hyden. *If Your Child Is Drinking*. New York: G. P. Putnam's Sons, 1981.

INDEX